MARY WILKINS FREEMAN

A Study of the Short Fiction

Also Available in Twayne's Studies in Short Fiction Series

Twayne's Studies in Short Fiction

Gary Scharnhorst and Eric Haralson,
General Editors

MARY WILKINS FREEMAN.
From Mary Wilkins Freeman's The People of Our Neighborhood
(Philadelphia: Curtis Publishing Company, 1898).

MARY WILKINS FREEMAN

A Study of the Short Fiction

Mary R. Reichardt
University of St. Thomas

TWAYNE PUBLISHERS
An Imprint of Simon & Schuster Macmillan
New York

PRENTICE HALL INTERNATIONAL
London Mexico City New Delhi Singapore Sydney Toronto

Copyright © 1997 by Twayne Publishers

Twayne Publishers
An Imprint of Simon & Schuster Macmillan
1633 Broadway
New York, NY 10019

Library of Congress Cataloging-in-Publication Data
Reichardt, Mary R.
    Mary Wilkins Freeman : a study of the short fiction / Mary R.
Reichardt.
      p.   cm. — (Twayne's studies in short fiction)
      Includes bibliographical references (p.   ) and index.
      ISBN 0-8057-4626-9 (acid-free paper)
      1. Freeman, Mary Eleanor Wilkins, 1852–1930—Criticism and
interpretation. 2. Women and literature—New England—History.
3. Regionalism in literature. 4. New England—In literature.
5. Short story. I. Title. II. series.
PS1713.R44   1997
813'.4—dc21   97-18464
                                                          CIP

10 9 8 7 6 5 4 3 2 1

Printed in the United States of America

Contents

Contents

Preface

Many readers who pick up this volume will have already encountered one or more of Mary Wilkins Freeman's short stories, perhaps the frequently anthologized "A New England Nun," "The Revolt of 'Mother,' " or "A Village Singer." Intrigued by the female protagonists' fierce dilemmas, the detached, ironic narrative stance, and the compact, forceful style, such readers may like to know more about the author and her works. If students of American literature, they may associate Freeman's name with other regional turn-of-the-century authors, in particular Sarah Orne Jewett. They may also be tempted to dismiss regional writing as a minor offshoot of American realism that is overshadowed by the more prodigious—and traditionally canonized—accomplishments of Mark Twain, Henry James, or William Dean Howells. These readers may therefore be surprised to discover that Freeman was one of the most prolific and popular writers of her time, successfully publishing novels, short stories, essays, children's works, plays, poetry, and even movie scripts throughout her nearly 50-year career. During much of that career, Freeman was quite literally a household name: any subscriber to *Harper's Monthly*, *Harper's Bazar*, *Woman's Home Companion*, *Ladies' Home Journal*, *Saturday Evening Post*, or more than half a dozen other influential publications both in the United States and in England was well acquainted with her work.

Though Freeman won acclaim for her extensive writing in other genres, her literary reputation was forged by and rests today primarily on her adult short fiction. In this area alone her output is remarkable. Between 1882 and 1928, she published approximately 250 short stories in a wide variety of magazines and newspapers. One hundred forty-seven of those stories were subsequently reissued during the author's lifetime in 14 collections, primarily by the Harper and Brothers firm with which she had a long-standing agreement. But sheer bulk of material, of course, does not an artist make. Since her name so readily sold a magazine, Freeman fielded numerous requests over the years from editors seeking holiday tales for their Christmas, Valentine's Day, Easter, or Halloween issues. Intensely pragmatic about the material benefits of her work, perhaps a result of childhood poverty, Freeman complied with those requests as often as her demanding writing schedule allowed. As a result, her oeuvre of short fiction contains at least 50 holiday stories, some of which are predictable in plot and overly sentimental in tone. Other Freeman stories, particularly those written late in her career, seem forced as well and leave the reader with little more than the sense that the author was scrambling to meet a deadline. And some of Freeman's tales are so dated in style or subject matter that they hold little interest for the modern reader; among these are a group of works featuring child protagonists and a handful of stories involving patriotic World War I themes.

Despite such obvious unevenness in her short fiction, Mary Wilkins Freeman authored a substantial number, 50 or more, of finely crafted stories, making her work worthy of the critical reevaluation it has received over the last several decades. No longer regarded as a merely transitional local colorist or regional writer, Freeman is now considered an influential contributor to the development of the American short story, particularly those written by and about women. Indeed, it is largely the author's concentration on female protagonists and feminine subject matter that led equally to the neglect of her writing throughout the middle years of the twentieth century and to the resurgence of attention her work, along with that of other "forgotten" women writers, now generates. The changing tenor of Freeman criticism over the years, in fact, makes for an interesting study in the vicissitudes of literary standards. But what is clear today is that Freeman's best stories have withstood the test of time; their renaissance is not merely a product of current literary fashion but a result of scholarship's increasing recognition of their artistry. That artistry is manifest in Freeman's characteristic combination of intense psychological probing of the secret inner lives—the frustrations and moral battles—of her characters; in an acute understanding of the delicate mediation necessary between the demands of the individual self and others; in ironic plot twists designed to undercut the typical domestic/sentimental story's "fairy tale" development; in ambiguous, open endings that prefigure modernist fiction; and in a sparse, dramatic style in which a single word, gesture, or object is positioned to provide crucial insight into the mental workings of the protagonist.

Freeman wrote superb short stories throughout her career, yet few readers know of her work beyond the handful of tales that appear regularly in anthologies. Of the several modern collections of her short fiction, only the most recent one brings together a substantial sampling of tales that represent her long and varied career; these include New England village stories, historical stories, symbolic stories, and ghost stories.[1] The purpose of this volume, therefore, is to provide the general reader as well as the student of literature with a road map for navigating through Freeman's oeuvre of short fiction. After an introductory overview of Freeman's influences and aesthetics that examines in detail two representative stories, part 1 discusses more or less chronologically the author's story writing in each of three stages of her career. Although Freeman's art did not develop noticeably over time—many of her finest tales are among her earliest—she experimented ambitiously with various kinds of short fiction throughout her life even as she continually branched out into other literary genres, such as plays and novels. "Early Village Stories, 1882–1891" considers those works, collected in *A Humble Romance* (1887) and *A New England Nun* (1891), that secured the author's fame and established certain themes that she would return to time and again throughout her lifetime. "Mid-Career Experiments, 1892–1903" explores the historical, supernatural, mystery, and symbolic nature tales Freeman wrote after her early success, fulfilling her stated desire to move from starkly realistic subject matter into that with more mystical resonance. And "Later Stories, 1904–1928" examines the new moods and subjects as well as the interrelated and child-protagonist stories that mark the final phase of her writing.

Of course, any attempt to generalize about the work of an author as versatile as Freeman is on some level a futile exercise in reduction. Too often narrowly classified in the past, Freeman's body of short fiction defies easy categorization: her outlook on human nature was broad, and her interests and moods were many. In particular, the hundreds of differing characters that people her stories are testimony to her remarkable grasp of the range of sensitivities, emotions, and relationships among folk in the rural New England where her stories most often take place. Still, certain subjects, themes, and techniques appear in any representative selection of her work. It is as possible, therefore, to identify the characteristic Mary Wilkins Freeman story as it is to indicate the typical Nathaniel Hawthorne or Ernest Hemingway tale. My objective in undertaking this study of Freeman's short fiction is to aid readers in recognizing her stories by describing characteristic works, some successful and some not, from each of the three periods of her career. Since Freeman's post-1891 work has often been too cavalierly dismissed by critics who deem it inferior to her earliest efforts, I have purposely given equal time to the mid-career and later writings. Some stories from each period necessarily receive brief mention only; others are discussed at length. I do not pretend to do full justice to Freeman's entire body of short fiction, but I hope that in part 1 readers will glean a useful overview of that corpus as well as an increased understanding of and appreciation for its craftsmanship.

Though often pressed to do so, Freeman rarely discussed her writing; her usual stance, in fact, was to sidestep reporters' and critics' questions by insisting that she had no influences and ascribed to no theories or trends. Thus her few elaborations on the origin, aims, and practice of her art are telling. Part 2, "The Writer," brings together nearly every important statement Freeman made throughout her career regarding her craft. Impatient with self-analysis, her voice here is often refreshingly down to earth, practical to the point of being utilitarian. She commenced writing, she tells us, because poverty forced her to earn a living, and pens and paper were cheaper than the supplies she would have had to purchase to fulfill her original dream of becoming a painter. She wrote truthfully and courageously only about the subjects she knew best and that most interested her, refusing to relinquish her independence by imitating others or taking criticism too seriously. And she unhesitatingly credits her own persistent hard work for her phenomenal success. In addition to these direct statements, part 2 includes other pieces that help shed light on Freeman's aesthetics. These include prefaces to *A Humble Romance* and *Pembroke*, an essay on Emily Brontë's *Wuthering Heights*, and excerpts from her personal correspondence.

Criticism of Freeman's short fiction has burgeoned during the last few decades of the twentieth century. Besides examining an increasing range of works, scholars continue to discover new aspects to the author's thematically ambiguous, or open-ended, stories. As in her own day, when the so-called "woman question" was hotly debated, Freeman's many stories about women's responses to and roles in a restrictive patriarchal society intrigue and disturb us today, engendering fervently argued interpretations. Part 3, "The Critics," presents four recent approaches to the well-known and controversial "A New England Nun." I believe that this side-by-side comparison of differing viewpoints on a single story serves to illustrate that her most skillful fiction contains several layers of meaning; it likewise provides a good indication of contemporary trends in Freeman criticism. Readers whose appetites are whetted for more will find a wide selection of critical studies on Freeman's stories listed in the bibliography.

Note

1. Mary R. Reichardt, ed., *A Mary Wilkins Freeman Reader* (Lincoln: University of Nebraska Press, 1997).

The date following each Freeman story cited in part 1 is the work's original magazine or newspaper publication date. Dates for the collections are listed in the Selected Bibliography.

Acknowledgments

I am grateful for permission from the following libraries and collections to reprint the excerpts from Freeman's letters found in part 2, "The Writer": The Andover-Harvard Theological Library; Fales Library Special Collections, New York University; Mary Wilkins Freeman Collection, Clifton Waller Barrett Library Special Collections Department, University of Virginia; Hamlin Garland Collection, Doheny Memorial Library, University of Southern California; Hayden Carruth Papers, Rare Books and Manuscripts Division, New York Public Library; The Rare Books Room, The Pennsylvania State University Libraries; Miller Library Special Collections, Colby College, Waterville, Maine; Edmund C. Stedman Papers, Rare Book and Manuscript Library, Columbia University; Rare Book and Special Collections Division, Library of Congress.

Part 1

THE SHORT FICTION

Influences, Aesthetics, and
Two Characteristic Freeman Stories

Mary Wilkins Freeman had already served a lengthy apprenticeship when, at age 30, she published her first short story for adults. In her school days in Randolph, Massachusetts, and later in Brattleboro, Vermont, where her family moved when she was 15, she dabbled in poetry, indulged if not encouraged by her parents, Warren and Eleanor Wilkins. Family members recalled how her father once proudly insisted on reciting one of those early efforts to an unimpressed group of relatives.[1] As a teenager, she showed a few of her religious pieces to the town minister and was informed that she had talent, but "fortunately," as she related years later, she never sought their publication.[2] Abandoning that strain, she turned to penning romantic children's poems and occasional pieces for adults, many of which were ballads based on the fairy tales she had loved as a child. She practiced, as did many a writer before her, by laboriously copying the styles of others. In her late twenties, her poems began to appear in such magazines as *Wide Awake, St. Nicholas, Century, Harper's Monthly*, and *Scribners*, and she continued to publish poetry sporadically throughout her career.

Because, as she once remarked, "no sane person can possibly call me a success in poetry," Freeman was soon also publishing works in a genre in which she excelled and that quickly afforded her a reputation as a fine teller of tales: children's stories.[3] Three collections of her juvenile writings, both poetry and stories, were published between 1883 and 1886; four more would follow during the next decade. This early concentration on the techniques of writing for children—use of a simple, direct narrative line, "read-aloud" dialogue, and vivid, concrete detail—exerted a significant influence on the adult short stories Freeman was also beginning to write. As well, her success in this genre introduced her into the world of late-nineteenth-century publishing: as a contributor to *Wide Awake*, for example, she joined company with such notable writers as Celia Thaxter, Mary Hartwell Catherwood, Edward Everett Hale, Rose Terry Cooke, and Oliver Wendell Holmes.

With the restless yet calculated ambition that was to characterize her nearly 50-year writing career, Freeman was already experimenting with adult short fiction as early as 1881. Why the short story? she was asked late in her life. "I think the answer is very simple," was her typically blunt reply. "The short story did not take so long to write, it was easier, and of course I was not *sure* of my own ability to write even the short story, much less a novel" (Kendrick, 382). Encouraged by the reception of her juvenile fiction, she studied publishing possibilities and began to send her adult pieces out to local newspapers, such as the *Boston Sunday Budget*, as well as to some top magazines of the day, among them *Lippincott's, Century, Atlantic Monthly*, and *Harper's Monthly*. The now-lost "The Shadow Family," a Dickens imitation, won a newspaper prize in 1882; Freeman was delighted not only with the story's publication but with the much-needed check for $50 that she received for it. But her writing career may be said to have truly commenced with the acceptance of "Two Old Lovers" for the March 1883 issue of *Harper's Bazar*.[4] Then as now a publication aimed at women readers, *Harper's Bazar* was edited by Mary Louise Booth, who, until her death in 1889, played an important role in the fledgling years of Freeman's career. A respected author and editor, Booth assisted Freeman in forging the skills necessary to produce successful magazine fiction.[5] Booth also promoted Freeman's stories within the Harper's firm and soon helped her gain entrée to the more prestigious *Harper's Monthly*, edited by Henry Mills Alden. Both Booth and Alden subsequently became her personal friends; the young author found the close relationships she formed with her editors and fellow writers to be a valuable benefit of writing.[6]

The *Harper's Bazar* publication of "Two Old Lovers" propelled Freeman quickly into fame. Responding to readers' acclaim, the *Bazar* went on to publish five more Freeman stories in 1883, one in each of its April, May, August, September, and December editions. The following year, an additional five stories appeared in the *Bazar*, and three appeared in *Harper's Monthly*. By that time, Freeman was already considered one of the best-selling protégés of the influential Harper and Brothers firm; her association with Harper's continued for the remainder of her life and resulted in the publication of 165 of her 247 adult short stories, 12 of her 14 collections, and 9 of her 14 novels.

Though Freeman insisted late in her career that she had "st[oo]d entirely alone," that there were no formative influences on her art, several personal and external factors help to explain the origin of Freeman's themes and techniques and account for her widespread popularity during the 1880s and 1890s (Kendrick, 382). However the artist may demur, no art stands in isolation; in Freeman's case, many of her influences are, in fact, readily discernible. We begin with the personal. Attempting to equate an author's life too closely with her writing rarely makes for good criticism, and Freeman's work has at times been subjected to an inappropriate degree of biographical scrutiny. That said, however, one can certainly look to significant events or conditions in an author's life that have contributed to the formation of his or her art. Although one cannot attest authoritatively to the existence of autobiographical elements in Freeman's fiction, her preoccupation with several themes—her writing and rewriting, time and again, of several story lines—mirrors some of her personal experiences and indicates her lingering desire to explore these issues from every possible vantage point.

Freeman's interest in poverty and its religious interpretation is the first of several such issues worth considering. Of genteel New England stock—both her parents could trace their lineage back to the country's founders—young Mary Wilkins knew firsthand about the acute need to keep up appearances as her family's financial circumstances worsened steadily during her late childhood and teenage years. In Brattleboro, necessity forced the Wilkins family to move four times in 10 years into a succession of smaller and shabbier homes and apartments; at times, too, they were forced to rely on charitable donations of food accepted by Eleanor Wilkins with stiff-lipped grace (Foster, 37). Far more important than the physical effects of poverty were its moral and emotional tolls. As Freeman's biographer Edward Foster remarks, in the orthodox Congregational theology the Wilkins family and many of their New England neighbors practiced, "it was always assumed that the poverty of the poor was punishment for sin" (Foster, 14). One cannot undervalue the effect of this statement when considering Freeman's repeated concern in her fiction with matters of poverty, pride, and the discrepancies between characters' assumed social fronts or faces and their actual circumstances. Despite the leavening influx of Unitarianism, the Congregationalism practiced in Freeman's New England yet required a conversion experience, a public demonstration of grace received.[7] This display made manifest to all, it was believed, the state of the individual's soul. As Perry Westbrook succinctly summarizes, the result was that "each person's sins and degree of grace were the concern of the entire community. . . . Small wonder that the villages seethed with gossip and that the church itself sanctioned and encouraged speculation as to the inner and outer life of each of its members or would-be members. No wonder that fears of what one's neighbors might think were pivotal in determining one's decisions. Always . . . one's conduct was an indication of the state of one's soul. . . . How desirable it was, therefore, that one's life appear Godly and prosperous!"[8]

In short, in the small villages where most of Freeman's stories are set, poverty, loss, and suffering—in fact, almost any "non-normal" situation or behavior—were considered evidence of an individual's wrongdoing and a mark of God's disfavor. Repeatedly in her fiction, Freeman portrays the inner anguish of those who are undergoing hardship but are convinced that they have done nothing to deserve it (for example, "The Strike of Hannah," "For the Love of One's Self," "A Poetess"); those who rail against a God who seems to have forgotten his covenanted promise to reward them for righteous living ("An Object of Love," "A Tardy Thanksgiving," "The Balking of Christopher"); those unrelentingly ostracized or slandered by gossip ("A Solitary," "About Hannah Stone," "The Witch's Daughter"); and those whose social and religious life has revolved around the church and who are now alienated from this lifeline ("A Village Singer," "A Moral Exigency," "A Conflict Ended"). Many other tales deal with related subjects, such as the delicate matter for the poor of giving and receiving with dignity ("A Mistaken Charity," "The Revolt of Sophia Lane," "Old Lady Pingree"); the consequences of outright rebellion against church, doctrine, or minister ("Life-Everlastin'," "An Independent Thinker," "The Bar-Lighthouse"); or the guilty, overscrupulous, or stubborn conscience that, as in some Poe characters, may border on mental breakdown or yield to the compulsion to confess publicly ("An Honest Soul," "A Stress of Conscience," "The Cloak Also"). Freeman always sympathized with the poor, the outcast, those who rebelled against the strictures and hypocrisies of formalized religion, and those who were forced to lead a type of double life in order to be accepted, or at least tolerated, by their neighbors.

Unwilling or unable to marry at the conventional age, Freeman also experienced personally the familial and social stigma attached to the single woman in a society in which marriage was still the norm. The only surviving child in a family that had buried three others by the time she was a young adult, Freeman was indulged and sheltered by her parents. But she must have felt that all of the family's hopes were now pinned on her: a good marriage, in particular, might reverse the family's financial, and attendant social, misfortunes. Many of her stories study close family relationships, especially those between mothers (or mother figures) and daughters; often, these intimate bonds are portrayed as tense, even cloying. A mother of a young woman in Freeman's world is usually preoccupied with securing a mate for her child, one who fulfills the mother's own desire for romance, material security, or social standing ("Louisa," "The Buckley Lady," and "Mother-Wings"). Another group of tales about family relationships focuses on the power differential between a dominant mother figure and a weaker, childlike person; the issue is often jealousy over romantic love ("Evelina's Garden," "The Long Arm," "Julia—Her Thanksgiving"). And in many stories, a long-standing family quarrel is resolved and harmony restored ("The Reign of the Doll," "The Revolt of 'Mother,' " "Billy and Susy").

Freeman examines all types of family relationships in her fiction. For many readers, however, the theme that best characterizes her stories is the exploration of the material and emotional consequences for a woman of marrying or of remaining single. Thorough in her scrutiny of the subject, Freeman is also honest and daring, even radical, in her conclusions. Defying conventional religious or social opinion and rejecting the Cinderella story line of much nineteenth-century fiction, she probes each situation she creates on its own terms. To the question each story poses, "Is it better for the woman to marry?" she asserts an emphatic "It depends." Her best work details with unflinching realism the severely limited options for women in the late-nineteenth-century New England village. Among other factors, widespread recession after the Civil War resulted in little money and, especially for women, little or no chance of obtaining gainful employment. Moreover, few eligible men remained in the region, as many had been killed in the war and others had left for better prospects in the growing factory towns or out West.

Against these external matters, Freeman weighs the individual character's personality: is the woman mentally strong and resourceful enough to remain unmarried and thus potentially alone, or is she too weak, dependent, or vulnerable to do so? Many stories highlight a young woman's dilemma as she ponders what she might gain or lose by marrying the man who is available to her ("A New England Nun," "Humble Pie," "The Chance of Araminta"). In another group of stories, the stereotypical blond and lovely but weak-willed woman of sentimental fiction competes with a levelheaded, plain, unromantic woman for a man's affections. Though the latter can often control the situation to her advantage, retaining or relinquishing the usually vacillating, childish man at will, she eventually—though not without some lingering regret— "gives up" the man to his more appropriate counterpart ("Juliza," "A

Moral Exigency," "Emmy"). A sizable body of stories examines the plight of the older woman who is alone, whether by choice or circumstance ("A Poetess," "An Object of Love," "The Balsam Fir"). How does she ward off poverty? Counteract the inevitable gossip about her "odd" or reclusive ways? Deal with isolation, loneliness, and monotony? And finally, a small but significant number of Freeman's short stories considers life after marriage for a woman. Inevitably, those who have opted to wed only after deliberation or only after first satisfying other pressing needs or desires get what they expect and are contented ("The Secret," "One Good Time," "Robins and Hammers"); those who awaited the fulfillment of a romantic ideal may find themselves bitterly disappointed ("A Tragedy from the Trivial," "Sour Sweetings").

Issues of poverty, religion, family relationships, and women's marital status are, then, the pivotal themes around which the majority of Freeman's short stories revolve. The same is true for Freeman's tales written in various subgenres—historical, supernatural, mystery, and symbolic—which she penned mainly in mid-career. That said, however, one must note that Freeman's diverse body of work also treats a variety of other themes (some adult stories, for example, examine the inner world of children) as well as admits the occasional subject (a visit to the Paris Exposition in "The Happy Day"; a "bedeviled" automobile in "A Guest in Sodom"). Yet her strongest and most characteristic stories, those that continue to compel us today, return time and again to her several basic themes. Although these issues parallel the broad outlines of some circumstances of her personal life, they are more remarkable for the firm hold they exerted on the author's imagination throughout her career. Clearly, Freeman discovered in them fertile sources for her art: striking deeply at well-forged patterns of belief, self-concept, and custom, they are calculated to engender intense interpersonal conflict as well as to disclose characters' psychological states, both hallmarks of Freeman's best fiction.

Besides the personal, several external factors help account for the type of fiction Freeman was producing in the last decades of the nineteenth century. It has long been conventional to place her writing in the local-color, or regional, period of American literature, a movement at the height of its popular appeal concurrent with her earliest writings. As is true of most labels, that of local color/regionalism is woefully imprecise. A kind of catchall category for fiction that emphasizes the shaping influence of place on character and theme, it has sometimes led to the inappropriate grouping of distinctly different authors, among them Bret

Harte, Sarah Orne Jewett, Mary Murfree, Grace King, Edward Eggleston, Kate Chopin, and Hamlin Garland. Since the definition of local color/regionalism can also carry pejorative connotations (some consider it a minor offshoot of realism that consists of sentimentalized, exaggerated sketches of local types and folkways), the term has, moreover, contributed at times to the devaluation of these writers' works. Even more detrimental may be some critics' lingering penchant to refer to these and other such writers as "transitional" figures in American literature, of interest only because their fiction bridges a gap between that of better known, more significant authors or movements. In fact, all authors—Freeman and her contemporaries included—are transitional only in that their work was influenced by that of earlier artists and that they themselves exert influence on succeeding generations of writers.

It is true that Freeman's apparent burst into fame in the 1880s was a product of the times, one that waved the standard of a "new realism" in fiction. But the problem then as now is one of definition. Just what constitutes realistic fiction? Experiments in a type of "clinical realism" in European fiction, such as works by Emile Zola, were intriguing but unworkable. William Dean Howells, despite his stance as one of realism's most ardent advocates, could pose only vague, conflicting definitions: "let fiction cease to lie about life," he exhorted, but only life's pleasant, or "smiling," aspects were appropriate as subject matter.[9] Howells's praise of Freeman's first collection, *A Humble Romance*, in the September 1887 "Editor's Study" column of *Harper's Monthly* was a triumph for the young author; no endorsement carried more weight at the time. Presumably, her earliest stories were fulfilling his agenda for American literature: they were dedicated, he wrote, to "the face of common humanity," were imbued with "a just and true respect for the virtues" of the lives they described, and exhibited a fresh "directness and simplicity" of style.[10]

By the release of her second volume, *A New England Nun*, however, Howells was not so sure. Mary Wilkins seemed at times to be producing a rather disconcerting admixture of realism and romance:

> We have a lurking fear at moments that Miss Wilkins would like to write entirely romantic stories about these honest people of hers; but her own love of truth and her perfect knowledge of such life as theirs forbid her actually to do this. There is apparently a conflict of purposes in her sketches which gives her art an undecided effect, or a divided effect, as in certain of them where we make the acquaintance of her

characters in their village of little houses, and lose it in the No Man's
Land of exaggerated action and conventional emotion. . . . It may be
that we shall always have to content ourselves with now a story of the
real and unreal mixed, and now one of unmixed reality, such as Miss
Wilkins alone can give us.[11]

Howells's assumption that Freeman was aiming at stories of "unmixed
reality" and half the time missing the mark reveals more about his own
agenda than about his understanding of the author's work. Nevertheless,
he succeeds in capturing here the essence of Freeman's sensibility: the
constant interplay of realism, romance, and sentiment that makes her fiction, along with that of other writers of the era, difficult to categorize.
Sarah Orne Jewett came the closest to defining what she, Freeman, and
others were producing in formulating her theory of "imaginative realism":
fiction grounded in the factual but suggestive, however vaguely, of a transcendent or spiritual realm beyond that of the senses. "It is," Jewett
wrote to a friend in 1897, "those unwritable things that the story holds in
its heart, if it has any, that make the true soul of it."[12] Though Freeman
advanced no theories of her own and in fact disliked speculating about her
art, she sometimes acknowledged her "strong inclination" for romance
and mysticism (Kendrick, 97). Her fiction blends hallmarks of realism—
ordinary characters in true-to-life settings, a dramatic revealing of plot
with detached, unobtrusive narration, an emphasis on social critique—
with the romancer's sense of "a certain latitude" in probing the ineffable
"truth of the human heart," whether in the use of imaginative events or
by symbolically evoking a transcendent world.[13] "A Symphony in Lavender" (1883), in which a woman has a mysterious, prophetic dream that
forever determines her course in life, is but one early example. Though
inclined toward romance, Freeman purposely avoided this strain in the
majority of her early stories, concerned that it would not sell. After the
success of her first two collections, however, she felt more at ease composing stories with strongly mystical or symbolic themes.

    In her infrequent statements about her writing, Freeman generally
echoed the realist's language of the literary era, claiming that she was
intent on "telling the truth" in her fiction. She told Hamlin Garland, for
example, that it was her only definite aim (Kendrick, 83). Yet she also
denied conscious allegiance to the realist school, wryly stating in a 1890
interview, "I didn't even know that I'm a realist until they wrote and
told me."[14] Around the same time, she acknowledged that "one can't
always tell what *true* is," and years later in a 1917 *Saturday Evening Post*

interview she averred that "sometimes incessant truth gets on one's nerves."[15] In the same interview, she stated that she lied in portraying the rebellion of Sarah Penn, the long-suffering wife whose husband refuses to build her a new house in "The Revolt of 'Mother.' " Though partly the petulance of an author justifiably weary of those who had been "insisting that The Revolt of Mother is my one and only work" for nearly 30 years, Freeman's apparent repudiation of one of her finest and most popular stories often poses a problem for her critics ("Who's Who," 75). But it need not do so. Freeman may very well have fibbed in this tale, exaggerating, as she implies, Mother's nerve in her rebellion or even her desire to revolt at all. By the standards of strict realism, Freeman maintains, the work is not true—but then, presumably, neither is much of her writing, since a woman's (or a man's) sudden revolt after years of patient endurance is one of her most frequent themes.[16]

Freeman's denial of the truth of "The Revolt of 'Mother' " points to her unwillingness to be confined to realist standards. Indeed, she repeatedly urged young writers not to imitate others but to "make [their] own patterns and found [their] own school."[17] The "truth" she was after was greater and more multifaceted than that acknowledged by many of the realists. Like some contemporary impressionists, such as Henry James, she believed that truth was myriad, consisting of not only the physical but the emotional, psychological, spiritual, mystical, and imaginative realms. Her work constantly moves from the concrete toward the expression of these more subtle domains. Whereas Howells and other critics have sometimes found Freeman's combined use of realism and romance disconcerting, others have rightly observed that this marriage of styles is a hallmark of her fiction and, when skillfully executed, her unique strength. Calling her an "idealist in masquerade," Charles Miner Thompson, an early critic, notes that "although she is ranked in the popular judgment as a realist, there is in her work the purest vein of romance and ideality, and even a certain touch of mysticism and allegory."[18] Another critic helps put these differing but not necessarily competing strands into proper relation: "Miss Wilkins wrote local color stories of an inner feeling at once romantic, naturalistic, and symbolic and of a surface texture realistic and impressionistic. And such, in so far as these terms are meaningful, was her way of voicing her truth, her own intensely personal interpretation of life and character in the New England village" (Foster, 91).

Besides elements of realism and romance, Freeman's fiction also employs features of the sentimental/domestic fiction still popular during the second half of the nineteenth century. As noted, courtship situations, marriages, and family relationships constitute her primary subject matter: they are the stuff of the ordinary women's lives she portrays. Like other realists, Freeman often uses these typical components of sentimental fiction for antisentimental purposes; that is, she twists them ironically to expose the falsity of sentimental conclusions. Rather than reward a long-suffering heroine with the perfect mate, for example, Freeman often focuses her stories on the plight of the deserving but rejected woman, the woman who has had no opportunity to marry at all, or the woman who has opted to remain single. Rather than extol the spiritual value of womanly self-sacrifice, her tales frequently explore the potential harm to others, the unnecessary loss, and even the death that may result from excessive self-abnegation ("A Taste of Honey," "A Modern Dragon," "The Witch's Daughter," "The Selfishness of Amelia Lamkin").

It is important to realize, however, that although many of Freeman's stories provide devastating critiques of sentimental ideology, others paradoxically uphold its tenets. In fact, a portion of her canon—her later work in particular—has been summarily dismissed as worthless by critics who are dismayed at the "happy ever after" weddings that conclude otherwise realistic narratives or are repelled when extreme self-sacrifice is praised or children and motherhood glorified. Though largely responsible for the recovery of Freeman's work over the last few decades, feminist critics have often failed as dismally as such earlier critics as Edward Foster and Perry Westbrook in dealing with Freeman's blatantly sentimental strain. "I found myself longing to rewrite beginnings and reshape endings of her stories or to manipulate details to fit my notion of a feminist model," one critic confessed.[19] Current work in revisionist criticism is encouraging in its effort to assess the writer's complex and varied use of the traditions available to her without imposing rigid or politically determined standards on them. Stuart Bradley Shaw, for example, has observed how such magazines as *Harper's Bazar*, in a drive to steer a conservative middle course, published articles that conveyed a host of conflicting messages about the emergence of the "new" versus the "true" woman in the late nineteenth and early twentieth centuries. Shaw concludes that the "sentiment" in Freeman's fiction that so disappointed Howells "can be read as successful contributions to the popular marketplace of women's fiction produced by a writer familiar with its conventions. . . . Freeman was a conscious and conscientious manipulator of the residual cultural and literary power of the sentimental tradition, rather than merely its victim."[20] Although the stories that appear to support sentimental ideology may not, in general, attract us today as they did their original readers, they are important to our understanding of Freeman as a skilled professional who knew her audience and who tailored her work accordingly. Moreover, they serve to demarcate the range of Freeman's thinking on a subject as vital and controversial as women's changing roles in society. Though some readers are frustrated by Freeman's apparent ambivalence on this issue, she actually achieves a provocative open endedness in her body of short fiction: refusing to prescribe or generalize about what course all women should adopt, she judges each of the myriad situations and characters she creates on an individual basis. Thus a woman's submission to a man, her sacrifices for her family, or the wedding bells heard at the end of the tale may be entirely appropriate to the needs of the individual involved or to the exigencies of the particular set of circumstances in which she is enmeshed.

Though "imaginative realism" may come closest to an apt descriptor of Freeman's work, we can also reclaim the term local color/regionalism if it is carefully refined. In recent years a tradition of women's writing in post–Civil War New England has been identified. Though produced by authors of widely differing skills and sensibilities, this body of literature exhibits both internal unity and a universality of theme that moves it far beyond mere superficial description of localized settings and indigenous characters.[21] Josephine Donovan has traced its lineage back to its British roots in the antiromantic, critical realist tendencies of such writers as Charlotte Lennox and Maria Edgeworth; there is no need to summarize her findings here.[22] It is important to state, however, that such artists as Harriet Beecher Stowe, Alice Brown, Elizabeth Stuart Phelps, Celia Thaxter, Rose Terry Cooke, and Sarah Orne Jewett were already established in this tradition by the time Freeman began sending out her first short stories. A number of these writers met frequently, corresponded, and read and criticized each other's works. All were linked as contributors to *Atlantic Monthly* or to the several *Harper's* publications, connections that amounted to a type of close family relationship in that era.

Though Freeman was never as intimately involved in this group as some, her writing shows the unmistakable influence of these New England women writers. Despite employing varying degrees of realist, romantic, and sentimental ideology in their fiction, these regionalists consistently explored the effects of gender, religion, and economics on New England women's lives. Their stories and novels scrutinize the impact of profound ideological and social changes that were occurring in the region even as they were writing. Post–Civil War New England was, indeed, in great flux as traditional ways of life began to be supplanted by newer forms. The area experienced widespread recession because of the war; able-bodied men who had survived the conflict left women, children, and the elderly behind on the farms and in the villages as they set out in search of brighter prospects elsewhere. The strong core of Calvinist belief had long been disintegrating, though its surface forms, most notably the church and its minister, remained influential forces in village life. In scholarly circles as well as in popular media, the "woman question" was earnestly debated; educated or not, women everywhere were aware that the older religious and cultural injunction that women be pious, pure, and submissive angels of the hearth was eroding before the demands of a new generation of women seeking independence, suffrage, and involvement in the wider arenas of political, business, and intellectual life. Both immersed in and keen observers of these ideological shifts, the New England women regionalists found the sources of conflict they needed for their fiction right at home.

Young Mary Wilkins had access to and followed closely the literary trends of her day. A fashionable spa, Brattleboro in the 1870s and 1880s was cosmopolitan, boasting a fine school system, an orchestra, and several libraries, book clubs, newspapers, and periodicals. The local newspaper, the *Vermont Phoenix*, regularly published recent fiction from *Harper's* and the *Atlantic*. With her parents, Mary attended lectures on literature and readings by well-known authors at the popular Brattleboro Lyceum. A bookstore adjoined her father's dry-goods shop in the center of town; she often stopped there on her way home from school. She read broadly, relishing equally the moral realism of Tolstoy, the romance of Scott, and the gothicism of Emily Brontë and Poe. She admired Dickens to the point of imitating his work in one of her first attempts at writing an adult short story. Several of her later tales, such as "Eglantina," "Evelina's Garden," "The Slip of the Leash," and "The Three Old Sisters and the Old Beau," echo those of Hawthorne, although Freeman once stated that she did not care for him (Kendrick, 385). She enjoyed Emerson and in mid-career penned a series of nature stories illustrating certain tenets of transcendental philosophy.

Moreover, we can assume that as Freeman commenced her career she perused with interest the work of the New England women writers who had published before her. Her early stories show the influence of Rose Terry Cooke and Sarah Orne Jewett in particular, both of whom were appearing in leading magazines when Freeman began writing adult fiction. Cooke's stories, such as "Mrs. Flint's Married Experience" (*Harper's*, 1880) and "Freedom Wheeler's Controversy With Providence" (*Atlantic*, 1877), often concern a woman's ordeal in marriage after her romantic illusion has been shattered by harsh reality. In Cooke's world, spinsters who finally marry soon long to return once more to the peace and independence of their single life. Cooke harshly indicts Calvinism for perpetuating women's oppression and effecting men's distortion into tyrants or stubborn brutes. Though Freeman's vision was rarely as dark as Cooke's, she no doubt found in the older author's work both the sanction and the inspiration for her own exploration of the intersection between formalized religion and women's roles. The two writers never knew each other well, but their careers and personal lives would prove to parallel each other to a remarkable degree. The stories Jewett was publishing in the late 1870s and early 1880s often treat the lives of single, sometimes elderly women who strive to maintain their independence despite opposition from the community. Among these are "A Lost Lover" (*Atlantic*, 1878), "A Bit of Shore Life" (*Atlantic*, 1879), and "Miss Becky's Pilgrimage" (*Independent*, 1881). As with Freeman's fiction, William Dean Howells was not always pleased with what Jewett produced: he rejected "Lady Ferry" (1879) and "A White Heron" (1886) for inclusion in the *Atlantic*, for example, because they were too romantic. Significantly, Freeman would later tell Jewett that she had never read a story that appealed to her more than "A White Heron" (Kendrick, 97).

Despite her claim to the contrary, then, Freeman's writing, like that of any author, was formed in part by a number of converging factors. Her life experiences as well as the artistic, social, and cultural temper of the times worked together to influence both her subject matter and her style; it is her unique combination of these factors that results in the excellence of her stories. Judging her the less important writer, however, critics have generally ignored the substantial influence Freeman's stories exerted on other major writers of her era. It is important to keep in mind just how phenomenally popular she was. Though she reached the height of her success in the early part of the 1890s, she continued to be a key figure on the American and British literary scenes for years to come. "Something like a craze" for her fiction endured up to World War I.[23] A skilled businesswoman, she negotiated payments and royalty terms carefully, and her stories at the peak of her popularity commanded the exorbitant price of $500 dollars each. She was often solicited for public lectures or readings, invitations she usually turned down, pleading overwork or ill health. Reporters flocked to her home for glimpses of the "New England nun" they expected to find, and newspapers monitored her personal activities closely, especially the several postponements of her marriage to Charles Manning Freeman, which took place finally in 1902.

It is safe to conclude that any established or emerging writer of the day knew of Freeman's work, at the very least by its reputation. Moreover, evidence suggests that a number of Freeman's contemporaries studied that work carefully and sought to imitate it. Though, as noted, Freeman no doubt learned from Jewett in her early career, the tide soon turned, and Jewett sometimes modeled stories on those first published by Freeman. Kate Chopin considered Freeman a "great genius"; her stories evince her thorough knowledge of both Freeman and Jewett.[24] Other writers whose work Freeman influenced to some degree include Henry James, Edwin Arlington Robinson, Edith Wharton, Robert Frost, Hamlin Garland, Willa Cather, and Sherwood Anderson.[25]

Freeman's Aesthetic: "Faithful, Hopeful, and Independent Work"

As discussed previously, Freeman claimed that her goal in writing fiction was telling the truth, though truth could be multifaceted and involve more than simple verisimilitude of setting and character. Above all, Freeman emphasized the importance of truth to the self, or artistic integrity. Endowed with a spark of talent, a young writer need only supply herself with the requisite materials—pens and ink, postage stamps, patience—and commence to write about "those subjects which she knows thoroughly, and concerning which she trusts her own convictions" ("Good Wits," 29). She should write "in her own way," both independently and courageously. Since "an editor is only human" and is usually not a creative writer, he or she may very well mistakenly underrate or overrate a story.[26] A young writer will do well, then, to "learn to be [her] own mentor" ("Girl," 272). After studying the needs of various magazines, she should send her work to the most likely publisher; if rejected, she should not become discouraged but should try again elsewhere, for "it is not conceited nor egotistical to believe in the merit of one's work" (272). And if she does achieve success, she should attribute it to nothing but persistence and hard work, her "own unaided efforts" ("Good Wits," 29).

The Yankee practicality that marks Freeman's comments about her writing is refreshing even as it is revealing. Not given to self-analysis and impatient with those like Hamlin Garland and Fred Lewis Pattee who tried at times to second-guess her motives and inspirations, she quickly cut through any mystification about the artistic process. "I sat down and wrote my little stories about the types I knew, they sold. That is really all. Very simple," she told Pattee brusquely toward the end of her career, refusing to elaborate much further despite his extended questioning.[27] Nevertheless, we can garner some details about her aesthetic from the seven prefaces and nonfiction essays she published during her lifetime as well as from portions of her letters. All of these pieces can be found in part 2, "The Writer."

Freeman distinguished between "sequential" writers—those whose work emerges organically, taking shape during the writing process—and authors who must have a "full-fledged plot and plan of action" even before picking up the pen: she judged herself to be of the former variety ("Girl," 272). Indeed, her letters reveal that tendency: speaking to one of her editors in 1897 of a holiday tale she had just begun, for example, she stated that "[it] is a story of three way-farers. I am not quite sure, myself, as to wither they will fare, except into some sort of a Christmas situation. I am sorry not to give you anything more definite, but I never know much about a story, myself, at this stage, and if I try to force the knowledge, and abide by it, I fear I shall spoil it all" (Kendrick, 195). She often sat down at her desk with no more than the germ of an idea gleaned from bits of family lore, village gossip, or her own observations of the people and places she encountered on her frequent visits, walks, and outings. Nothing escaped her: "I suppose it seems to you as it does to me that everything you have heard, seen, or done, since you opened your eyes on the world, is coming back to you sooner or later, to go into stories," she wrote to Jewett in 1889 (Kendrick, 99). Sympathy for a chained dog she saw at an elderly neighbor's birthday party provided the impetus for "A New England Nun," for example, and a family story about a lover's quarrel resulting in an unfinished house forms the central conflict for the novel *Pembroke*. Certain fancies, such as that of the "forlorn little girl" that "had been in my head a matter of a dozen years," haunted her until she exorcised them by writing them into stories (Kendrick, 97). Thus commencing her writing with only slight impressions and ideas, she allowed them "to grow and formulate and expand into a full garden" as she wrote ("Girl," 272). Since she conceived of her writing primarily as a task to be accomplished ("it is never from anything but a sense of duty that I commence to write"), the virtue she found the most necessary was discipline (Kendrick, 58).

Therefore, she strove to maintain a strict working schedule throughout her career and kept to her room daily until she had written at least 1,200 words, at times much more.

Ascribing to the realist's goal of avoiding an intrusive or moralizing narrator, Freeman considered it imperative that a writer "leave herself out of the whole proposition. Her own emotions and personal experiences are intensely interesting to her and a doting few, but the world at large cares nothing whatever for them. They are looking for the work and not especially for the worker" ("Girl," 272). In an essay on *Wuthering Heights* that, like Melville's "Mosses from an Old Manse," betrays as much about herself as a writer as it does about her subject, she praises Emily Brontë in particular for her objective narrative stance. Tellingly, she conceives of the technique in gendered terms, equating it with the author's boldly "masculine" portrayal of reality:

> *Wuthering Heights* from first to last is an unflinching masterpiece. There is evident no quiver of feminine nerves in the mind or hand. The utter fearlessness of the witness of the truth is upon [Emily Brontë]. She hedges at nothing. . . . The personality of the author is entirely in the background. . . . She wrote about [the characters], that was all. She was not in the least responsible for their wild rebellion and revolt against the existing order of things. . . . *Wuthering Heights* gives the impression of impersonality on the part of the author, if ever a book did. It is far different in that respect from Charlotte Brontë's work. There is the nervous throb of a woman's heart through *Jane Eyre* and *Shirley*, but in *Wuthering Heights*, if the throb be there we do not feel it.[28]

For the most part, Freeman adhered to her own standard. Especially in her early stories, she makes effective use of a dramatic style in which events unfold primarily through dialogue. Necessary background information and summary is given briefly by a narrator possessing, typically, only limited omniscience; that is, the narrator knows certain thoughts of some characters but is not privy to the whole truth. Overt moralizing is absent; still, we are made aware, by well-chosen words or phrases, of the bent of the narrator's sympathies. Freeman usually succeeds, therefore, in "staying out" of her fiction: one feels an empathetic presence in her stories, but the author herself remains elusive. This accounts, perhaps, for some of her original readers' seemingly frenetic desire to search out and disclose the "real" Mary Wilkins Freeman.

Freeman further commends Brontë for her uncompromising depiction of "offensive, even repulsive" characters and situations: "she handles brutality and coarseness as another woman would handle a painted fan" ("Brontë," 88). But though such portrayals give *Wuthering Heights* unquestionable power, they fall short, to Freeman, of the ideal. Some element of redeeming light in the darkness is missing; some aspect of ineffable serenity in the resolution is lacking that might have afforded the work a more universal appeal. "Had [Brontë] lived longer," Freeman speculates, "she might have become equally acquainted with the truth and power of grace; she might have widened her audience; she might have attracted, instead of repelled" (89). Although she was fascinated with the novel's "savageness," Freeman's own ethic, derived, as she admitted, from her inexorable New England conscience, required a certain degree of moral restraint. Though fiction should be committed to telling the truth, "even the truth must be held back unless it is of a nature to benefit and not poison" ("Girl," 272). Freeman's moral agenda for literature here echoes, of course, that of Howells and other realists. An ardent patriot, moreover, she reiterates in the same article Howells's appeal for a national literature, one that expresses the positive aspects of the United States and thus enhances its world reputation. Such an ethic accounts, in part, for Freeman's frequent comic endings. As noted, a significant number of stories and novels end with a marriage. *Pembroke* (1894), a kind of peculiarly American *Wuthering Heights* in its frank yet restrained depiction of passion, sexuality, and physical and emotional cruelty, is resolved by not one but four marriages. Many other stories tie up ends in ways that signal if not material triumph, then at the very least the achievement of a kind of transcendent peace or satisfaction— no doubt the "grace" of Freeman's idealism.

Freeman insisted on clarity in writing. She enjoined budding authors to "write even about difficult themes in such a way that a child can understand" ("Girl," 272). One hears in this statement her editors' advice from her apprentice years as a children's author. When she began writing stories for adults, Freeman struggled with the tendency to overwrite, to "mention everything" in order to ensure that she had conveyed her point (Kendrick, 61). Mary Louise Booth's counsel in these formative years seems to have been invaluable. Under the editor's tutelage, Freeman learned to simplify her sentence structure and add more visual detail. She also mastered other elements of effective magazine fiction: for example, opening with a provocative "hook," moving the plot rapidly to its dramatic climax, building in a surprise or ironic reversal, and concluding on a satisfactory note. Importantly, she learned to do all this in just a few pages, keeping her stories short and focused. Later in her career, Freeman deviated from this style in some of her longer stories that adopt the stilted diction and full-blown style of romance; these are, as a group, less successful than her more concise tales.

Part of the burgeoning mass-media market, one "actively creat[ing] both [its] product and audience through aggressive managerial and marketing techniques," Freeman was among the first of the American female authors to conceive of her art in essentially professional terms, as both a profitable and personally rewarding career.[29] Forced by necessity in her early years to produce stories that would sell, Freeman exhibited in the remainder of her career an awareness of the continual balance needed between the supply and demand of the marketplace, between the writing and selling of her wares. Many of her stories were commissioned and hence expressly written to meet a particular magazine's stipulations. Though seemingly at odds with her statements calling for artistic integrity and independence, she apparently found little contradiction in producing hackwork to support herself while simultaneously working on the fiction she wanted to write. She expressed only occasional misgivings about such commissioned writing. Once, for example, she confided to Booth that she had concluded a story for a religious magazine with the requisite "neat allusion to church" and that "[she] wouldn't write these [stories] if [she] did not like the money" (Kendrick, 66). But she did like the money, and her early need of it set a pattern for the rest of her career. Even when quite wealthy (her estate amounted to an astonishing $111,807 at her death in 1930), she never ceased to write on demand, haggle over prices and royalties, and work long hours in order to earn as much as possible. It did not matter to Freeman, finally, *why* an author wrote as long as the work, once undertaken, was conscientiously and steadily performed. "In reality," she stated, "a man may write something which will live for the sake of something rather ignoble, and a woman may write something for money with which to buy a French hat. I personally do not believe it matters why the must, as long as it is must" ("Girl," 272).

Two Characteristic Stories

So far, we have examined at some length Freeman's influences and aesthetic and have noted some of her typical themes and techniques. In the rest of part 1, we will see how these elements apply to the stories in each of the three stages of the author's career. Because Freeman's canon of short fiction is large and diverse, however, it is appropriate to conclude this section with detailed analyses of two highly characteristic stories. I have purposely chosen two lesser-known pieces here: "An Object of Love" (1885) was one of Freeman's earliest tales, and "Juliza" (1892) appeared in the second phase of the author's career. I classify both as "village" tales, an admittedly imprecise rubric that I have adopted merely to distinguish this particular type of story from others Freeman penned, such as ghost, mystery, historic, and symbolic stories.[30]

"An Object of Love"

"An Object of Love" was commissioned by *Harper's Bazar* for the Valentine's Day 1885 issue, and Freeman complied with a "love" story that deliberately and delightfully subverts the hackneyed romantic sentiments that the editors of the magazine probably expected. Freeman told Booth that the germ of the story was inspired by "a striped and white cat" she had once owned who was "extravagantly fond of squash" (Kendrick, 61). Sarah Orne Jewett thought the work was "exquisite," a perfect model of short fiction.[31]

Like many Freeman stories, the plot of "An Object of Love" is slender and provides enough scaffolding only for Freeman's true interest, probing the inner self of the protagonist, Ann Millet. One of Freeman's many elderly and poor village women living a monotonous life alone in a white clapboard house, Ann one day loses her beloved cat Willy; at the conclusion of the story, Willy is discovered in the cellar, where Ann to her chagrin has inadvertently locked him. The story's main focus is what happens to Ann emotionally and spiritually during the time Willy is missing. Narrated with a skillful mixture of ironic detachment and empathy, Ann's crisis over her lost pet is at once endearingly comic and profoundly serious. As the magnitude of the crisis is revealed, we learn much about Ann Millet; Willy's absence, we discover, is only the tip of the iceberg, the catalyst for the crystallization of many years of repressed loneliness and resentment.

Willy is gone, and Ann rebels. Her rebellion consists of several small acts but has, as do the actions of many Freeman characters, one underlying target: God, or more properly, a religious doctrine that has molded Ann's thinking about God in such a way as to provide her with the means of revolt she believes appropriate to the situation. Having all her life attended church services with the utmost regularity, a predictable routine that extends even to her sitting in precisely the same place and greeting the minister in precisely the same manner week after week,

Ann suddenly does not show up to meeting after Willy is missing. Midway through the story, the laconic narrator relates no more than "The next Sunday Ann was not out at church," and we understand directly the extremity of the woman's situation, her fierce sense of injustice, and the convergence of her spiritual state with the cat's disappearance.[32] We have been forewarned, for Ann has already been revealed to us as a woman who conforms outwardly to religious practices but inwardly cannot make sense of religion's tenets; they do not touch her heart. Full of suppressed inner conflict, she distances herself from her true feelings in an attempt to do what she ascertains is her duty; her only prayer is that she'd "orter be thankful," "orter hev more patience," and "never orter complain" (*HR*, 266, 267, 268). Calvinism has given Ann the only concept of God she knows, he of the covenant who has promised to reward those who strictly adhere to his commandments. Ann's dilemma, then, is clear: no one has been more careful to keep the letter of the law than she, yet God has seemingly failed to uphold his end of the bargain. He has left her alone in the world and taken away, as a final insult, her "object of love," the only being Ann cherishes and that helps her endure her isolation during the long winter. "I mean jest what I say," she angrily informs her neighbor Mrs. Stone; "I ain't never goin' to meetin' agin. Folks go to meetin' to thank the Lord for blessin's, I s'pose. I've lost mine, an' I ain't goin' " (273). Moreover, the narrator informs us, we are to understand that this rebellion, however humorous it may appear on the surface, is no laughing matter: "Ann Millet, in spite of all excuses that could be made for her, was for the time a wicked, rebellious old woman. And she was as truly so as if this petty occasion for it had been a graver one in other people's estimation" (276).

No one comprehends the nature and magnitude of Ann's spiritual upheaval. To Mrs. Stone, she borders dangerously on heresy. "Why, Ann Millet," the neighbor scolds, "it's downright sinful fur you to feel so. Of course you set a good deal by Willy; but it ain't as ef he was a human creature. . . . I don't understand any human bein' with an immortal *soul* a-settin' so much by a *cat*. . . . I thought the Lord would be a comfort to you" (273–74). But the Lord in his distant heaven is not a comfort to Ann. "I'm *here*, an' I ain't *thar;* an' I've got hands, an' I want somethin' I kin touch," she retorts fiercely (274). As often in her fiction, Freeman employs here the "normal" village woman, the conventionally religious and married Mrs. Stone (whose name indicates her density and insensitivity), as Ann's foil. In contrast to Mrs. Stone's complacency, Ann's sudden revolt, the veritable explosion of that which has long been simmering just beneath the surface, is all the more heavily underscored.

At a loss as to how to deal with Ann, Mrs. Stone summons the minister, Mr. Beal, but as is true with all of Freeman's clergymen who arrive to discipline wayward women, "it was a case entirely outside his experience, and he did not know how to deal with it" (277). He is, after all, a man of no particular talents or sensitivities, only a "dull, middle-aged preacher in a dull country town" (271). The religion he professes fails him; fearing to say the wrong thing, he says nothing at all and quickly takes his leave.

The story's ironic conclusion is cleverly foreshadowed. When visiting Ann, both Mrs. Stone and Mr. Beal imagine they hear a cat's faint meow. Ann is hard of hearing, however—a condition she conveniently uses to her advantage when she does not wish to respond to Mrs. Stone—and thus is not aware that Willy has been trapped in the basement all the time. Only when she chances to open the cellar door a week later does she discover his whereabouts. As the cat streaks by her, a "white, awed look" comes over her face, and she initially seems stricken with remorse. "Thar he was all the time," she mourns, "jest whar I put him; an' me a-blamin' of the Lord, an' puttin' of it on him. I've been an awful wicked woman" (278). But though it appears that the story might turn into a pious tale of repentance at this juncture, it does not do so. For Ann's expression of guilt, like her prior "thanksgiving" for blessings received, is not heartfelt. As such, Freeman maintains Ann's integrity and deepens our interest in this passionate and complicated but repressed individual. Despite the crisis's happy outcome, Ann once again evokes mere duty in this scene rather than venting her true emotions: "I hadn't orter hev anythin'," she mutters to herself; "I'd orter offer up Willy" (278). Freeman thus rewrites the typical sentimental story of the heroine's conversion: despite the depth of Ann's trauma, her religion remains superficial; she experiences no life-changing spiritual alteration, and the reader feels no corresponding pious uplift.

But Ann does change in one way as a result of Willy's disappearance, and here is where the story moves decidedly beyond the mere comic or pathetic. In a masterful ending wrought by calculated understatement—a characteristic of Freeman's best stories—Ann returns to church after Willy is found but, contrary to her habit, does not go up after the service to greet Mr. Beal. Instead, for the first time, he is forced to come down from his pulpit to seek *her* out. Probably assuming that his visit has been instrumental in her return, he greets her effusively. But in a razor-sharp retort, which as the story's last line gives the effect of stunning and silencing the man, Ann thoroughly disillusions him of that fancy:

> "I am rejoiced to see you out, Miss Millet," said the minister, shaking her hand.
> "Yes. I thought I'd come out to-night."
> "I am so happy to see you are feeling better."
> "The cat has come back," said Ann. (279)

In Ann's final remark can be seen the full extent of her bargaining relationship with God: God has returned the cat, justice has been restored, and she will therefore resume his worship—for now. The last line of this open ending also raises serious questions about the nature of God's providence and about religion's injunction to submit meekly in all matters. Perhaps most importantly, however, Ann's statement poses a powerful challenge, even a threat, to both God and the minister in its implication that she will attend church only as long as Willy remains with her. The tables have turned, albeit subtly: Ann has seized control of the situation, and the minister has already begun to defer to her. This "solemn, spiritual-looking old woman," to all appearances a godly pillar of the church, is in reality impenitent and defiant (270). To Ann, the issue is simple and unequivocal: no cat, no church.

Does the narrator approve of Ann Millet's rebellious spirit? Of limited omniscience, the narrator provides us with just enough information to allow us to sympathize with but not fully comprehend Ann's plight. We are not sure, for instance, why she adheres so rigidly to the outward forms of a religion in which she does not truly believe, but we can certainly guess. Since she has no family, the church and its activities are a social lifeline for Ann, who otherwise would be completely separated from her fellow villagers. Because she is unmarried, elderly, and alone, she is already deemed odd and "uncanny" by others who "complained of feeling nervous when Ann looked at them" (267). In short, she is not far from being branded a witch, the usual fate of isolated or outcast women in Freeman's world. With little money, no kin, and nowhere else to go, she has to fit into the community on some level; her very survival depends on it. The extreme disparity between Ann Millet's inner and outer selves is typical of many Freeman women who find conforming to the village norm necessary to some degree yet whose deepest self rejects and even scorns that norm.

Nevertheless, although the story indicts the villagers' moribund religion and intolerant attitudes, it also makes clear that Ann's conformity and superficiality in spiritual matters stems in good measure from her own narrow personality. We applaud the gumption she displays in rebelling, but she is not necessarily a character to be admired and certainly does not represent a feminist ideal of strength and independence. For having retired from her trade of dressmaking, Ann has simply "stopped just where she was"; she is, in short, one of Freeman's many New England characters who have become set in their ways through stubborn willfulness or mere lack of imagination (271). Ann's outdated clothing provides an effective metaphor for her stunted spirituality: having "never gone a step further in fashions" since the day she laid aside dressmaking, she "treated her old patterns as conservatively as she did her Bible" (270–71). The ironic pairing of Ann's fashion with her Christianity in this line sums up the story's exploration of inner and outer forms of piety, of religion's substance versus its style. Moreover, Ann's narrow personality, her habit of "look[ing] alike at everything," puts into perspective both the unwontedness and the magnitude of her rebellion at Willy's disappearance; clearly, she has long suppressed the outrage that now so forcibly erupts (267). Still, her revolt remains a limited one: for all practical purposes, at the story's conclusion she is back where she started, at odds with her deepest self in practicing a religion that apparently has little or nothing to offer her. Freeman's analysis of Ann Millet is complex, admitting no easy solutions. The contradictions inherent in her character—her long submission and her sudden rebellion, her clinging to religion and her heresy, her seeming self-reliance yet childlike dependence on her pet—render Ann, finally, not a stereotype but a fully realized human being in all the mystery of that creature's ingrained patterns of thought and behavior.

"An Object of Love" is one of Freeman's many tragicomedies, balancing moments of extreme pathos—Ann's breaking into sobs in front of Mrs. Stone, her frantic calling for Willy in the dark and cold night—with moments of pure comedy, such as when sympathetic neighbor children shower Ann with stray cats, hoping to compensate for her loss. The emphasis on Ann's inordinate appetite is humorous as well, especially when coupled with the odd eating habits of Willy, the cat who relishes squash. Her recent harvest of squash, in fact, occasions a further comical moment when Ann, who has labored to bring the heavy pile into the kitchen, hurls it outside again as part of her revolt; it is this wantonness with God's bounty that most horrifies Mrs. Stone.

Besides the humorous touches, other elements of the tale mark it as typical of Freeman. Though not as pronounced as in other stories, the use of natural imagery in "An Object of Love" is effective and lends us additional insight into Ann's dilemma. Freeman generally uses nature to mirror her characters' psychological states, as she does here. The story's setting in a bleak November landscape with the threat of frost in the air reflects Ann's colorless existence. The sudden, glorious display of northern lights in the sky on the first night she searches for Willy points to the intensity of her emotional upheaval even as it reinforces the sense of her cosmic and spiritual isolation. She is, after all, only a "little thin, shivering old woman standing out-doors, all alone . . . in the great universe in which she herself was so small" (272). In both theme and style, "An Object of Love" is a characteristic Freeman story, consisting of many building blocks the author would continue to employ in her short fiction.

"Juliza"

Although her oeuvre presents a wide panorama of female characters, Freeman most often focuses on the elderly or the very young. "Juliza" is typical of her many stories concerning young women who live at home and have reached marriageable age. To Freeman, the situation is an uneasy one: clashes occur frequently between the daughter and a parent, usually the mother, over differing values and expectations. Though the mother may embrace romantic ideals and the daughter decidedly more modern or practical views, some Freeman stories reverse this pattern, and the girl awaits a knight-errant while the mother simply tries to wed her daughter to any man who will support her. Friction also arises between the young woman and her suitor because they have little opportunity for physical contact and even less for communication. Fueling such tension is the prevailing material and social compulsion in the Freeman village for women to marry. Women who stay single by either choice or circumstance risk poverty and, as in "An Object of Love," isolation and ostracism. Yet there were simply not enough men left in post–Civil War New England villages to go around. The expectation that all young women marry, the consequences of not doing so, the limited number of men available, and the family conflict that arose from such situations supplied Freeman with a rich vein of material as she explored women's attitudes and responses toward the looming prospect of marriage.

"Juliza" is structured around a series of confrontations between the title character, her supposed fiancé, Frank Williams, and her mother, Mrs. Peck. The story opens with a social affair held in the church vestry, a sewing circle of older women who at dusk rearrange their chairs to accommodate the town's youth for supper and entertainment. Though the same age as the young people present, Juliza commands respect the moment she enters the room: heavyset, calm, and mature, she looks and acts much older than her peers. Moreover, she is held in considerable repute by all the townsfolk because of her abilities as an orator. Her dramatic recitations at parties and public events delight her audiences and often move them to tears. As the entertainment for the evening, Juliza delivers three enthusiastically received speeches.

At 10 o'clock the sociable breaks up, and Juliza expects to be escorted home by her longtime beau, Frank. When he complies only reluctantly, she presses him for the reason. After hesitating a bit, Frank blurts out that he is weary of caring for his sickly mother. "There ain't but one thing to do," Juliza replies promptly; "I'll get married to you right away, and come over to your house. That'll settle it. I'm a good cook and a good housekeeper: mother says I am."[33] But his response to her offer astonishes her. Embarrassed by her indiscretion—for she, a woman, has done the unthinkable in proposing marriage before he has—Frank informs Juliza that he no longer wishes to marry at all and deposits her at her doorstep. Once inside, Juliza bluntly submits the matter to her mother: " 'Mother,' said she, suddenly, 'what do you suppose the reason is that Frank don't want me to marry him?' " (*UNC*, 26). When Mrs. Peck learns that Juliza has initiated the subject, she scolds her furiously: "Do you know what you've done? . . . You've made yourself a laughin' stock all over Stony Brook. . . . Don't you know girls don't tell young men they'll marry 'em unless they're asked?" (27).

The next day, a second round of confrontations takes place. Her mother having gone shopping, Juliza beckons Frank into the house when she sees the young man pass by. She demands he tell her the truth, and he confesses what she has suspected, that he has fallen in love with Lily Emmons, a girl from a neighboring town. Discovering, after further interrogation, that Frank has had little opportunity to talk with Lily, Juliza offers to aid him in his courting. "I think you had better see her," she advises him. "I'll tell you what I'll do. You get ready an' go to Hillbrook, an'—I'll stay with your mother while you're gone" (32). Surprised and gratified by her generosity, Frank prepares to visit his sweetheart. Meanwhile, Juliza tells her mother of the plan. Enraged,

Mrs. Peck attempts to prohibit it until Juliza, "display[ing] art which would have done credit to a diplomat," convinces her that such a move will alleviate the inevitable town gossip: folk will, naturally, assume she has rejected Frank if she helps him woo another girl (33). Juliza spends a week at Frank's home, caring for his elderly mother. As predicted, Frank returns from his week in Hillbrook engaged to Lily; they are married six weeks later. The entertainment for the wedding reception is a recitation by Juliza Peck.

As in "An Object of Love," the plot of "Juliza" is slight. Characterization, however, is rich and complex, and the theme subtly but powerfully manipulated. Since the narrator of "Juliza" is not omniscient, we must deduce the characters' motivations and emotional states from the facts reported. Juliza Peck is revealed as a young woman who has been controlled and molded all her life by her domineering mother. Depicted in regal terms, Mrs. Peck rules the household. She is concerned with material goods and social appearances, so much so that she has even "judiciously" named her only child for two aunts, Julia and Eliza, so that Juliza will inherit both their estates. Mrs. Peck's first reaction to her daughter's breakup with Frank, as noted, is fear that Juliza will now be a "laughin' stock" around town. In addition, she waxes indignant that a man such as Frank Williams has had the gall to refuse a Peck. "I should like to know what [Frank] thinks he is," she scolds. "[T]he Williamses warn't never much; they've picked up a little late years, but I remember the time when they was jest as poor an' low down as they could be. Your father an' me look a good deal higher than he for you; I can tell him that" (28). Mrs. Peck regulates all aspects of Juliza's recitations, from selecting the pieces to drilling her daily in performance. She refuses to allow her daughter to turn what is described as a real skill into a career: "I'm willin' she should speak to accommodate as she does here in town, but I ain't willin' to have her go round speakin' in public," she informs a neighbor. "It ain't a woman's place" (23).

A dutiful daughter, stolid Juliza conforms unquestioningly to her mother's strictures. As is typical of Freeman's works, however, the story's primary focus is on the young woman's sudden and uncharacteristic spate of rebellion. Minor as they may seem to the modern reader, Juliza's several acts of resistance are immense steps for her. She willfully tramples on the social dictate that prohibits a woman from proposing marriage, even when that marriage has long been assumed to be inevitable by both parties. Moreover, although others are embarrassed by her overstepping of prescribed gender boundaries, she refuses to accept blame. "I don't see why it's any worse for a girl to speak than 'tis for a man. . . . I don't see a single thing to be ashamed of," she retorts when Mrs. Peck accuses her of immodesty, adding, "I think it's you that's immodest, mother. I'm too modest to see how I wasn't" (27). Defiantly, she proceeds to break a further social taboo by helping the man who jilted her woo his new lover. She even elects to perform bridesmaid's duties at Frank and Lily's wedding.

Though seemingly unflappable throughout the ordeal, Juliza betrays to the reader a few subtle indications of her emotional turmoil. Prior to summoning Frank into her house on the day she learns of his involvement with Lily, she "bore down heavily" while brushing her hair, then she sits stiffly and silently for an hour, deliberating (28). When Frank appears on the road outside, she "rush[es] to the window, and pound[s] on it," then wrenches the door open with a "desperate jerk" (29). Once at Frank's home, she assumes such an exhausting round of housework and care for his feeble mother that she "had little leisure to grieve, if she had wished to, even at night" (34). The intentional ambiguity of this statement is characteristic of Freeman, who, similar to Hawthorne, often provides "multiple choice" narrative commentary in her stories. It is left to the reader, finally, to infer the actual state of mind underlying Juliza's perpetually dignified, calm demeanor. Subtle hints continue throughout the tale: when Frank returns triumphantly from Hillbrook, for example, he is greeted by a "pale" but "steady" Juliza, who, after ushering him into his mother's room, "open[s] the door softly and spe[eds] out" of the house undetected (35).

Juliza's true feelings about Frank's rejection are most apparent in the story's final paragraphs. As she recites poetry at the wedding feast, Juliza, who has previously been unable to coordinate her body movements gracefully to her speech ("You plank your arm up an' down like a pump-handle," her mother has reproached her), now performs "as she had never done before. Her gestures were full of fire; every line of her form and face seemed to conform to the exigencies of the situation; her voice rang out with a truth that was deeper than her own personality" (28, 36). Suppressed anger, one can assume, so well hidden on the surface, fuels the newfound passionate "fire" of her art and results in a splendid performance. Ironically, her masterful oration eclipses the wedding itself: "the bridal couple were forgotten" (36). In a final act of covert rebellion, then, Juliza has succeeded at least momentarily in seizing control of the party, displacing attention from Frank and Lily. With her usual composure, she afterward accepts the newlyweds' congratulations, but the last lines of the story are telling. When Frank leans over to whisper an apology for his past behavior, Juliza accepts it graciously but with "the same proud lift to her head, that she had had when reciting" (36). The implication is, of course, that she is still performing an act.

What, finally, can we make of "Juliza"? Though little known because it was not included in any of Freeman's original collections and has only recently been reprinted, the story is comparable to the familiar "The Revolt of 'Mother,' " "A Village Singer," and "A New England Nun" as well as to the many other Freeman works that examine the necessary balancing act, for women in particular, between social or familial restrictions and individual fulfillment. In "Juliza," Freeman effectively employs metaphors of voice and silence to develop this theme. Though Juliza's talent as an orator is without dispute in the story, the substance and style of her art are, ironically, purely imitative. Describing "heroic deed[s] and "tragic death[s]," the poems she recites are not only penned by others but uphold sentimental ideals that little pertain to life as Juliza has experienced it (23). Moreover, she has evolved her skill by copying her mother's voice and gestures. Thus at the wedding reception, when she delivers her most powerful recitation ever, she is also paradoxically most fully aping Mrs. Peck, whose theatrical "backward fling" of her head and "sweep of her great arms" lend her "energetic fire" whenever she speaks (28). Because she is a woman, the story suggests, Juliza's speech—her voice—is acceptable, however imitative or false, only when exercised within a tightly controlled, socially proper framework, symbolized here by conventional, sentimental verse. She is silenced and shamed if she presumes to breach that boundary, even when addressing such a practical and important matter as the likelihood of marrying a man who has been courting her for years.

In "Juliza," then, Freeman reverses the typical sentimental/domestic plot by focusing not on the "blushing" and "pink" Lily but on the plain, ungainly Juliza, who openly rejects, at one moment of her life at least, the expected female role of demure ingenue. At the same time, the story illustrates just how thoroughly Juliza has already been molded by the very standards she is attempting to resist. The irony of the situation is typical of Freeman, who often portrays women's lives as overwhelmingly determined though admitting of small, sometimes ineffective moments of free decision or action. Juliza's unwarranted act of helping Frank court Lily is one of the tale's masterful ambiguities and suggests the narrow arena in which women are permitted to operate. On the one hand, Juliza's self-sacrifice and submission to the man's desires are quintessentially "feminine" gestures. On the other hand, her act is a means with which to oppose her nagging mother and, perhaps above all, to preserve her essential dignity, for she will neither plead with nor cajole Frank. Her calm control of the situation may very well be Juliza's greatest performance of all time, but the story never allows us to be completely sure.

In Freeman's stories, women like Juliza Peck and Ann Millet who resist social and religious codes often end up deeply reenmeshed in the very confines that have prompted their revolt in the first place. As noted earlier, readers searching for models of independent or powerful women sometimes find this aspect of Freeman's fiction disappointing.[34] I find it, rather, one of the author's chief strengths. For in examining women's lives in the late-nineteenth-century New England village, Freeman refuses to judge her characters against an ideal, feminist or not. Caught up in webs of relationships, family expectations, social mores, and the limitations of their own personalities, Freeman's characters wage their personal battles for autonomy, dignity, and self-expression. Each woman's response to her situation depends on many intervening factors, some of which she is unaware of. Necessarily, her struggles are often ineffective and sometimes fail utterly. Freeman's work moves us to consider the constraints on individual expression and action, in particular those on women, in our own time and place. Social, cultural, and religious standards may have shifted, but these stories remain a relentless reminder of the extent to which all human beings are shaped by forces beyond any one individual's control.

Early Village Stories, 1882–1891:
A Humble Romance and *A New England Nun*

Freeman wrote 69 short stories for adults between 1882 and 1891. Of these, 58 were published in the three Harper's periodicals (*Harper's Bazar, Harper's Monthly,* and *Harper's Weekly*), and the rest appeared in various other magazines and newspapers, including *Ladies' Home Journal, Century, Lippincotts,* and *Boston Sunday Budget.* Freeman worked with the Harper's firm to gather 52 stories into her first two collections, *A Humble Romance and Other Stories* (1887) and *A New England Nun and Other Stories* (1891). Critics received both volumes enthusiastically, citing in particular the stories' realistic depiction of the New England landscape and character, use of commonplace events, depth of understanding of the human condition, and original, spare style. An 1891 *Critic* review is typical:

> What can we say that will express our sense of the beauty of Miss M. E. Wilkins's *A New England Nun and Other Stories?* So true in their insight into human nature, so brief and salient in construction, so deep in feeling, so choice in expression, these stories rank even with the works of Mrs. Stowe and Miss Jewett. It is the marvelous repression of passion and feeling in the New England character that Miss Wilkins has drawn with such technique. Beneath the icy surface of demeanor she has looked into the heart of this strong, self-contained people and has seen boiling and bubbling wells of fervency.[35]

Her contemporaries were correct in praising these collections, for they contain a number of the author's finest and perennially popular stories, such as "The Revolt of 'Mother,' " "A New England Nun," "A Village Singer," and "A Poetess." These works are central to Freeman's canon of short fiction because they represent early and skillful variations on themes she returned to throughout her career: poverty and pride, the plight of the elderly, revolt against religious or social codes, women's decisions in courtship and marriage, and manifestations of the stubborn New England will. In a tribute to their excellence, these stories have attracted frequent scholarly attention during the last few decades.

Rather than restate the tenor of that criticism, my purpose in this section is to discuss these tales somewhat briefly before turning the focus on lesser-known pieces that also exemplify Freeman's early themes and techniques. Readers who move beyond the handful of stories that are regularly anthologized will discover others equally intriguing, finely crafted, and deserving of analysis. The great majority of Freeman's short fiction is, in fact, just beginning to be rediscovered.

It is hardly an exaggeration to state that Freeman explored from every conceivable angle the issue of courtship and marriage in the New England village as she knew it. Most of her early stories involve at least one male-female romantic situation along with its attendant misunderstandings, tensions, separations, and decisions. Among these are works that concern long-parted lovers who, upon reuniting, must determine whether or not to marry; circumstances in which a character must distinguish between true love and romantic infatuation; and stories that focus on a young adult's strife with a parent over a courtship or impending marriage.

In "A New England Nun" (1887), Joe Dagget and Louisa Ellis have been parted for 14 years while Joe has been in Australia earning his fortune. Now in middle age, the reunited couple attempt to renew their courtship out of a sense of duty toward each other and out of faithfulness to the promises they made years earlier. Despite his lengthy time abroad, Joe is little changed. Louisa appears to him "every whit as attractive as ever," and he is eager to pursue the "old winds of romance" that yet "whistled as loud and sweet as ever through his ears."[36] But the case is quite different for Louisa. Never as ardently in love with Joe as he with her, she has merely, like most girls, "seen marriage ahead as a reasonable feature and a probable desirability of life" and acquiesced to her mother's urging to accept the offer of her first suitor (*MWFR*, 43). Those romantic winds, so strong in Joe Dagget's ears, "had never more than murmured" in Louisa's (44). Now, many years later, they have completely abated. Louisa's first reaction to Joe's return is, therefore, consternation. In marrying him now, she realizes that she will lose all that has given her a sense of calm order, gentle grace, and peaceful tranquillity for well over a decade. She will have to tolerate his "coarse masculine presence in the midst of all [her home's] delicate harmony": for instance, the dirt he tracks in and his awkward upsetting of her carefully arranged items (45). Moreover, in moving in with Joe, she will be forced to leave the home in which she has "felt like a queen" in her independence, ruling her dominion and doing whatever pleases her, whether it

be distilling rose essences, sewing and resewing a linen seam, or beauti-
fully ordering the contents of her bureau drawers (49). Her duty as a
married woman will be to clean and cook for Joe, to care for his "domineering, shrewd old matron" of a mother, and to entertain company
(44). But despite all these unpleasant prospects, Louisa never considers
reneging on her promise to Joe.

An unexpected turn of events provides her, however, with an opportunity to do so. Though also intent on honoring his vow to Louisa, Joe
finds he has fallen in love with his mother's housekeeper, Lily Dyer.
Upon overhearing Joe and Lily's conversation one day and discovering
their attachment, Louisa asks Joe to release her from their engagement
because, as she states truthfully, "she had lived so long in one way that
she shrank from making a change" (49). Clearly, both are relieved, and
they part for the last time with more fondness than they have experienced since Joe's return.

Slight in plot, "A New England Nun" is masterful in the ultimate
"undecidability," to use Elizabeth Meese's term, of its exploration of
whether Louisa should proceed in her marriage to Joe Dagget.[37] In
probing both Louisa's character and the exigencies of the situation, the
narrator declines to judge conclusively but builds a strong case for the
desirability of her remaining single. Louisa's lack of real love for Joe, the
surrender of the lifestyle she cherishes, the toil she will have to assume
as Joe's wife, and of course the fact that Joe loves another woman are
advanced as matters of serious consideration. Against these factors,
however, the story invites and entertains the inevitable opposing view,
one championed by readers in Freeman's day as well as in our own.
Louisa's solitary existence is completely self-centered, her work socially
useless. She has grown so inflexible in her routine that it is implied that
she might even die if wrenched from it. Compared to a nun in her con-
finement, she is actually much unlike a nun in that she has no spiritual
end to her contemplation, no sacrifice of a worldly life for the love of
God. Evidently, Louisa does not attend church, care for friends or family, or participate in any aspect of the town's social life. Like Thoreau,
therefore, she apparently does not hold to conventional ideas about the
social or religious purpose of life, but unlike Thoreau she is not con-
ducting an experiment in her self-imposed isolation, nor will she leave
her hermitage when the experiment is finished.[38] So completely is
Louisa set in her ways that the only possibility for change in her life, the
story implies, is the forced alteration that will occur by marriage to Joe.

Whether that marriage is desirable has proven to be a provocative issue for each succeeding generation of the readers of "A New England Nun." The articles in part 3, "The Critics," illustrate the range of that controversy and also raise other matters in the story of critical interest.

Stronger and more animated female protagonists than Louisa Ellis appear in "Louisa" (1890) and "A Moral Exigency" (1884). In both stories, an added complication to the question of marriage is the parents' intervention. Like Juliza, Louisa Britton in "Louisa" must endure her mother's scoldings, but her situation is far more dire. The Brittons are impoverished to the point of starvation, and Louisa's marriage to her well-off suitor, Jonathan Nye, seems a providential solution. Moreover, Louisa's mother so entirely approves of Jonathan that "she herself was in love with him" (*MWFR*, 143). To her mind, he is the prince who has come to claim the princess and restore the kingdom, the fulfillment of a fairy tale she can live vicariously through her daughter once she is "installed in [Jonathan's] large white house as reigning dowager" (143). In Louisa's rejection of Jonathan—for she is not at all attracted to the man—she must consequently bear the full brunt of her mother's disappointment over the spoiled fantasy as well as her own guilt for not being able to support her needy family. By the story's conclusion, however, Louisa has acquired not a husband but a teaching position, and Mrs. Britton, hearing through town gossip that she would not have been welcomed into Jonathan's home even if he had married her daughter, denounces the man as ardently as she once promoted him.

Eunice Fairweather in "A Moral Exigency" does not need to contend with her parents' unfulfilled dreams as much as with their concerns that they are aging and, because her father is a poor minister, that they have little to leave their daughter should she not marry. An even greater influence on Eunice's decision about marriage is the moral and religious legacy she has inherited from her parents, which she tries in vain to suppress. The story presents Eunice with two contrasting courtship situations that between them suggest the narrow range of options women in general may have in marrying. The first is when her well-meaning father strongly advises that she accept the suit of a middle-aged, widowed fellow minister with four children, convinced that this man's interest is the work of providence on his daughter's behalf. But Eunice, who despises her role as a minister's daughter even as she dutifully fulfills its tedious round of demands, indignantly, even bitterly refuses the clergyman's offer.

Her father roused himself then. "My dear daughter," he said, with restrained eagerness. . . . "Mr. Wilson is a good man; he would make you a worthy husband, and he needs a wife sadly. Think what a wide field of action would be before you with those four little motherless children to love and care for! You would have a wonderful opportunity to do good."

"I don't think," said Eunice, bluntly, "that I should care for that sort of an opportunity."

"Then," her father went on, "you will forgive me if I speak plainly, my dear. You—are getting older; you have not had any other visitors. You would be well provided for in this way—"

"Exceedingly well," replied Eunice, slowly. "There would be six hundred a year and a leaky parsonage for a man and woman and four children, and—nobody knows how many more . . ."

"The Lord would provide for his servants."

"I don't know whether he would or not. I don't think he would be under any obligation to if his servant deliberately encumbered himself with more of a family than he had brains to support." (*HR*, 224–25)

In rejecting Mr. Wilson, who, as she correctly surmises, is looking primarily for a capable mother for his children, Eunice defies the notion of marriage as women's moral duty, a kind of missionary undertaking that provides them with an arena for good works. For an otherwise obedient minister's daughter, the refusal is tantamount to the type of rebellion typical of Freeman's characters, the sudden assertion of the self after years of repression or compliance to others' desires. And as is true with many of Freeman's rebels, Eunice's self-assertion both frightens and disorients her; it becomes, in fact, a "horror" (232). So strong is her resultant inner turmoil that it begins to distort her perceptions and renders even familiar household items frightening and full of "dumb accusations." "The change was in herself, not in them," the narrator explains. "The shadow that was over her own soul overshadowed them and perverted her vision" (232).

The full extent of this change in vision occurs after Eunice's second and more devastating act of revolt, for which the first has been the catalyst. At a Christmas Eve party on the day she has refused Mr. Wilson, Eunice receives unexpected attention from Burr Mason, a boyishly handsome man she is acquainted with but has never spoken to at length. Though a relative newcomer in the village, Burr is already popular and is known to be courting Ada Harris, the daughter of the most wealthy and influential man in town. Eunice is aware of Burr's engagement to Ada, a former schoolmate of hers, yet she defiantly accepts and encourages the man's visits despite her parents' remonstrances and the news that Ada is prostrate with grief.

Burr is, in many ways, the direct opposite of the widowed minister, Mr. Wilson. Like Wilson, however, he also does not love Eunice. A "terribly vacillating" young man, his attraction to her is merely "some sudden fancy," and he even cautions her that Ada's pretty face might at any moment tempt him back (229, 228). Sensible and intelligent, "her head not turned, in the usual acceptation of the term," Eunice is aware on some level of that lack of love and of Burr's complete unsuitability for a woman like her (228). She too is not in love with him. But a sort of fascination has seized hold of her, momentarily suspending her reasoning and suppressing her usual moral scruples. "How this sober, conscientious girl could reconcile to herself the course she was now taking, was a question," the narrator muses. "It was probable she did not make the effort; she was so sensible that she would have known its futility and hypocrisy beforehand" (229). To "steady, homely" Eunice, a man like Burr "seemed almost as much out of her life as a lover in a book" (228). But the novelty of the romance compels her forward and allows her, for once in her life, to forgo duty for pleasure, submission for resistance. Even when the distraught Ada comes to plead with Eunice, she remains haughty and unmoved in the face of the younger girl's hysteria.

However, Ada's accusations soon force Eunice from her fantasy back into the reality of her true self that she cannot escape. For Ada has charged her not only with cruelty but also with selfishness in her refusal to give Burr up: "It is all for yourself—yourself!" she screams at Eunice (231). Though having previously indulged her "selfishness" in rejecting a man who desires only a housekeeper, Eunice proves unable to bear the burden of continued self-assertion. After Ada leaves, her "strong will broke down before the accusations of her own conscience," which has been formed by a long moral training in self-sacrifice that, finally, is impossible to suppress (232). Impelled by the pleasant memories of Ada's friendship in their school days, Eunice decides to "return" Burr to her.

As Leah Blatt Glasser has pointed out, Freeman makes effective use of mirror imagery in "A Moral Exigency" to indicate the blurred vision and distorted perceptions that arise from Eunice's divided inner self.[39] The "double picture" of herself she views in the glass one evening suggests her simultaneous desire to rebel from and to obey the moral imperatives ingrained in her personality. A part of her envies Ada, who, as the "pretty blonde of average attainments," is her opposite and double (228). Yet another part of her pities and even scorns the impassioned and emotionally fragile female, the type of woman who could be satisfied with a weak, fickle man like Burr. Eunice can no more fit into this stereotyped role for a woman than she can into that of the submissive housekeeper-wife: neither role provides her with the kind of fulfillment she seeks. But there is no third alternative. Thus Eunice finally surrenders her hold on Burr under the threat of losing the only substantial love she has likely ever known, the mother-love she once felt for Ada. Her last utterance is a poignant indication of her awareness that there may, quite simply, never be adequate fulfillment for a woman of her sensibilities and longings: " 'Love me all you can, Ada,' she said. 'I want—something' " (233).

As she does in "A Moral Exigency," Freeman often employs the technique of doubling characters to depict the limited roles open to women as well as the inner division that may result from such severely restricted options. In "A Conflict Ended" (1886), two couples are paired, and the women's responses contrast those of the men as well as each other. We are on familiar ground here with typical Freeman subject matter: religious controversy, male/female relationships in courtship, the obstinate, or set, New England will, and the mending of a long-standing quarrel. Adhering to his vow, Marcus Woodman has sat on the church steps every Sunday morning during meeting for 10 years in order to protest the installation of a new minister. Incensed by his mulish behavior and unwilling to marry the town's laughingstock, his fiancée, Esther Barney, broke their engagement soon after he began his weekly vigil. By the time the story opens, Esther has created a satisfactory life for herself as a prosperous dressmaker. She employs a young apprentice, Margy Wilson, who shares her home. Margy, courted by George Elliot, one day severs her relationship with the man because he insists that his mother live with them once they are wed. "If George Elliot thinks more of his mother than he does of me, he can have her. I don't care. I'll show him I can get along without him," Margy tells Esther, but her brave words fail to disguise her frustration and anguish (*MWFR*, 17). Sympathizing with the girl, Esther breaks her usual reticence and relates the tale of her former engagement to Marcus and the distress his obstinacy subsequently afforded her. "Well, it's all over now, as far as I'm concerned," she concludes. "I've got over it a good deal, though sometimes it makes me jest as mad as ever to see him setting there. But I try to be reconciled, and I get along jest as well, mebbe, as if I'd had him—I don't know. I fretted more at first than there was any sense in, and I hope you won't" (19).

Despite Esther's counsel, Margy soon weakens in her resolve, returns to George, and submits to his will—only to discover that he has known for some time that his mother now plans to live elsewhere. "I thought it was your place to give in, dear," George simpers—and Margy agrees with him (20). Back at home, the elated girl suggests to Esther that Esther's similar capitulation to Marcus might mend their relationship. "Don't you believe," asks Margy, "if you was to give in the way I did, that he would [give in also]?" "Oh, I don't believe he would. You don't know him; he's awful set," Esther responds sharply, but giving in is something she's never considered, and a seed is planted in her mind (21). Over the next several weeks, she contemplates what she might stand to gain or lose if now, after all these years, she were to wed Marcus. She must consider many aspects of such a union, not the least of which is her reluctance, like that of Louisa in "A New England Nun," to disturb the "peace and pride" of the comfortable life she has created for herself (21). But when Marcus's mother suddenly dies, the thought of the "dreadful babyish" man trying to keep house for himself compels her to make an overture to him. When she does so, Marcus breaks down sobbing; he confesses his love for her and the misery he has endured over the years. But he also warns her that he cannot and will not relinquish his habit of sitting on the church stairs. Esther agrees to marry him anyway. On the Sunday following the wedding, when she is to "come out bride," Marcus prepares to take up his customary position, only to find that Esther is determined to join him on the steps. Her "last weapon" employed, she calculates—and hopes upon hope—that Marcus's love for her will make him unwilling to subject her to the mockery and gossip he has had to endure (24). Against all odds, her gamble pays off. Though propelled by a nearly overwhelming force to resume his station, Marcus resists, "st[ands] up straight, like a man," and enters the church (24).

On the surface, "A Conflict Ended" seems to be an object lesson in, as George informs Margy, the fitness of women submitting to men. Certainly, the story can be read this way, which makes its theme virtually unacceptable to the majority of today's readers. One does well to remember, however, that this subject would have been equally controversial to its original *Harper's Monthly* audience, a readership inundated by arguments in the popular media that weighed the relative merits of the "true" woman against those of the "new" woman. Moreover, by the time "A Conflict Ended" was published, Freeman was already known for her stories about independently minded women who forgo marriage or maintain their beliefs in the face of opposition. As with other finely crafted Freeman stories, the reader must therefore fully scrutinize "A Conflict Ended" to appreciate the subtle complexities of the women's decisions in the tale. For Freeman deliberately creates her ostensibly reactionary subject in order to make profound statements about the necessity of compromise in relationships and about the heroic strength of those who are able to rise above petty or self-serving concerns to enact that compromise. With few exceptions, in Freeman's world only women possess such fortitude.

Although we never learn the exact nature of the religious controversy, the story's introductory paragraphs explain that Marcus Woodman's dispute with his Congregational church stems from the engagement of an "undoctrinal" minister. In fact, the issue has been so divisive among the church's members that nearly a third of them have moved to the Baptist church across the street. Ten years after the conflict, old animosities still reign; each Sunday members entering one church make it a point to mock those entering the other. Put into this perspective, Marcus's quarrel is merely one manifestation of the entire town's stubborn refusal to make peace. In fact, he may be viewed as more admirable than many for adhering to his stance without resorting to his neighbors' mean-spiritedness. Week after week, he silently endures their mockery without returning it. Like some of his fellow New Englanders, however, Marcus possesses a will so obdurate that over time it has warped his whole person. After 10 years, his sitting on the stairs is no longer a protest—he confesses that he doesn't object to the minister anymore—but an addiction. Esther is correct when she compares his behavior to "the way other men take to smoking and drinking," for Marcus is truly incapable of overcoming the habit through his own volition (23).

Now comprehending Marcus's condition and motivated by a love that, as is often true with Freeman's women, seems more motherly than romantic, Esther decides that "giving in" to Marcus may be the only possible catalyst for his change and that doing so may also lead to an overdue reconciliation between them. She is aware that she does not need him for a full and happy life; she conjectures, no doubt correctly, that marrying him may even diminish what she has. She deliberates among her options, forms a resolution, and then moves ahead swiftly with her plan, steeling herself against the onslaught of inevitable gossip.

Her prolonged, mature reasoning is much unlike Margy's hasty and emotional submission to George: unlike Esther, Margy cannot survive without her man. Margy thus becomes the usual Freeman sentimental foil, comparable to Lily Emmons in "Juliza," Lily Dyer in "A New England Nun," and Ada Harris in "A Moral Exigency"; her attitudes and responses serve to highlight, by way of stark contrast, those of the protagonist. The story's irony is effected when the wiser Esther believes she is imparting instruction in persistence and endurance to the younger woman, only to discover that she herself has received a more valuable lesson, one in the art of compromise.

On a larger scale, Freeman's message, although embedded in controversial issues of women's roles, is clear. Women, not men, usually possess the healthy and flexible will necessary to alter circumstances in positive ways. Freeman was continually fascinated by the potential healing of the stubborn will or dogged conscience: the theme appears, to a greater or lesser degree, in most of her short stories and novels. Her preface to an 1899 edition of *Pembroke*, in which she alludes to "A Conflict Ended," is revealing: the novel, she states, "was originally intended as a study of the human will in several New England characters, in different phases of disease and abnormal development, and [was] to prove, especially in the most marked case, the truth of a theory that its cure depended entirely upon the capacity of the individual for a love which could rise above all considerations of self."[40] Marcus's love for Esther finally allows him to break his stair-sitting habit, but Esther's more powerful and active love initiates not only the process of "making a man" of the helpless Marcus but also, the story implies, the healing of an entire town. For as Marcus enters the meetinghouse with Esther on his arm, the villagers' gibes suddenly and unexpectedly cease: they display some fellow feeling—empathy—for the first time in years. "The people followed [Marcus and Esther]," the narrator relates. "Not one of them even smiled. They had felt the pathos in the comedy" (24).

Freeman does not always achieve such a high level of technical skill or depth of theme in her many stories concerning courtship and marriage. Less successful are such early works as "A Souvenir" (1885), which turns on the characteristic Freeman plot of lovers parted by misunderstanding and parents' interference; "A Lover of Flowers" (1886)—one of only six stories in Freeman's first two collections that feature a male protagonist—in which a lonely man is deserted by the young woman he is about to marry; and "The Scent of the Roses" (1887), in which a woman believes her former lover is now courting her younger sister. In the words of an early critic, such pieces as these tend to be no more than "slight, reminiscential, pleasing, sometimes entertaining, occasionally revelatory of human nature."[41] Though nearly every Freeman story has moments of sheer delight, for example in a character's unexpected witticism or in a lovingly detailed description of household items, these tales lack the smooth integration of plot strands, the ironic twists, and the psychological complexity that mark Freeman's more accomplished works. More skillful stories about courtship and marriage in *A Humble Romance* and in *A New England Nun* include "A Conquest of Humility" (1887), in which a woman who was jilted by her fiancé publicly humiliates him in turn, and "Amanda and Love" (1890), in which a woman who is jealous that her sister has a lover is forced to learn a lesson in humility and acceptance.

In addition to issues of romantic love, Freeman's early stories frequently focus on characters' conflicts with religious doctrine, church, or minister. More than half of the stories in her first two collections turn on such tensions, including "The Revolt of 'Mother' " (1890), "A Village Singer" (1889), and "A Poetess" (1890). Though criticism of "The Revolt of 'Mother' " usually centers on Sarah Penn's—Mother's—bold defiance of her husband, Adoniram, in moving her family into the barn when he refuses to build them a larger house, Sarah's rebellion is less against Adoniram than it is about taking measures to rectify an unjust providence, a familiar Freeman theme and one we have already seen in "An Object of Love." As she tells her daughter Nanny, Sarah "reckon[s] men-folks in with Providence" as well as with the weather; she accepts what comes yet still exerts her right to seize at "loop-holes" when "not provided with large doors" (*MWFR*, 124, 125). Convinced that her position is a righteous one, she several times confronts her husband about the family's pressing need for more space. In doing so, she takes care to imitate "the humble fashion of a Scripture woman" (126). Moreover, Sarah's appeal is mainly to Adoniram's religious duty: in her opinion, he has been unfaithful to his God-given role as provider. "I want to know if you think you're doin' right an' accordin' to what you profess," she demands (127).

Met only with stubborn silence in return, Sarah bides her time for months until she receives her "loop-hole" in the form of Adoniram's three-day absence for a business trip. "Unsolicited opportunities are the guide-posts of the Lord to the new roads of life. . . . It looks like a providence," she concludes (130). Less worried about Adoniram's reaction than determined to act on the God-given chance, Sarah hastily sets up housekeeping in the large new barn. She asserts her right to the religious independence that stems from her Protestant heritage even when the town minister arrives to correct her frowardness. "I believe I'm doin' what's right," she informs him sternly. "I've made it the subject of prayer, an' it's betwixt me an' the Lord an' Adoniram. . . . I think it's right jest as much as I think it was right for our forefathers to come over from the old country 'cause they didn't have what belonged to 'em. . . . I've got my own mind an' my own feet, an' I'm goin' to think my own thoughts an' go my own ways, an' nobody but the Lord is goin' to dictate to me unless I've a mind to have him" (132–33). As is typical of Freeman's ministers, this one finds the woman's case completely beyond his experience.

Similar to Esther's choice at the end of "A Conflict Ended," Sarah's decisive action brings the results she calculates on and hopes for. Adoniram, astonished on his return to find his family ensconced in the barn, acquiesces to his wife's desire. What is unexpected in both stories is the extent of the men's emotional breakdown—their heartfelt sobbing and Marcus Woodman's throwing himself down on his knees ("You look ridickerlous," Esther duly informs him [22]). A man's obstinate, inarticulate demeanor merely masks his truly sensitive and often weak nature, Freeman implies, and a woman need only use the "right besieging tools" to break down a "fortress whose walls had no active resistance" (135). In Sarah's case, the necessary tool is a resolute following of her own religious sensibility, for which the story rewards her. Like that of most Freeman women, Sarah's rebellion is limited in scope, for she has no intention of abandoning her customary submissive roles as wife and mother. But she *will* follow the lead of providence in righting a perceived injustice. As such, she is one of many Freeman women who determinedly grasp at life's "loop-holes" when not given "large doors." What such women lack in opportunity and resources is more than outweighed by their native wit and willpower. As one critic puts it, "[These women's] demands may be small, but it is impossible to renege on them. . . . The issues change in each story, each circumstance, but the ability to evaluate, choose, and then act according to inner convictions remains essential."[42]

Sarah Penn has "done her duty" by Adoniram for 40 years before her sudden revolt, the biblical measure for an extensive period of time. Similarly, Candace Whitcomb of "A Village Singer" has performed as church soloist for four decades before the congregation deems her voice too "cracked" to continue in that position. The story opens with Candace seeking revenge: from her house next to the church, she plays her parlor organ and sings at the top of her voice during service in order to drown out her replacement, Alma Way. Church members are stunned by her behavior; Alma and her fiancé, Wilson Ford, who is Candace's nephew and heir, are indignant, and Mr. Pollard, the minister, soon knocks at the elderly woman's door to admonish her.

Bitterly resentful over her perfunctory dismissal, Candace unleashes the full extent of her fury on the clergyman. Himself a 40-year veteran of the church who also has a mildly unsteady voice ("he had a slight hesitation of speech, not an impediment"), Mr. Pollard is an apt target for Candace's rage at the church's prejudicial treatment of older women versus older men (*MWFR*, 82). She is hardly subtle in her equation of "an old singer an' an old minister":

> I want to know what you think of folks that pretend to be Christians treatin' anybody the way they've treated me? ... My voice is as good an' high to-day as it was twenty year ago; an' if it wa'n't, I'd like to know where the Christianity comes in. I'd like to know if it wouldn't be more to the credit of folks in a church to keep an old singer an' an old minister, if they didn't sing an' hold forth quite so smart as they used to, ruther than turn 'em off an' hurt their feelin's. I guess it would be full as much to the glory of God. S'pose the singin' an' the preachin' wa'n't quite so good, what difference would it make? Salvation don't hang on anybody's hittin' a high note, that I ever heard of. (85)

Despite the decline of Mr. Pollard's preaching, the congregation has no intention of letting him go. Nor do they complain of the aging voice of the male soloist, the "old bachelor tenor" William Emmons, who was once Candace's beau. But Candace, despite her many years of faithful service, has been ousted in a humiliating and underhanded manner. "There they come here last week Thursday, all the choir," she relates scornfully to Mr. Pollard, "an' pretended they'd come to give me a nice little surprise. . . . When they'd gone I found this photograph album on the table ... an' I opened it, an' there was the letter inside givin' me notice to quit. If they'd gone about it any decent way, told me right out honest that they'd got tired of me . . . I wouldn't minded so much" (86).

Unlike other Freeman stories about women's defiance, "A Village Singer" does not have a positive ending. So acutely does Candace feel her slight and so violent is her response that she soon succumbs to a fever. Freeman uses fire imagery to suggest how all-consuming the elderly woman's passion is to her otherwise fragile being. Before taking to her bed, Candace observes both a stove fire as it reduces kindling to ashes and, in the distance, a forest fire that threatens the new spring foliage. But she herself "was in the roar of an intenser fire; the growths of all her springs and the delicate wontedness of her whole life were going down in it" (90). On her deathbed, she shows signs of making peace, apologizing to Mr. Pollard for her outburst and reinstating her nephew Wilson, whom she had cut off, in her will. In an apparent final act of atonement, she even importunes Alma to sing "Jesus, Lover of My Soul" for her. A hesitating Alma complies. But although Candace seems to capitulate in all the ways expected of a dying elderly Christian woman, her last words, "You flatted a little on—soul," constitute a sharp though veiled rebuke to Alma and the other listeners (92). With the remark, Candace asserts her authority by judging the younger woman's voice inferior. She simultaneously decries the "flatting" of souls—the narrow-minded, self-serving behavior—of the congregation that has so rudely and unfairly displaced her from a position that was vital to her existence. And finally, as Marjorie Pryse has noted, Candace renders a warning to her rival, "reminding Alma not only of the inevitable decline of her voice, and therefore the congregation's potential dissatisfaction, but also of her own mortality."[43]

Like that of "A Village Singer," the plot of "A Poetess" concerns an older woman's separation from meaningful work at the hands of a meddling minister. Betsey Dole is esteemed among her neighbors for her verse making. Commissioned by Mrs. Caxton, who is grieving the loss of her son, Betsey spends many hours at her kitchen table composing a memorial poem, forgetting even to eat and sleep in the effort. A woman of considerable empathy—her face, for example, unconsciously takes on others' expressions when she speaks with them—Betsey is confident that she "can enter into [Mrs. Caxton's] feelin's considerable," even though she herself has never been a mother (*MWFR*, 112). She succeeds admirably; Mrs. Caxton weeps over the finished product, declaring it "beautiful, beautiful . . . jest as comfortin' as it can be" (114). To Betsey, such praise more than justifies her arduous toil. "It was to her as if her poem had been approved and accepted by one of the great magazines," the narrator comments. "She had the pride and self-wonderment of recognized genius" (114).

The joy Betsey feels at her accomplishment is short lived, however. Through gossip, that all-pervasive carrier of blessing or damnation in the Freeman village, Betsey learns that the village minister, Mr. Lang, scorns her poem, that he has called it, in fact, "jest as poor as it could be" (a direct contrast to Mrs. Caxton's "jest as comfortin' as it can be";

115). So anguished is Betsey upon hearing this verdict, even though it has come to her thirdhand, that she, like Candace Whitcomb, virtually gives up the struggle to live at once. Alone in her house, she querulously addresses God and his apparent injustice: "I'd like to know if you think it's fair. Had I ought to have been born with the wantin' to write poetry if I couldn't write it—had I?" (117). Then she proceeds methodically to burn all the poems she has carefully saved over the years, both those she has written and those she has clipped from newspapers. Shortly thereafter, she falls ill. When Minister Lang, who "did not once suspect his own connection with the matter," pays his final call, he agrees to honor the dying woman's request to bury the ashes of the poetry with her (119). Though bewildered, he assents as well to her request that he compose an elegy about her after she is gone. "I've been thinkin' that—mebbe my—dyin' was goin' to make me—a good subject for—poetry," Betsey whispers to him. "If you would jest write a few lines" (120).

"A Poetess" illustrates the harmful, even devastating effect a callous remark may have on a sensitive nature. That the snub comes from the town minister, whose work is to heal souls and not to destroy them, illustrates poignantly the power patriarchal religion was yet able to exert in that time and place over such a devout, demure old woman as Betsey Dole. But the fact that Mr. Lang also writes poetry—and has even published some in a magazine—adds a level of complication that elevates the story into a wry and insightful commentary on the nature of art and on changing standards for literature in the late nineteenth century. Such critics as Perry Westbrook and Barbara Solomon make a typical mistake in assuming that Betsey's poetry amounts to no more than sentimental drivel, the New England equivalent, for instance, of Emmeline Grangerford's "Ode to Stephen Dowling Botts."[44] Westbrook calls it "mawkish," and Solomon insists that the story "wants us to be certain ... that indeed Betsey writes dreadful, sentimental verses."[45] In "A Poetess," however, as in her many other "undecidable" stories, Freeman deliberately withholds the exact nature of what appears to be the key to the story's interpretation, forcing her audience to construct a plausible reading from the stock of assumptions and prejudices it brings to the work. Is Betsey's poetry necessarily "mawkish" and "dreadful" because it is written by a pious elderly maiden lady, one who dresses in many-turned faded gowns, lives with a caged parakeet as her only companion, and whose experience of life is no broader than the circumference of her carefully tended flower garden? Are the minister's verses necessarily better because they have been accepted by a magazine and composed by a man of supposedly greater education, wider outlook, and deeper understanding of human nature? Can one therefore assume, as Westbrook does, that Mr. Lang possesses "some discrimination" in literature and evaluates Betsey's poetry correctly (Westbrook, 48)? The story confirms none of these suppositions. Freeman qualifies her language cautiously when describing Betsey's efforts (she "*looked like* the very genius of gentle, old-fashioned, sentimental poetry. *It seemed as if one* . . . could easily deduce what she would write" (111; emphasis mine). We are never made privy to the final product. Moreover, we are informed of the minister's poetry writing only through the gossip of Mrs. Caxton, who might well be telling the truth when she heatedly declares that "maybe his [poetry] ain't quite so fine as he thinks 'tis. Maybe them magazine folks jest took his for lack of something better" (116). Through Mrs. Caxton, we also learn that Mr. Lang probably had mixed motives in criticizing Betsey's poetry, not the least of which was to win the approval of his sweetheart, Ida, with whom he was conversing at the time.

"A Poetess" questions, then, readers' judgments about the relative merits of "spinster" and "minister," at least in terms of what kind of art each is capable of creating. On another level, the story also reflects Freeman's keen awareness of the changing literary scene of her day and of the extent to which standards of taste were increasingly market driven in a growing mass culture. No matter what type of poetry Betsey or the minister writes—the story suggests that it doesn't really matter—the fact that Mr. Lang's has received public approbation through publication outweighs Betsey's more modest claim of having successfully touched the heart of her patron, Mrs. Caxton. Betsey's verse making is based on a typically female ethic of compassion and care giving; her writing serves to heal others as well as to validate her as a woman and a creative artist, "one born with the wantin' to write poetry." As Juliza Peck's recitation and Candace Whitcomb's singing do for them, Betsey Dole's poetry provides her with a useful and respected role in the community; it is her lifeline to social interaction. She is rewarded fully when she accomplishes her goal of "enter[ing] into [others'] feelin's considerable."

By contrast, the minister demonstrates little ability to empathize with others. Even when Betsey attempts to stimulate his dormant sympathy by requesting that he write an elegy about her, he remains stiff and confused. Though only a "country boy who had worked his way through a country college," he has arrogantly assumed the role of arbiter of taste in the village, and he judges others accordingly (118). His art is based on traditionally masculine characteristics of individualism, competition, and marketplace commodity, all increasingly prized values in American society in the 1880s and 1890s. "A Poetess" thus achieves its force from opposing, in starkly gendered terms, the radically differing standards of literary merit operative in late-nineteenth-century America. It is both ironic and tragic that the tale's women—Betsey, Mrs. Caxton, Ida—accept with little or no hesitation the masculine standard as correct. Linda Grasso, who also assumes Betsey's poetry is sentimental, reads the story as an ominous death knell for women's writing and culture. "By casting the representative of the 'new' [that is, the minister] as a murderer oblivious of his crime," Grasso states, "Freeman suggests that an aesthetic based on blinded individualism and 'unfeeling standards' has literally obliterated the more socially empathetic, culturally useful aesthetic of sentimentality."[46] A simple, even pathetic, tale in its broad outline, "A Poetess" is actually one of Freeman's most complex and skillful stories in its examination of power differentials and gender, the nature of true ministering versus the institutionalized ministry, and the relative standards for art in a given society.

As we have seen, Freeman's stories are often about the strong force the outward forms of a spiritually moribund Calvinism wielded on post–Civil War New England villagers. Church services are attended several times a week, and the town minister is deferred to and his affairs eagerly discussed. But few Freeman characters concern themselves with debating doctrine, spreading the gospel, or reading their Bibles (though the book is prominently displayed on every parlor table and regularly dusted). In short, the majority of villagers do not seem to equate their rigorous religious training with their deepest selves, nor does it take precedence in their daily lives. As in "A Village Singer," the result is a rampant hypocrisy that only a very few struggle to expose or counteract. When a Freeman character takes her spiritual and moral life seriously, it is nearly always in glaring opposition to established religious and social protocol. Such is the case in "An Independent Thinker" (1887), in which an elderly deaf woman knits at home to raise money for her destitute neighbors rather than attend a Sunday service she cannot hear. Until her good deed is revealed, she is ostracized for her behavior by the very persons she has been secretly supporting. Such is also the case in "A Meeting Half-Way" (1891), a story that has never been reprinted since its first appearance in *Harper's Bazar*. Intriguing for its portrayal of a woman minister (she has purchased a near-deserted church and holds services for anyone who will come), the tale concerns two women who rise above their individual allegiances to particular denominations, in this case Congregational and Episcopal, in order to overcome their differences and solidify their friendship. When they are finally united in common worship, "it was as if the ancient strife had ended for both in a better Church than either had ever known."[47]

Freeman frequently evokes this "better church" through her female characters' actions and decisions. By following the dictates of conscience despite the reproach of others, such women effectually replace the incapable or weak minister by performing acts of loving service that are testimony to their beliefs. Though ignored in recent criticism, "Life-Everlastin' " (1889) features such a strong female protagonist. Middle-aged Luella Norcross is as much out of place among the vain, hypocritical folk in her village as her odd-looking house is relentlessly "out of plumb." Her sister Maria Ansel confesses to being "mortified to death" because Luella insists on wearing an outdated bonnet, refuses to attend church, and performs such "unseemly" acts as feeding and sheltering tramps. "If I was you I'd act a little more like other folks, or I'd give up," Maria scolds (*MWFR*, 67). Although misunderstood, Luella persists in her daily round of good deeds, including harboring a feeble-minded woman, paying rent on a house for an insolvent man, and giving what she has to anyone who requests a handout. As a result, the narrator relates, "if she was not in full orthodox flavor among the respectable part of the town, her fame was bright among the poor and maybe lawless elements, whom she befriended" (70). Luella's charity even extends to the town miser, Oliver Weed, who is too cheap to call a doctor for his asthma. Though all despise and shun the rich man, Luella views his stinginess as a moral affliction in as much need of healing as is his physical illness. "Mebbe [he] can't help bein' close any more'n we can help somethin' we've got. It's a failin', and folks ought to help folks with failin's, I don't care what they are," she maintains (69). While Maria fusses over the current fashion for correct bonnet placement, Luella calmly stitches a pillow stuffed with healing life-everlasting blossoms to help old man Weed get his rest.

Exasperated, finally, by Luella's failure to conform, Maria convinces the minister, Mr. Sands, to have a talk with her sister. "I don't see you at church very often, Miss Norcross," the nervous young man blurts out after exchanging the customary pleasantries. "You don't see me [there] at all," Luella counters sternly, adding, "I'm not a believer, an' I won't be a hypocrite" (71–72). Having never before encountered an outspoken agnostic, Mr. Sands is seized by "amazement and terror" as he hastily tries to construct an argument that will sway the gentle but firm woman sitting before him (72). "Your soul's salvation," he says, gasping, "do you never think of that?" "I ain't never worried much about my soul's salvation," Luella returns; "I've had too many other souls to think about" (72). Other attempts to reason with her prove equally useless. Though Mr. Sands has rehearsed a speech beforehand and has studiously assumed a solemn tone and patronizing manner, Luella, who considers him "very young," soon quiets him as she would a tiresome child, filling his pockets with apples and sending him on his way.

The story's turning point comes when Luella finds the murdered bodies of Oliver Weed and his wife on the morning she enters their house to deliver the life-everlasting pillow. The murderer is obviously the stable hand John Gleason, a former tramp whom Luella once fed and sheltered. After reporting the crime and watching a flurry of sheriff's men and gawkers converge on the Weed home, Luella discovers that Gleason is hiding in the empty house next door to hers, a building she owns. Torn between horror at the crime and compassion for its perpetrator, she endures sleepless nights and anxious days agonizing over whether to turn Gleason in to the authorities. A "pity that was almost tenderness" overwhelms her when she realizes that the man is trusting in her mercy, for he accepts the food she covertly places at the house's door after nightfall (76). Disturbingly, she envisions "the whole crew of her pitiful dependents . . . pleading [with] her to keep faith with their poor brother" (76). On the other hand, she recoils at Gleason's cold-blooded killing of the Weeds and recalls that the man is wanted for another murder as well. Her greatest fear, however, comes when she contemplates what Gleason's fate will be *after* he is hung for his crime. A believer in God ("I ain't a fool," she has told the minister), Luella worries that Gleason's actions have earned him a place in eternal hell (72). "Have I got to give him up to be hung?" she mourns to herself. "What's goin' to become of him then? Where'll he go to when he's been so awful wicked?" (76). In compassion, she resists serving as the instrument that would lead to a fellow human being's damnation. So wrenching is her dilemma that she even decides to give Gleason the opportunity to rob or murder her by keeping her front door ajar during the night and prominently displaying her money and silver. At least then, she reasons, either she wouldn't feel such compunction in handing him over or she would no longer be alive to do so.

After long deliberation and uttering "one great sob," Luella finally turns Gleason in to the sheriff the following morning. On the Sunday after he is apprehended, she appears in church for the first time in 25 years. Everyone is astonished; predictably, Mr. Sands smugly congratulates himself for her return, and Maria Ansel is outraged that Luella has failed to dignify the occasion by purchasing a new bonnet. On the walk home, Luella confides the reason for her return to church to a neighbor woman. She does so with characteristic reticence and dignity: " 'I ain't got much to say about it . . . but I'm goin' to say this much—it ain't no more'n right I should, though I don't believe in a lot of palaver about things like this—I've made up my mind that I'm goin' to believe in Jesus Christ. I ain't never, but I'm goin' to now, for'—Luella's voice turned shrill with passion—*I don't see any other way out of it for John Gleason!* " (79).

A conversion story, "Life-Everlastin' " is similar to a number of other Freeman tales, such as "A Tardy Thanksgiving" (1883), "The Bar Light-House" (1883), and the later "The Balking of Christopher" (1912), in which characters achieve a greater understanding of spiritual or moral matters after undergoing a crisis. "Life-Everlastin'," however, is the most specific story in Freeman's canon as to the nature of the doctrine that the protagonist converts to; that is, Christianity. Despite its conventional surface form—didactic conversion narratives were a hallmark of sentimental/domestic writing as well as of the Puritan tradition—"Life-Everlastin' " evinces Freeman's unique interpretation of the issue in its focus on an independently minded protagonist who chooses, finally, to participate in organized religion but only on her own terms. As is true with many of Freeman's outcasts, Luella is heroic in her ability to prevail over petty meanness and vicious gossip. In fact, Freeman paints here one of her bleakest and most cynical portraits of village life. The hypocritical Maria Ansel, the miserly Oliver Weed, the childish Mr. Sands, the selfish Clara Vinton (the minister's fiancée, who refuses to marry him because he doesn't have a parsonage), the bumbling sheriff and his men, the murderer John Gleason—all serve to throw into sharp relief the wise, generous, and loving woman who is more at ease with the downtrodden and the homeless than with her relatives and neighbors.

Luella is no less than visionary in manifesting a "broad charity which was quite past the daily horizon of the village people" (69). Not based on theory or doctrine, her charity springs from her intrinsic empathy for others and is fueled by her ability to act on principle despite severe censure. Luella's profession of Christianity at the end of the story is therefore neither complacent nor conventional: she does not convert to win others' approval or for personal gain (she has, in fact, told Mr. Sands that it would be "dreadful piggish" to profess Christianity merely to be assured a place in heaven (72). Rather, Luella's conversion is a conscious act of will motivated by love; she "made up her mind" to become a believer through compassion for John Gleason. Knowing Gleason faces execution, she considers the doctrine of Christ's mercy—so like her own mercy—to be the only possible hope for the man's eternal fate. "Unreasonable" Christianity thus becomes reasonable to her not through a minister's preaching or others' coercion but through direct experience of the need for a superhuman source of forgiveness. Luella is, in effect, a Christ figure who cannot believe in Christ until she realizes the human limitations to her own generosity. The life-everlasting pillow, a symbol of Luella's natural, earthbound healing of others, takes on supernatural import as her instinctive leniency finds depth and affirmation in the healing compassion of Christ. In recognizing the ultimate sense of that which "don't seem sensible," Luella (whom the villagers consider devoid of sense) in effect recognizes herself (72). Her God is not the ruthless Calvinist God who damns or saves at whim but a God who understands and sympathizes with human "failin's" and who graciously allows for second chances.

Luella's return to church after Gleason's arrest is not, therefore, a concession to the hypocritical standards of her community but an acknowledgment of a newfound shared belief with professing Christians. True to that belief, as she is to all dictates of conscience, she can no longer separate herself from other worshipers. Similar to Nicholas Gunn in "A Solitary" (1890), an isolated man who makes a decision to reenter society because "men's tracks cover the whole world, and there ain't standin'-room outside of 'em," Luella's reintegration into the church community is a move that has positive repercussions, such as the end of her alienation from mainstream social life.[48] Moreover, there is reason to believe that her presence will begin to operate as leaven on the congregation's bankrupt Christianity. Mr. Sands proffers such hope in his sermon, which that particular Sunday contains, unusually, "considerable honest belief and ardent feeling" (78). Above all, the story makes it clear that Luella has not surrendered her independence of mind by returning to church: for example, she still repudiates her sister's shallow, "feminine" values by refusing to elevate fashion to any degree of importance in her life. Rather, Luella brings her "better church" to a community in desperate need of the lessons she can teach, those of tolerance, magnanimity, forgiveness, care giving, and heartfelt conviction. It is significant that Luella's final act of kindness in the story is, graciously, to house the minister and his new bride in the vacant home located between her own house and the church, the very place where John Gleason hid. The act suggests that Luella now provides not only the physical but, by extension, the spiritual structure for the future of Mr. Sands's profession: sandwiched between the church on one side and Luella on the other, the naive but good-hearted Mr. Sands will continue to benefit from Luella's humane mediating influence on a doctrine that has all but ceased to foster spiritual or moral growth in the villagers' lives.

Besides themes of courtship and marriage, and religious or church controversy, many of Freeman's early stories concern the plight of impoverished and elderly persons. Attempting to survive on tiny stores of food—a lettuce leaf, a few potatoes, a teaspoonful of jam, a cup of tea—the poor struggle to conceal their poverty from others while simultaneously striving to avoid the shameful measures of placing a mortgage on their home or being carted off to the almshouse. The poorest of the poor in the Freeman village are women. Women without husbands or fathers are often destitute and have little or no means of income. Younger women sometimes find employment: Louisa Britton teaches school in "Louisa"; Louise Durfree sells china figurines in "A Study in China" (1887); and in "Calla-Lilies and Hannah" (1887) Hannah Redman sews boots at home for a factory, an occupation familiar to residents of Randolph during Freeman's early years in that town. But older women and those raising children alone have no recourse but to take in occasional mending or sell the meager produce they eke out of their kitchen gardens. The daily struggle for survival never ceases. Thus, well into their 70s or 80s, Freeman's women still wage a continuous battle against starvation and for adequate clothing and shelter.

Freeman's sympathy for such women no doubt resulted from her own experience of poverty. She never forgot, in particular, its emotional consequences. Asked in a 1903 magazine interview what she would do with a million dollars, she responded that she would seek out the "unacknowledged poor" as recipients of her charity, "those who in many cases are not actually suffering physically for what money can do, but who have much mental distress over the prospect of an unprovided-for old age, and who lack the little amenities which redeem life from a sordid grind. . . . There are so many who own little homes, who have maybe just enough to pay the taxes, but not a cent besides, and are too old to work as once they could."[49] Freeman found ample material for her art in her exploration of the mental agony unrelenting poverty caused and, especially, of the tensions springing from the heightened sense of pride that often accompanies it. A number of Freeman's stories, for instance, deal with the delicate issue for the poor of receiving handouts or gifts. In "Old Lady Pingree" (1885), an elderly woman accepts regular donations of food only if a neighbor hides the basket in the entryway corner for the needy woman to "discover." "This was the code of etiquette, which had to be strictly adhered to," the narrator relates. "Gifts or presents openly proffered her were scornfully rejected, and ignominiously carried back by the donor" (*HR*, 153). The story's conflict arises when Nancy Pingree must decide whether to give the small hoard of money she has carefully saved for her funeral to a woman even more impoverished and proud than she.

"A Gala Dress" (1888), based on an actual incident Freeman heard related by Brattleboro gossips, involves two genteel elderly sisters who "starved daintily and patiently on their little income" as they labor to ward off prying eyes by taking turns appearing in public in the single black silk dress they own between them (*NEN*, 44). When it is her turn to wear the dress, each sister attaches a different trim to its hem, thereby fooling others into believing they own two separate dresses. Catastrophe strikes when the dress is inadvertently singed one day by firecrackers. In "A Mistaken Charity" (1883), the elderly, handicapped Shattuck sisters are terrorized by a "do-gooder" who insists they will be better off in the town's poorhouse, thinly disguised as an old-ladies' home. Violently uprooted from all they have known, the sisters manage to escape and return to their slovenly but comfortable home. "Sister Liddy" (1889) is set in the almshouse itself, where indigent women, the insane, and orphan children share close quarters. Possessing nothing whatsoever in life to brag of, old Polly Moss invents the memory of a beautiful and wealthy sister in order to compete with the others who pass the time by indulging in verbal one-upmanship. And in "A Church Mouse" (1889), homeless and unwanted Hetty Fifield does not even have a poorhouse to retreat to, for the village has none. Fighting fiercely for her survival, she barricades herself in the town meetinghouse until she finally gains permission from the authorities to live in the edifice as church sexton. There is, quite literally, no other place for her to go.

"An Honest Soul" (1884) is another interesting early example of Freeman's preoccupation with issues of pride and poverty. Elderly Martha Patch, true to her name, makes her living by piecework, quilting bedcovers and weaving rag carpets for her neighbors. Her experienced eye quickly translates bags of scrap fabric into dollars: the story opens, in fact, with Martha calculating how long she will be able to survive on the money earned from her most recent task, stitching quilts for two village women. We are informed in some detail how Martha has arrived at this near-desperate state and also why her house has no windows or doors but only a blank wall facing the main street. Martha's father, a stubborn and penurious New Englander, refused to buy anything on credit; in particular, "a mortgaged house was his horror" (*MWFR*, 4). Grubbing for a living all his life, he was never able to provide his family with more than the L portion of a projected two-story house. His meager savings, moreover, covered only his funeral expenses when he died. After her mother's death, Martha, who never married, inherited the family cause of keeping the dreaded mortgage at bay even if it meant never having the means to cut a window into the front of the house. As she sews all day long, Martha's only diversion is the activity on the street; she thus feels keenly the lack of a view. "When the minister's prayin' for the widders an' orphans he'd better make mention of one more," she states feistily, "an' that's women without front winders" (5).

Resentful of her fate, Martha is nevertheless bound by the fetters of her extreme scrupulosity to play it out. When she errs by mixing up the women's fabric as she pieces their quilts—to her dismay, not once but twice—she entertains no option but to rip the seams and spend many more days tediously restitching them. "If I'm goin' to airn money I'll airn it," she tells herself unequivocally. "I'll hev them quilts right ef it kills me!" (6, 8). The effort nearly does kill her; running out of food, she collapses from near starvation and fatigue just as the work is completed. Martha's extreme honesty is important to her self-concept: the blank wall she is forced to stare at as she sews is adorned, fittingly, by a large portrait of George Washington, that great nemesis of all untruth. But the narrator makes it clear that such rigorous honesty is excessive, even neurotic. Not only would Martha's clients not care about the mismatched quilts, but had they known of her condition they most certainly would have provided her with sustenance. However, they do not know, for Martha's pride will not permit her to accept anything for which she cannot pay. The narrator rightly questions, therefore, whether "there were any real merit in such finely strained honesty, or whether it were merely a case of morbid conscientiousness. Perhaps the old woman," the narrator muses further, "inheriting very likely her father's scruples, had had them so intensified by age and childishness that they had become a little off the bias of reason" (8).

A neighbor, Mrs. Peters, discovers Martha lying helpless on her kitchen floor; the old woman soon revives after accepting, though with reluctance, a little of Mrs. Peters's food and a cup of tea. Quickly deducing Martha's sorry state of affairs, Mrs. Peters not only provides her with "reinforcements" from her own larder but arranges that very day for her husband to put in a front window on Martha's house. At first suspicious of the offer, Martha hesitates when Mrs. Peters insists that it would actually be charitable of Martha to use up the old sash material and glass cluttering the Peters's barn. But Martha gives in only when the neighbor further suggests that she pay for the window by performing some additional sewing work for the Peters family in the ensuing months. Martha rejoices like a child when she realizes she can obtain a front window and "that her pride might suffer it to be given to her and yet receive no insult" (11).

A grim, ironic humor pervades "An Honest Soul," from Martha's assertion that the minister ought to rank women "without front winders" with orphans and widows to her last line, in which she declares, in self-deprecating understatement—for no one yet knows of her trouble with the mismatched fabric—that she is "kinder sick of bed-quilts somehow" (12). The surface humor relieves the tale's otherwise tragic implications. An isolated spinster, Martha seems to be merely a "patch" on the landscape of life. Her very existence is a type of crazy quilt pieced from scraps of food, bits of money, and other meager means for physical survival. What has become lost—buried—in such unrelenting daily toil is the soul or spirit, the leisure to pursue life's higher goods. Like the biblical Martha, Martha Patch has forgone the "better part" by concentrating all her energy on her sewing and housework. In fact, housekeeping has become one of the few pleasures "which enlivened her dulness and made the world attractive to her"; even as she lies prone on the kitchen floor from weakness and exhaustion, she is distressed to see dust on a chair (8). But unlike her biblical counterpart—and this is Freeman's point and the story's real tragedy—Martha Patch has not chosen her condition. Trapped by the excessive pride and conscientiousness she inherited from her New England father as well as by his legacy of financial insecurity, Martha has had no option but to adapt herself to the severely restricted life of a woman who not only must provide for herself but whose pride demands she disguise from others any sign of need. Indeed, it is not surprising that Freeman's work has sometimes been linked with that of the naturalist school because of its complex analysis of the powerful inner and outer forces that determine character.

Bounded by a blank front wall, Martha's physical and metaphorical horizons seem completely obstructed. Still, at age 70, her spirit craves

more than the suffocating routine to which she has always been subjected; one can only wonder how the younger Martha reacted to her vir-
tual imprisonment as she sewed day in and day out at her mother's side.
Though she cannot realize its symbolic import, Martha's desire for a
"winder" on the world becomes an effective metaphor for the human
need to liberate the spirit. Her subconscious longing for that freedom is
seen as well in her observation of a bright patch of grass in her yard
under which, she speculates, something may have been buried. Upon
learning that she will get her window, Martha notes with joy that the
spot of grass has burst into bloom with a profusion of dandelions and
clover; considered not weeds in Freeman's day but edible and medicinal
plants, the dandelions and clover are emblems here of the growth and
renewal of life. The comic ending averts our attention, but Freeman's
story invites deep consideration of elderly New England women whose
lives are greatly circumscribed by a combination of economic depriva-
tion, social isolation, and pernicious character traits inherited from their
Puritan ancestors.

Norma Johnsen interprets "An Honest Soul" as a possible mirror of
Freeman's early writing life. Johnsen explains that Mary Wilkins, according to her earliest biographer, not only loathed "writ[ing] in her down-
stairs room because the window looked out on the blank wall of a neighbor's house" but also, as she states of Martha Patch, "seized eagerly upon
the few objects of interest which did come within her vision, and made
much of them" (*MWFR*, 5). "Martha's desire for interesting sights parallels Mary's interest in the details of village life that inspired her stories,"
Johnsen concludes, "and suggests as well the similarity between 'piecing'
bits of material into a quilt and 'seizing' details and fragments of memories and 'making much of them.' . . . Wilkins shows her sense that writing
is piecing. . . . [Her] collections of stories, most notably *A Humble Romance*
and *A New England Nun*, are especially quilt-like in that her stories are
remarkably consistent in color and form—a quality noted by some of her
earliest critics."[50] Indeed, all of Freeman's tales written in her early career
strike the reader as variations on only a few major themes. Read independently, each story's handling of those themes is unique, almost always
intriguing, and often brilliant. Read consecutively, however, these early
stories are pervaded by a sameness that disgruntled some of her reviewers
after the publication of *A New England Nun*. Motivated partly by this criticism and partly by her desire to grow artistically, Freeman embarked after
1891 on the second phase of her career, during which she penned longer
forms of fiction and short stories in particular subgenres.

Mid-Career Experiments, 1892–1903: Historical, Supernatural, Mystery, and Symbolic Stories

The years between 1891 and 1903 were extremely productive for Freeman. Approaching financial independence after the success of her first two volumes of stories, she felt more at liberty to pen longer fiction, both drama and novels. She wrote two plays, *Red Robin, A New England Drama* and *Giles Corey, Yeoman,* in 1892, and her first novel, *Jane Field,* which she also attempted unsuccessfully to dramatize, was published in 1893. A steady succession of novels followed: *Pembroke* (1894), *Madelon* (1896), *Jerome, a Poor Man* (1897), *The Jamesons* (1899), *The Heart's Highway* (1900), and *The Portion of Labor* (1901). Freeman's range of subject matter in these works manifests her determination to move beyond her usual vein of work, one she feared she may have worked too long. For example, *Giles Corey* is based on events surrounding the Salem witch trials, *The Heart's Highway* is a historical romance that takes place in seventeenth-century Virginia, *The Portion of Labor* is a social-protest novel about class inequities in a New England factory, and *The Jamesons* is a slender "city mouse/country mouse" comedy. In general, all of Freeman's novels received mixed reviews but sold admirably well nonetheless. Though praised for interesting characterization, they were just as often criticized for improbable plotting. Critics noted accurately that the novels often read like a series of loosely integrated short stories: "Miss Wilkins . . . thinks in the length of the short story," stated one; "[s]he has never been able to see the larger proportions of the novel in their proper perspective" (Thompson, 672). Then as now considered her most skillful novel, *Pembroke* is the clear exception, for in this dark tale of the obdurate strength of the New England will Freeman successfully unites several plot strains involving the families of four married sisters.

Despite the fact that her primary energy was focused on writing novels and that her personal life was unsettled (after many delays, she married Charles Freeman in 1902 and moved to his home in Metuchen, New Jersey), Freeman's output of short stories remained remarkably high in this period as well. She continued to write children's tales, publishing three volumes: *The Pot of Gold and Other Stories* (1892), *Young Lucretia and Other Stories* (1892), and *Comfort Pease and Her Gold Ring* (1895). She also published 89 adult short stories, about half of which were subsequently reissued in six collections. As with her novels, Freeman experimented widely in these stories, trying her hand at various subgenres: interrelated village tales (*The People of Our Neighborhood*, 1898); stories with historical settings (*Silence and Other Stories*, 1898, and *The Love of Parson Lord and Other Stories*, 1900); symbolic and nature-mysticism stories (*Understudies*, 1901, and *Six Trees*, 1903); and ghost stories (*The Wind in the Rose-Bush and Other Stories of the Supernatural*, 1903). This section discusses Freeman's ventures, sporadic throughout her career but concentrated in this second phase, into historical, supernatural, mystery, and symbolic short fiction.

Historical Stories of Past New England

A descendant of the original Massachusetts Puritans on both sides of her family and a student of the Calvinist legacy, Freeman perused early American history avidly. Family tradition associated the Wilkins name with Bray Wilkins, one of the judges at the Salem witch trials, although when asked to verify the connection Freeman would not do so (Kendrick, 384). A number of her earliest children's verses and stories are set in the Puritan past, including those in *The Adventures of Ann: Stories of Colonial Times* (1886). Released to coincide with the 200th anniversary of the Salem witch trials, *Giles Corey*, as Westbrook notes, demonstrates Freeman's thorough familiarity with Charles Upham's multivolume *Salem Witchcraft* (1866) in its portrayal of the circumstances that led to Corey's execution for refusing to testify at his own trial (Westbrook, 100–101). Freeman was fascinated by the old man's unyielding will as well as by the atmosphere of gossip and innuendo that led to the conviction of the innocent by their own relatives and neighbors. She probably also knew Longfellow's drama *Giles Corey of the Salem Farm* (1868), but her retelling of the story is noteworthy, as a recent critic has pointed out, for its psychological analysis of the Puritan mindset in "its love of unity and display of power, its outbursts of enmity, its ready response to the phenomenon of superstition and fear, of trance and hypnotism, and even insanity."[51]

As noted earlier, Freeman often explored the condition of women labeled witches by the community. In "Christmas Jenny" (1888), for example, eccentric Jenny Wrayne is suspected of sorcery by those to whom "everything out of the broad, common track was a horror. . . . [a] characteristic which was a remnant of the old New England witchcraft superstition" (*MWFR*, 59). Around the time she was writing *Giles Corey,* Freeman also composed a number of stories set in the past that examine the roots of the superstitious New England character. One of these, "The Little Maid at the Door" (1892), studies the escalation of fear in Joseph and Ann Bayley, a prominent Puritan couple, as they journey through the woods on horseback during the witchcraft hysteria (most of the names in the story are historically accurate). Man and wife are whipped into near frenzy as they imagine herds of "black beasts" and the dreaded "black man" himself behind the trees. As Joseph urges the horse on, to their horror the Proctor house suddenly looms into view; Elizabeth and John Proctor and their two older children have recently been jailed for "consorting with the devil." As they ride past the house, Joseph is convinced he perceives the specters of the Proctors hovering outside. When his wife reluctantly glances in the direction in which he points, however, she spies what her husband cannot see, a little child crying on the doorstep. Her fright inexplicably dissipated, Ann begs her husband to stop. When he refuses, she contrives to lose one of her expensive shoes in order to be allowed to get down from the horse and backtrack through the woods in search of it. Joseph refuses to accompany her; rather, suspicious "dark thoughts came into his mind" about his wife's motives.[52]

Ann consoles and feeds the little girl, then is forced to rejoin her husband. The youngest Proctor, Abigail, who has been left to fend for herself after her family's arrest, was "deemed too young and insignificant to have dealings with Satan." She therefore was "left alone in the desolate Proctor house in the midst of the woods said to be full of evil spirits and witches, to die of fright or starvation as she might. There was but little mercy shown the families of those accused of witchcraft" (*S*, 239). Cruel neighbors, moreover, have pillaged the house and barn for the livestock and the remaining food on which the child might have been able to survive. Always sensitive to children's inner worlds (which accounts for her successful juvenile fiction), Freeman traces young Abigail's thoughts and actions in the days following the arrests as she comforts herself by sleeping in a nest of her parents' clothing and hallucinates about food. When her sister Sarah is released from prison in a few days' time, Abigail is already so weakened from fear and hunger that she dies despite Sarah's efforts to revive her. The framed story closes with a reiteration of its opening scene: the Bayleys wend their way through the forest once again but this time bravely, since they are accompanied by Cotton Mather and other magistrates and ministers. As the caravan passes the Proctor house, Mather notices the young woman Sarah Proctor standing outside but, blind to her beauty, can only speculate as to whether she bears the likeness of a witch. Ann Bayley's sight is different, however. The sole woman of the group, she alone perceives the "little maid" in the doorway once again, but this time she is pleased to observe that Abigail is rosy cheeked and smiling, with shining face and hair and dressed in a lovely white gown.

A ghost story, "The Little Maid at the Door" is one of several Freeman wrote about abused children returning from the dead to haunt their abusers; these are discussed as a group later. As a historical tale about witchcraft in Puritan Salem, "Little Maid" succeeds in rendering palpable the terror Salem residents suffered during this time of great stress. Freeman, like Hawthorne in "Young Goodman Brown," locates the source of evil in the individual psyche's tendency to deceive itself under extreme duress. "There was epidemic [in Salem] a disease of the mind which deafened and blinded to all save its own pains," the narrator states early in the story (226). This blindness toward all but one's own self and survival transformed a once close-knit, homogenous community into a set of individuals isolated from and distrustful of others. Family relationships were terribly distorted as husbands turned against wives and parents were separated from children.

"Little Maid" is a horrifying story about the results of such blindness and delusion. High-ranking and godly Puritans, Joseph and Ann Bayley are nervous and superstitious in the face of the witchcraft scare. Freeman adds an important complicating factor to their already strained mental states in that they have recently lost a child themselves. Grief and fear combine, therefore, as they battle both inner and outer demons: Joseph's tense face, for example, "show[s] not only the spirit of warfare against his foes, but the elements of strife within himself" (229). Like Cotton Mather at the tale's conclusion, husband and wife thus see and hear only what they dread—or desire—to see and hear; the landscape becomes a projection of their overwrought imaginations. As they gallop by the Proctor house, Joseph perceives what Ann cannot, the ghosts of the older Proctors who are jailed, and Ann perceives what her husband cannot, a child who looks like her dead Susanna crying for her mother. Although Ann responds sympathetically to little Abigail, the story's irony lies in the fact that the Bayleys themselves are complicit in the Proctor family's arrest and in the girl's starvation, for Joseph is a court magistrate. A woman in Puritan society and Joseph's wife, Ann is helpless in the situation. Her delusive final vision of the happy, well-fed child thus serves to mitigate both her guilt over Abigail's death and her grief over her own child's death even as she proceeds with her husband toward the next witch trial: "See! see! she is smiling!" she exclaims. "I trow all her griefs be well over" (254).

Freeman's historical stories, like "Little Maid," succeed when complex psychological character analysis combines with setting in an integral way. The Salem witchcraft scare, with its basis in religion and its profound individual and social consequences, provided her just such material. In addition, "Little Maid" is an accomplished piece structurally. Freeman balances the breathless pace of the Bayleys' horseback ride in the opening scene with the slow-moving, painfully detailed middle section, which depicts Abigail fretting and starving throughout the long, silent days. Of the other tales collected in *Silence*, "A New England Prophet" (1894) is likewise skillful in illustrating the delusion and the damaged relationships resulting from religious fanaticism, in this case the Millerite hysteria that occurred in Randolph in 1843 and 1844. Freeman no doubt based the story on her parents' and neighbors' recounting of the sensational affair. Here, as in much of her writing, she expresses her concern for those who harm the vulnerable through the abuse of power, religious or otherwise. Solomon Lennox predicts the imminent end of the world in the fantastical figures his retarded son draws on a slate. He holds the entire village in thrall as he proclaims his vision, commanding them to abandon all activities but the making of white gowns in anticipation of the community's translation to heaven. Children go to bed hungry; cattle and horses starve in the barns.

Meanwhile, Solomon's brother Simeon is one of only a few townsfolk who discredit the prophecy. He slyly suggests that if the world is about to end as his brother predicts, Solomon should have no qualms about signing away all his property to Simeon. Solomon hesitates for only a moment, then does so. With the initiation of this subplot, Freeman softens the tale's grim tenor and turns it into a wry comedy of sorts. The appointed time for the end of the world comes and goes, and a humiliated Solomon leads his exhausted, bedraggled disciples back home after their all-night vigil on a hilltop. But Solomon and his family have no home to return to, for Simeon has already gleefully taken possession of it. When convinced that his brother's proud spirit is now chastened, however, Simeon reverses his claim to the property on the condition that Solomon's wife bake him mince pies, a request she has haughtily denied him in the days when the disciples were fasting and praying. Freeman thus contrasts the villagers' religious frenzy, a harmful product of obtuse, unyielding spirits, with Simeon's mundane but wholesome insistence on regular daily food. Although he regains all of his possessions, Solomon Lennox, the story suggests, is never the same after his failure. Like Hawthorne's Young Goodman Brown, he sulks alone for the remainder of his life, "sadly within himself: a prophet brooding over the ashes of his own prophetic fire" (*S*, 224).

"Silence" (1893), "Catherine Carr" (1899), and "Lydia Hersey of East Bridgewater" (1891) are less effective historical stories, although each features the type of strong, outspoken young woman protagonist more frequent in Freeman's later fiction. The first story captures the horror of the 1704 Deerfield massacre ("the dark sweep of the tomahawk, the quick glance of the scalping-knife . . . infants dashed through the air, and the backward-straining forms of shrieking women dragged down the street"), but the young woman Silence's lapse into insanity over her missing lover is not convincing (*S*, 17). "Catherine Carr" concerns a woman who saves both her town and her lover from the British during the War of 1812, but the characterization is weak, and Catherine's actions seem merely the whim of a naive, mischievous child. Set in Puritan times, "Lydia Hersey" has little to do with its historical context but retains interest in the relationship between male and female it portrays. Though the banns of their marriage have been posted, imperious Lydia refuses to marry her fiancé, Freelove Keith, because she considers his cavorting with a raucous band of friends to be childish behavior. Angry when Freelove resists her commands, she takes revenge by humiliating an infatuated student, Abel Perkins; she compels the eager young man to wear an apron, tend her garden, churn butter, and spin. Soon growing sick of her own scheme, however, she rails at him furiously: "If you are not ashamed for yourself, I am ashamed for you," she cries. "No man can make a woman like him by doing everything she tells him to; she only despises him for it. You remember it next time" (*S*, 274–75). Lydia is reunited with Freelove in the end when, on the last day of the wedding banns, he returns to her and she readily agrees to marry him that very day. As in "The Secret" (1907), a later story with a contemporary setting, "Lydia Hersey" builds tension in its depiction of the impasse wrought by the battle of wills between two headstrong, uncompromising individuals. In both stories, unlike in "A Conflict Ended," it is the male who makes the first overture toward the couples' eventual reconciliation.

Later Freeman stories with historical settings include "Josiah's First Christmas" (1909), "Honorable Tommy" (1916), and "The Witch's Daughter" (1910). The first two are Christmas stories about children who contrive to celebrate the holiday despite their Puritan elders' disapproval. The third is a short piece about a mother and daughter who live in New England after the witch trials are over but who still are victimized by the legacy of prejudice and suspicion. Old Elma Franklin's unusual appearance is the cause: though withered and lean, she has piercing blue eyes and long blond hair, ample evidence, in popular opinion, to be convicted of black magic. When her daughter Daphne's lover is scared away by Elma's reputation and the girl grows ill, the desperate Elma decides she will indeed turn to sorcery to aid Daphne. Freeman studies the psychology of the self-fulfilling prophecy here: though she is not a witch, "much brooding upon the suspicion with which people regarded her had made [Elma] uncertain of herself. . . . [I]f she were indeed witch as they said, she would use witchcraft" (*UNC,* 127). She does so with tragic results, her own death.

Around the time she was creating stories with specific historical settings, Freeman also composed a series of lengthy tales located in the vaguely defined past, a conducive setting for their romantic themes. These include "Evelina's Garden" (1896), "The Tree of Knowledge" (1899), "The Love of Parson Lord" (1899), "Eglantina" (1902), "Amarina's Roses" (1905), and "The Fair Lavinia" (1907). Although the plots' complications differ, the stories are alike in their focus on the quest for ideal love or on the failure of those who try to manipulate another's pursuit of love. Instead of being poor and humble, the protagonists in these works are mainly members of the gentry. In addition, the stories are related in their narrative style: Freeman uses complex sentences, archaic diction, inverted word order, and other literary devices to indicate a romantic past era. Unfortunately, this style frequently comes across as awkward and stilted. Freeman's use of archaic speech is far more believable when it imitates the speech patterns of an actual historical period; for example, the language of *Giles Corey* and "Little Maid" seems true to Puritan times and is thus both convincing and unobtrusive. Clearly, Freeman was experimenting with her technique in these stories; it is hard to imagine prose further removed from the direct, terse simplicity of her trademark New England village tales. She attempted this elaborate style in *Madelon* as well, a novel about which she expressed considerable anxiety due to its being "such a deviation from [her] usual line of work" (Kendrick, 187).

Despite their contrived style, several of these stories are thematically intriguing and warrant the recent critical attention they have received.[53] "The Tree of Knowledge" and "Evelina's Garden" return to a familiar Freeman subject, one woman's restriction or usurpation of another's love affair. Freeman wrote many stories on this theme, including the earlier "The Scent of the Roses" (1887), "A Pot of Gold" (1888), "Amanda and Love" (1890), and "The Long Arm" (1895), and the later "The Gift of Love" (1906), "Dear Annie" (1910), and "Sarah Edgewater" (1916). In contrast to the near-hostile relationship between sisters in "Amanda and Love," in which one jealously attempts to drive the other's lover away and "weeps bitterly" when the plan fails, for example, both "The Tree of Knowledge" and "Evelina's Garden" feature compassionate women who, disappointed in love themselves, wish to shield their more vulnerable female relatives from a similar fate. Cornelia Pryor in "The Tree of Knowledge" sends "uplifting" letters signed with a fictitious male name to her sister Annie "to fill her mind with such a pure ideal. . . . to show what a man worthy of her affection should be, that she might love no other."[54] The benevolent intention backfires when Annie falls in love with a thief, believing him to be the letters' author. Her love serves to ennoble the man, however, in a conclusion that unabashedly celebrates in fairy tale fashion—these romantic works often read like fairy tales—the triumph of ideal love.

In "Evelina's Garden," Evelina Adams specifies in her will that her younger cousin, also named Evelina, is to remain single if she wishes to inherit the older woman's considerable estate. Moreover, the will stipulates that young Evelina must tend the exquisite flower garden that Evelina Adams has devoted her life to nurturing, since family pride kept her, years earlier, from marrying a man of lower social class. When young Evelina's fiancé, Thomas, a poor minister, learns the terms of the will, he forsakes her, convinced it is in her best interest to retain the estate. Nevertheless, love wins out; in a dramatic scene, young Evelina kills the garden with boiling water to assure Thomas of her sincere affection. But to their wonder and delight, the reunited couple then discovers that Evelina Adams's love has anticipated theirs. A sealed portion of the will reveals that, upon Evelina's marriage, the estate is to be transferred to Thomas—and thus, by extension, back to his new wife, Evelina. "This do I," Evelina Adams's will explains, "in the hope and belief that neither the greed of riches nor the fear of them shall prevent that which is good and wise in the sight of the Lord, and with the surety that a love which shall triumph over so much in its way shall endure" (*MWFR*, 192).

"Evelina's Garden" was a favorite of Freeman's and its original readers: after being collected in *Silence,* it was reissued by Harper's in 1899 as a separate book. It inspired much fan mail, including one note to which Freeman playfully responded, "Thank you very much for your kind letter about Evelina's Garden, and though I have been very tardy in telling you so—it grew again, the next spring" (Kendrick, 189). In recent criticism, Josephine Donovan has paired this story with Jewett's "A White Heron" in illustrating her thesis that turn-of-the-century women had to choose whether to remain in a "prepatriarchal" nature-identified, female world or to enter a patriarchal society characterized by heterosexual marriage. In contrast to "A White Heron," Donovan concludes, "Evelina's Garden" "signifies the triumph of 'male-identified' culture over feminine nature" in young Evelina's voluntary "destruction of the feminine realm and the roots of women's culture."[55] Donovan's feminist analysis provides a provocative point of departure for comparing the two works; as noted earlier, Freeman found Jewett's story appealing and may have had it in mind when she wrote her tale. However, "Evelina's Garden" also bears a more than cursory resemblance to Hawthorne's "Rappaccini's Daughter," in which a father poisons his daughter in order to ensure that she remain forever in his garden. Each story involves a parent figure who seeks to control the affections of a younger person, and each presents a crisis that serves to test the nature of authentic love, both that between parent and child and that between male and female. The stories' conclusions are, of course, very different. Freeman may well have been responding to Hawthorne's tragic ending, in which an arrogant male's scientific experiment goes horribly wrong, by creating an alternative version in which a wise and loving woman's foresight provides even after death for her young relative's greatest good. As such, "Evelina's Garden," like a number of other Freeman stories, illustrates the narrator's statement in "The Tree of Knowledge" that "the tenderness of one woman for another is farther reaching in detail than that of a man, because it is given with a fuller understanding of needs" (*LPL,* 98).

Freeman discouraged the frequent correlations made between her work and Hawthorne's. Besides those linking "Evelina's Garden" with "Rappaccini's Daughter," however, parallels can be found between "The Slip of the Leash" (1904) and "Wakefield"; between "The Three Old Sisters and the Old Beau" (1896) and "The Wedding Knell"; and between "Eglantina" and "The Birthmark." The connection between the latter two stories is particularly intriguing, for once again Freeman rewrites Hawthorne's tragic ending, which results from a male's pride—Aylmer's quest to perfect his wife's appearance—into a positive conclusion that emphasizes the ultimate blindness of genuine love. When Roger Proctor regains the eyesight he lost in childhood, he is still in love with Eglantina, who, like Georgiana in Hawthorne's tale, has a prominent birthmark on her face. Eglantina, however, fears that Roger will renounce her once he sees her face; she flees from him and is convinced only at length that his love is sincere. The "wrong vision" of the story turns out to be not the man's, as in "The Birthmark," but ironically the woman's. An especially pernicious type of pride makes Eglantina run from love; she refuses to accept that another can cherish her for her essential self and not for her looks alone. Not imitations of Hawthorne's stories, "Evelina's Garden" and "Eglantina" are rather counterparts to them, providing alternative solutions to dilemmas concerning loving human relationships. In these pieces, as in the entire group of short stories set in a hazy past era, Freeman consistently promotes, albeit in idealistic ways, what one critic has referred to as her "ethic of love": situations in which "characters have learned or are learning the priority of human love before human will."[56] Viewed in this manner, these romantic mid-career stories, sometimes dismissed as overly sentimental, are consistent with Freeman's earlier realistic fiction, which explores the same complexities of human relationships but just as often depicts the poignant dissolution of love rather than its triumphant achievement.

Supernatural and Mystery Stories

According to her biographer Edward Foster, Freeman speculated that every New England village harbored some mystery or crime (Foster, 83). Convinced of the "hidden darkness of human nature," she often used her fiction to uncover the subtle but destructive dark forces—stubbornness, jealousy, self-righteousness—operating in seemingly respectable, churchgoing folk (Brontë, 89). It is, in fact, a surprisingly small step from Freeman's starkly realistic tales of everyday village life to her stories of supernatural occurrences in the same towns and among the same people. Her ghost stories extend her lifelong concern with issues of isolation and community, poverty and pride, frustrated hopes and repressed desires, and to a lesser extent, the failure of conventional religion. Eschewing the machinery of claptrap gothicism (stormy nights, clanging chains, and the like), Freeman is far less interested in the actual existence of ghosts or uncanny events than she is in the psychological condition of the persons who witness them. If, as is sometimes stated, the root of all gothic fiction is the cosmic struggle between good and evil, Freeman locates that struggle inside humans who, until forced to confront what they cannot rationalize, are unaware of their own potential for evil. Even after their encounter with the supernatural, many Freeman protagonists remain blind to that potential, which makes these tales among her most pessimistic.

As with her historical pieces, Freeman wrote ghost and mystery stories throughout her career but worked particularly in these genres between 1892 and 1904. She joined many of her contemporary realists, including Jewett, Henry James, and Edith Wharton, in experimenting with supernatural fiction. Over the years, her ghost stories have generated widely differing critical opinions, ranging from out-of-hand dismissal to praise for their unique contribution to the genre. One of their earliest admirers stated that "[Freeman's] ghost stories in *The Wind in the Rose-Bush* are among the best New England has ever produced—unconventional, unexplained, unreduced, yet seemingly natural and wholly convincing."[57] Recent scholarship shows signs of rediscovering this often misunderstood genre, which around the turn of the century was dominated by women writers both in the United States and in Britain. Freeman's supernatural stories deserve the renewed attention they have received. Deceptively simple on the surface due to the author's remarkably restrained narrative style, the majority of these tales employ the doubling of characters, or even multiple sets of doubles, to render complex psychological portraits of those who are haunted. Several are told by a gossiping, first-person narrator, whose unreliability due to her own fixations is soon revealed; her story thus turns back on her and exposes her motives in its telling. Moreover, like the best of Freeman's short fiction, these stories remain open ended, compelling readers to carry away a heightened sense of the uncanny lurking just beneath the surface of the ordinary and, most importantly, a deeper distrust of what may be hidden in the recesses of their own hearts.

Freeman's earliest collections, *A Humble Romance* and *A New England Nun*, contain several supernatural stories. In "A Symphony in Lavender" (1883) a woman is warned by a mysterious dream to reject a man she is about to wed; in "A Far-Away Melody" (1883) two spiritually minded elderly sisters hear heavenly music presaging their deaths; and in "The Twelfth Guest" (1889) a benign ghost appropriately named Christine appears to a family on Christmas Eve. Also among her earliest works is "A Gentle Ghost" (1889), the first of the author's series of tales about neglected or abused young girls. Freeman told Jewett that she felt compelled to exorcise "that forlorn little girl" who "had been in my head a matter of a dozen years" by working her first into a poem and later into a story (Kendrick, 97). Evidently, however, the ghost-child did not disappear, for Freeman went on to rewrite the girl's story four more times. Beth Wynne Fisken has noted how "A Gentle Ghost," "The Little Maid at the Door" (1892), "The Wind in the Rose-Bush" (1902), and "The Lost Ghost" (1903) escalate in horror. "The School-Teacher's Story" (1894), an uncollected piece that Fisken does not mention, completes the series. Fisken theorizes that Freeman's preoccupation with the subject might have resulted, among other factors, from her envy of her talented and popular sister Anna and from her guilt when Anna's sudden death at 17 left her the only remaining child in a family that had already suffered the loss of two other children. Freeman herself dated her obsession with the haunting little girl to approximately 1876, the year of Anna's death.

Whatever the source of Freeman's preoccupation with the child's story, I agree with Fisken that there exists an undeniable "personal element that haunts some of these stories and evidently haunted [Freeman] as well."[58] The first in the sequence, "A Gentle Ghost," is not actually a ghost story, since the child's moaning that haunts Mrs. Dunn and her daughter Flora, who are mourning the death of Jenny, Mrs. Dunn's daughter and Flora's sister, turns out to be that of an orphan from the nearby asylum. Nevertheless, the story is a chilling study of the close association of grief, fear, and superstition as mother and daughter cling to each other for comfort in the days following Jenny's burial. Described in detail earlier, "The Little Maid at the Door" also concerns a mother who has recently lost a little girl. She is haunted by the ghost of an abused child, a crime, as noted, for which she and her Puritan magistrate husband are partly responsible. In "The School-Teacher's Story," the ghost girl appears to a middle-aged schoolteacher. Related in the first person, the woman's narrative betrays a fierce determination of will that has resulted in the suppression of the anger and loneliness she has felt since being rejected by her fiancé years earlier. Though she declares that she does not like children and takes pains to describe herself as detached and cynical, the unnamed protagonist has taught school competently for 44 years. After accepting a new position at a country school, she is haunted by the spirit of a child who was murdered there 60 years before; the wan little girl repeatedly asks the teacher to find her doll and hear her lessons. "It seemed to me, somehow," the woman states in a moment of candid self-reflection, "as if all the wants I had ever had myself, sounded in that child's voice, and as if she was begging for something I had lost myself."[59] Although she has steeled herself against all emotional involvement, she finds herself softened by the ghost child, sews her a doll, and eventually learns of her sad history when she follows her to the cemetery plot where she was laid to rest long ago.

The fourth and fifth stories in the series, "The Wind in the Rose-Bush" and "The Lost Ghost," collected in *The Wind in the Rose-Bush*, are the most disturbing, for in each the abuser is the child's mother (stepmother in "Wind"). Alfred Bendixen has stated perceptively that the primary "source of terror in most of [Freeman's] supernatural tales is the perversion of the home, the distortion of normal family relationships."[60] Indeed, these two portrayals of depraved motherhood represent the ultimate corruption of the Victorian ideals of true womanhood and of the sanctity of the home. In "The Wind in the Rose-Bush," young Agnes evidently died because her stepmother, Mrs. Dent, withheld from her some necessary medicine. Agnes has already been dead a year when the story opens with Agnes's aunt Rebecca, who is not aware of her niece's death, arriving from Michigan to claim the child. For several days, Mrs. Dent attempts to conceal the fact of the girl's death from Rebecca. Meanwhile, Rebecca grows increasingly frustrated with the delay in seeing Agnes; she also becomes unnerved by weird occurrences that seem to indicate that the girl is present in the home. The mothering instincts of Rebecca, a middle-aged spinster, have been repressed but now emerge suddenly in her longing to care for her dead brother's child. At one point, for example, she "unconsciously held her shawl, rolled up in a canvas bag, on her left hip, as if it had been a child" (*WRB*, 4). Rebecca's anguish comes when she finally comprehends that she has arrived for Agnes too late, that her last opportunity for motherhood, one she has unaccountably delayed in grasping, has been wrenched from her—and in the most horrifying manner.

The most appalling abuse of a child occurs in the last of Freeman's stories about the "forlorn little girl." In "The Lost Ghost," the child is locked in a room and abandoned by her vain and cruel mother, who runs off with her lover while her husband is away on an extended business trip. The little girl starves and freezes to death. Her ghost, incessantly wailing, "I can't find my mother," haunts two childless widows who operate a boardinghouse in the home years after the dreadful event. One of them, the maternal Mrs. Bird, so pities the apparition that, apparently, she wills her own death in order to tend to the girl in the spirit world. Her departing spirit is seen "walking off over the white snow-path with that child holding fast to her hand, nestling close to her as if she had found her own mother" (*MWFR*, 276). Thus, in this final version of a theme that haunted Freeman for nearly 30 years, mother and child are united for eternity in the netherworld. The move must have settled the ghost child in Freeman's imagination, for she never again returned to the subject.

Of the other stories in *The Wind in the Rose-Bush*, "The Southwest Chamber" (1903) and "Luella Miller" (1902) are fine supernatural tales and good examples of Freeman's technique of doubling in order to disclose a character's psychological state. In the former piece, two sisters who have inherited their aunt's home and converted it into a boardinghouse realize that one of the bedrooms, that in which the mean-spirited Aunt Harriet died, is haunted by her ghost. First the younger sister, Amanda, experiences odd happenings in the bedroom—a dress out of place, a pitcher of water inexplicably drained—then the schoolteacher who has rented the chamber flees from it after likewise seeing strange phenomena. Other boarders offer to sleep in the room, but one by one they become unnerved by the presence lurking there. Finally, Amanda's older sister, Sophia, encounters the ghost and immediately decides to dismiss the boarders and put the place up for sale.

The story focuses on each individual's reaction to the supernatural occurrences. The characters who experience the greatest fear are those who are hardheaded and unimaginative, who tolerate no disorder and who take pride in firm control over themselves and their environment—in other words, Freeman's typical New England Yankees. When they are forced to confront that which threatens to dislodge their narrow but stable world view, such characters are at once overwhelmed by self-doubt and react with terror and defiance. After the encounter with Aunt Harriet's ghost, the schoolteacher, though "masterly" and "dignified," begins "straightway . . . to wonder if there could be anything wrong with her mind. She remembered that an aunt of her mother's had been insane" (*WRB*, 130). Horrified at the possibility of her own madness, she suffers the nervous breakdown she has long been near. Then a haughty widow who scoffs at the supernatural moves into the bedroom, declaring, "if I saw things or heard things I'd think the fault must be with my own guilty conscience" (133). Her words subsequently turn back on her when she is nearly strangled during the night by mysterious hands. Protesting that no true Christian can believe in ghosts, a minister then attempts to enter the chamber but, resisted by an unseen force, discovers that he is prevented from even setting foot in it. "Doubting, raging, overwhelmed with spiritual agony as to the state of his own soul," he is shocked from his self-complacency and forced for the first time to confront the existence of spiritual evil (158).

Finally, Sophia, who as proprietor of the boardinghouse is naturally reluctant to admit that one of its rooms is haunted, sleeps in the bedroom herself. To her horror, she becomes possessed by Aunt Harriet's malignant spirit and sees in the room's mirror the old woman's face instead of her own, "scowling forever with unceasing hatred and misery" (162). The narrator has informed us earlier of the bitter feud that has divided the family; as a result of that quarrel, Sophia never met Harriet. But when she sees Harriet's image mirrored back to her as her own double, Sophia understands that the power of hatred can persist past the grave and down through generations. She realizes her own potential for inheriting that hatred and takes the warning to heart, at least to the extent that she sells the house and distances herself and Amanda from Harriet's evil influence. Like the schoolteacher, the widow, and the minister, Sophia is obliged for the first time to admit her inability to control forces both inside and outside of herself. For a stubborn, nononsense New England businesswoman, the lesson is one in the nature of fear itself.

"Luella Miller," one of Freeman's best stories, pairs as doubles the title character with the woman who relates her story. Ostensibly about the vampirelike Luella, who appears to cause the death of all those who care for her, the story more subtly exposes the character of Luella's neighbor Lydia, who, we discover through her telling of the tale, resents Luella for marrying a man she herself wanted. The women are reverse images of each other: Luella is an unusual type in New England, a "slight, pliant" woman with "little slender, clinging hands, and a wonderful grace of motion," and Lydia is the typical Freeman spinster, plain, sharp-edged, "straight as an arrow . . . recently let loose from the bow of life" (*MWFR*, 249). Lydia recounts the frightening story of Luella's life. It seems that everyone who came in contact with Luella worshiped her, eagerly served her, and horrifyingly, eventually died from the effort. Incapable of domestic work, Luella cannot even brew a pot of coffee; her husband, Erastus, did all the housework before he suddenly weakened and died not long after they were married. Erastus's teenaged sister Lily then volunteered to keep house for Luella, but she soon succumbed to a mysterious wasting disease, as did Luella's aunt, the next to tend the helpless, babyish woman. Others who stepped into the position met with a similar fate.

Lydia is clearly obsessed with Luella's story. Though she is proud of having resisted becoming one of Luella's victims, ironically, her preoccupation with the other woman renders her one at last. Importantly, we are privy only to Lydia's version of Luella's life; Lydia alone testifies to Luella's power to kill those who love her. As Lydia relates her narrative, her envy of the other woman is apparent. For one thing, she is particularly at a loss to account for others' unwavering devotion to Luella, affection Lydia herself does not naturally elicit. Long after Luella has died, Lydia keeps the tale of the vampire woman alive for new generations of villagers, thereby ensuring that she will receive attention from those who are fascinated by it. The story's effect is only enhanced when Lydia is found dead one day, stretched out on the ground in front of Luella's house. A woman who "never spared the truth when she essayed to present it," Lydia leaves her listeners half believing that she has exaggerated the story and half believing in the existence of a woman so charming yet utterly useless that she literally sucks the life out of those who fall under her spell (249). Bendixen observes that "the sharp contrast between Lydia and Luella, between the frustrated old maid and the dangerously dependent wife, dramatizes the unsatisfactory alternatives too often offered women" in Freeman's time (*WRB*, 251–52). In her doubling of women characters, Freeman frequently places those alternatives in opposition but perhaps never as starkly as in this piece. An eerie ghost story, "Luella Miller" is even more disturbing as a study of the lives of two warped and distorted women: the passive, selfish woman whom others must cater to and the equally self-serving woman who forges an entire career out of relentless, malicious gossip.

After the publication of *The Wind in the Rose-Bush*, Freeman continued writing occasional supernatural tales, including "The Hall Bedroom" (1903), a fascinating epistolary account of a down-and-out man's venture into a sensual, fifth-dimension realm; "The Jade Bracelet" (1918), an inferior story of a man who becomes possessed by an evil Chinese person's spirit when he places a bracelet on his wrist; and "The White Shawl" (undated), an intense, compelling tale about a crippled woman who through love and faith evokes a miracle as she manages to guide trains through a dangerous crossing during a blinding storm. In manuscript form at Freeman's death, "The White Shawl" resembles the early "The Bar-Lighthouse," although in this story the mysterious event turns out to have a natural cause. At the end of "The White Shawl," a character observes that "sometimes the partition walls [between the natural and the supernatural] are very thin for certain souls, perhaps transparent and there may be entrances for them under certain stress, of which you and I know nothing" (*UNC*, 316–17). This statement can serve as a summary of Freeman's thesis in all of her supernatural fiction: ghosts and uncanny phenomena arise from troubled hearts, those burdened by unfulfilled desires, family tensions, suppressed jealousy or anger, or despair. Freeman's portraits of characters whose overwrought mental states propel them to penetrate the partition between the natural and the spiritual worlds show her remarkable knowledge of human psychology. These stories also demonstrate the author's significant skill in manipulating material to reveal the *unheimlich* in the homey or the uncanny in the ordinary, the hallmarks of effective supernatural fiction.

Freeman employed the typical technique of mystery writing in much of her short fiction: a gradual, carefully foreshadowed revelation of the circumstances that have led to a present condition. The early "Calla-Lilies and Hannah," for example, follows this formula; the reader does not learn whether the protagonist is a thief until the tale's climactic moment. Two mid-career stories present more elaborate mysteries. A favorite of Freeman's original readers, "The Gold" (1904) is set during the turbulent years of the American Revolution. Catherine Duke, incensed that her husband, Abraham, refuses to disclose where he hid his recent inheritance of gold before he sets off for war, spends every waking moment after his departure scouring the house in search of it. Her obsessive toil, which eventually warps her mind, is in vain: she is murdered—possibly by Abraham himself, more likely by someone who has heard her brag about the gold—before she locates it. Like the purloined letter in Poe's tale, the gold turns out to be so obviously situated as to completely escape her attention. Although the solution to the mystery of the gold's whereabouts is neatly contrived, the focus subtly shifts in the latter part of the story to the miserly Abraham Duke's tragic predicament. Widely suspected of killing the only man in town who might have betrayed the gold's whereabouts to his wife, Abraham, upon his return from the army, is unable to obtain any cash for his precious metal. Freezing and hungry in his wreck of a house, he dies a miserable death, "starved with his wealth glittering in his eyes" (*MWFR*, 344).

"The Long Arm" (1895) was written in conjunction with newspaper columnist Joseph Edgar Chamberlin, one of Freeman's close friends. A frequent visitor to Chamberlin's Boston home, Freeman met many fellow authors there as well as her future husband; she frequently was called on to entertain the group by telling ghost or mystery tales around the open hearth. When the Bacheller syndicate announced a short-story competition, Freeman invited Chamberlin to collaborate on an entry with her. He suggested they take as their model the Lizzie Borden slayings, still unsolved and thus widely discussed three years after they had occurred, in 1892, in the nearby town of Fall River. As Lillian Faderman has noted, "The Long Arm" may also be based on the equally sensational Alice Mitchell case of the same year, in which a mentally disturbed Tennessee woman murdered her lesbian lover to "make it sure that no one else could get her."[61] Freeman wrote the story in a few days, and Chamberlin helped tailor it to the contest's requirements. The story won the $2,000 prize, appeared in the syndicate's many newspapers before being collected in *The Long Arm and Other Detective Stories* (1895), and gained Freeman widespread popularity. Writing not long after Freeman's death in 1930, Foster notes that "some of the very old people think of Miss Wilkins chiefly as the author of this story."[62]

"The Long Arm" is the first-person journal account of a young woman who has been arrested for murdering her father but released from prison for lack of evidence. Popular opinion is against her; thus, upon returning to her village home, she feels "condemned to something infinitely worse than the life-cell or the gallows."[63] Moreover, she is plagued by self-doubt, for she had reason to hate her father when he swore he would disinherit her if she married a man she loved. Sarah commences her journal with the goal of examining the case's facts as thoroughly and impartially as possible. The few clues available seem to make little sense when added together, but the oddest element of the crime and the one most damaging to her is the fact that all of the house's doors were locked from the inside when the murder occurred. Sarah and her father were alone in the house that night. The arrival of a sympathetic detective impels the second half of the story to its intriguing conclusion. With Sarah's help, the detective determines that the town seamstress, Phoebe Dole, is the culprit; she used her unusually long arm to reach the inside door latch by means of the leather-flapped cat door. Once accused, Phoebe readily confesses to the crime. Her motive was her fear of losing her longtime companion Maria Woods, whom, she discovered, was secretly planning to marry Sarah's father. Phoebe also admits that she prevented Maria from marrying the same man 40 years earlier. "This time," she explains, "I knew I couldn't [stop her] unless I killed him. She's lived with me in that house for over forty years. There are other ties as strong as the marriage one, that are just as sacred. What right had he to take her away from me and break up my home?" (*LA,* 61).

   Though the subject is open to speculation, no hard evidence exists to confirm that Freeman had a lesbian relationship with Mary John Wales, the woman she lived with in Randolph for nearly 20 years, from 1883 to 1902. Freeman's fiction, however, certainly indicates her vital interest in intense, sometimes cloying relationships between women. These pairs often consist of a domineering and controlling woman who holds a weaker, subordinate, sometimes much younger woman in her thrall. Though Freeman hedges at describing the exact nature of the more volatile female-female relationships she portrays, such stories often echo the broad plot outline of "The Long Arm" in their portrayal of one woman who jealously tries to prevent the other from marrying and moving away. Two other pieces with this theme are the uncollected "Two Friends" (1887) and "Julia—Her Thanksgiving" (1909).[64] The novels *The Portion of Labor* (1901) and *The Shoulders of Atlas* (1908) also present relationships that can be viewed as quasilesbian. The lesbian overtones in "The Long Arm," a satisfying if not particularly suspenseful mystery tale, establish this story as one of Freeman's boldest examinations of the subject.

Symbolic and Nature-Mysticism Stories

Comprising a final category of Freeman's mid-career experiments are the 18 stories collected in *Understudies* and *Six Trees* that explore the psychic connections between the natural world and human beings. These works represent Freeman's fullest expression of the symbolic and mystical elements she desired in her fiction but avoided in her early career because she thought they might not appeal to the public. Closer to sketches than to fully plotted stories, they are premised on the Emersonian theses that "nature is the symbol of spirit," that all elements of the natural world bear correspondence to each other, and in particular, that nature can exert moral influence on individuals, "unlock[ing] a new faculty of the soul."[65] As a young woman in Brattleboro, Freeman read and discussed Emerson's essays with her friends. She was also greatly affected by the region's "marvelous beauty"; in fact, she attributed the impetus for her "try[ing] to achieve anything" in life to it (Kendrick, 381). Long after she had left Vermont, she recalled, "I used to stand . . . and look at [Mount Wantistiquet] and its brethren along the horizon, giving to all who were willing to receive, colors wonderful enough to transform lives, no matter what troubles were in store for them" (Kendrick, 396–97). Elsewhere she voiced her firm belief that "everywhere in New England we more or less clearly sense a strange atmosphere of spirit beyond the material."[66] Not incompatible with the Puritan view of nature as a metaphor for the divine, transcendental thought was an integral part of Freeman's New England heritage. It provided her with the means to expand her psychological inquiry into the New England character through a more overt use of symbolism than she had heretofore employed in her fiction.

The 12 stories that comprise *Understudies* appeared more or less alternately in *Harper's Bazar* and *Harper's Monthly* between May 1900 and January 1901: 6 animal tales were published in the *Monthly*, 6 flower tales in the *Bazar*. According to several letters she wrote to Harper and Brothers at the time, Freeman originally wanted to combine animal and insect stories in one collection and flower and tree stories in a second. She acquiesced, however, to her publisher's request to release the animal and flower stories together as *Understudies*. The tree stories, published in the *Bazar* from September 1901 through January 1903, were issued separately as *Six Trees;* the insect stories were never written. Although Freeman distinguished the animal stories as "psychological" and the plant stories as "symbolic," each differs only in the natural item employed as metaphor and in the extent to which the human protagonist is aware of that item's parallel to himself or herself and is receptive to its potentially transforming powers. "Who shall determine the limit at which the intimate connection and reciprocal influence of all forms of visible creation upon one another may stop?" the narrator of "The Great Pine" rhetorically queries (*MWFR*, 241). Freeman's intent in these symbolic stories is to probe that limit in individuals of widely differing sensibility.

As in her early stories, Freeman's protagonists here are primarily the solitary, the outcast, or those who have become embittered by harsh circumstances or by a deadly monotony of life. A certain self-centeredness attends such conditions, imprisoning the characters in the confines of their own constricted outlooks on life. "To speak truly, few adult persons can see nature," Emerson stated; appropriately, then, to the degree that Freeman's protagonists can escape self-preoccupation and perceive nature, nature in turn provides them with models of endurance, stability, self-sufficiency, and providential care (Emerson, 23). Misunderstood or rejected by human society, sensitive individuals find a source of companionship and healing in the natural world. Their identities strengthened and their spirits enlarged by such contact, some can subsequently turn outward and begin to care again for those around them. Others remain wrapped up in themselves, largely unaware of nature. Yet they too are revealed as its beneficiaries; they too are shown to be "part and parcel" of it. In each story, therefore, nature serves to illuminate character. Freeman's insistence in her fiction on a wide variety of individual personalities and responses to life finds its parallel in these tales in nature's diversity and munificence. These works thus also respond to the transcendentalist imperative that "there may be as many different persons in the world as possible . . . each one be[ing] very careful to find out and pursue *his own* way" (Thoreau, 48).

Both *Understudies* and *Six Trees* were well received in Freeman's day, and *Six Trees* in particular has garnered praise from modern critics. With only a few exceptions, each of the stories in the two collections is carefully drawn and, because open ended, thought provoking. Two or three from each volume can be rated among Freeman's finest work. Of the animal stories, "The Cat" (1900) and "The Parrot" (1900) are exceptional pieces. Freeman had a special affinity for animals; her letters are replete with descriptions of her various pets, and she once acknowledged to a friend that "all my life I have discriminated between animals as between people" (Kendrick, 332). It was natural for her to choose as her subject for the first work of the series the animal of which she was most fond. "That Cat lives in the White Mountains. . . . I have met him," she replied when a reader complimented the tale (Kendrick, 241). Her lifelong observance of cats' behavior no doubt accounts for the detailed focus in "The Cat" on the animal itself rather than on a human protagonist, as occurs in the other tales in *Understudies*. Left alone by his master during the winter to forage for himself, the cat lives in a deserted cabin and hunts for food. When a squatter, "an outcast among men for his poverty and lowly mystery of antecedents," takes over the dwelling, the cat unquestioningly welcomes the company and shares his prey with the elderly, sickly man.[67] Though the newcomer's "experience with men had not been pleasant, and neither had the experience of men been pleasant with him," the man treats the cat with affection, and they live devotedly together throughout the long, harsh winter (*U*, 10). Spring arrives, and the stranger one day vanishes, leaving the cat plaintively wailing "that cry of the animal for human companionship which is one of the sad notes of the world" (14). Soon, however, the cat's old master returns to take up summer residence in the cabin, and the cat greets him, rubbing against his legs and purring.

When the master misses his store of tobacco and realizes that some other person has been occupying the space, he is both perplexed and perturbed: "his rough forehead knitted, and he and the Cat looked at each other across that impassable barrier of silence which has been set between man and beast from the creation of the world" (16).

Each a loner and a forager, the two men and the cat are similar in their unremitting struggle for survival in a harsh, grasping, and competitive world. The law is simple in such an environment: man and animal alike seize as rightfully theirs whatever comes their way—a rabbit as food, another man's cabin as shelter. Softening the ostensibly deterministic theme, however, is Freeman's probing of the benevolent, providential, yet mysterious relationship between humans and some kinds of animals. Such bonds often have the power (as we increasingly realize today) to console and heal those who for some reason do not or cannot respond to other people. Nevertheless, the relationship between humans and animals remains ultimately inscrutable; an "impassable barrier" of otherness separates one species from the other. Though she ascribes a limited sensibility to the cat, Freeman is careful not to anthropomorphize it; in fact, none of the six animal stories devolves into mere sentimentality, the genre's usual pitfall. Rather, "The Cat" leaves readers looking afresh at the animals that share their lives, musing about the bonds that unite humans and beasts as well as about the enigmatic, impenetrable wall that forever divides them.

"The Parrot" is, interestingly, the only animal story that features a female protagonist. Freeman's subject matter here is characteristic: Martha, a minister's daughter and a spinster who lives a solitary, colorless life, is courted but then rejected by a young man, also a minister. Martha's owning of a parrot, however, refigures this typical plot into an intense psychological study of the manner in which a human's repressed emotions may be projected onto a pet and, in turn, mirrored back to the human. As is true of many of Freeman's female protagonists, such as Ann Millet of "An Object of Love" and Eunice Fairweather of "A Moral Exigency," Martha is a severely divided woman, "with the influence of a stern training strong upon her, and yet with a rampant force of individuality constantly at war with it" (*MWFR*, 211). Her house reflects her rigidly controlled demeanor: it is "sharply angled," has a "clean, repellent glare of windows" beneath "stiff parallelograms of white curtains," and is surrounded by a yard of "evenly slanted" grass (211). Her strict Calvinist upbringing has resulted in her dreading any release of the strong, sexually charged passion that churns within her: her onetime attendance of a concert, for instance, caused her to feel "contaminated for days," and even the lush elm tree on her property lends her "a vague and unreasoning sense of immorality" (212, 211). Inexplicably even to herself, Martha owns a parrot, an exotic, half-tamed creature that is both her nemesis and her double in its uncanny ability to express her most deeply hidden longings. Trapped in his wire cage, as his mistress is in her restricted life, the parrot shrieks profanities and inarticulate speeches "with a seemingly diabolical comprehension of the situation," leaving Martha to speculate—guiltily, because of its religious unorthodoxy—whether or not the bird possesses a soul (212).

Martha is surprised but elated when a young minister begins to wait on her. After a year of his weekly visits she expects they will marry, but she abruptly learns through gossip at the church sewing circle that he has kept a fiancée in a neighboring village all the time. Not once betraying her emotions in public, she makes her solitary way home after the meeting and there throws herself to the floor, releasing "all the floodgates of her New England nature" as she wails aloud in grief and wrath (217). She is startled when, from the parrot's cage, "a cry of uncanny sympathy and pain and tenderness outside the pale of humanity" arises, a cry that once again seems to point to a consciousness beyond animal instinct in the bird (217). Still, Martha doubts that the parrot actually possesses such a faculty. But several weeks later, the final episode in her relationship with the minister convinces her otherwise. Arriving at Martha's house with his new bride to pay the customary wedding visit to each member of his congregation, the minister and his wife are seated in Martha's immaculately clean, orderly parlor. Suddenly the parrot, unaccountably left uncaged for once and wild with freedom, swoops in and furiously pecks the bride's bonnet to shreds. A scene of fright, confusion, and anger ensues; the couple hastily exits. Alone with the parrot, Martha now recognizes clearly "in the fierce bird a comradeship and an equality, for he had given vent to an emotion of her own nature, and she knew forevermore that the parrot had a soul" (218). Though we are not privy to her life after the event, the story seems to offer the hope that Martha might now be able to relax somewhat, if not break through, the barriers of religion, family heritage, society, and self that have so restricted her emotional needs: her recognition of her kinship with the parrot signals both a new acceptance of her own half-tamed passion and a defiance of the religious tenet that deems ascribing a soul to an animal tantamount to the worship of idols. Henceforth, we assume, Martha may allow or even encourage the parrot to act out her long-repressed emotions—a first step, perhaps, toward the healing of her divided sensibilities.

In Freeman's flower and tree stories, the title plant serves either as a metaphor for the protagonist or as a symbol of the positive qualities that he or she lacks and aspires to. The best of these, "Arethusa" (1900), pairs the "rarest and most beautiful," "maiden" orchid arethusa with Lucy Greenleaf, a dainty, ethereal, "fluttering" young girl (*MWFR*, 219). Her daughter having reached marriageable age, Mrs. Greenleaf wishes Lucy would respond to the attentions of her one suitor, Edson Abbot. She cannot understand the girl's complete disinterest in the man, for she herself "had been insensibly trained by all her circumstances of life to regard a husband like rain in its season, or war, or a full harvest, or an epidemic, something to be accepted without question if offered, whether good or bad, as sent by the will of the Lord" (222). Half in love with Edson herself, Mrs. Greenleaf speaks persuasively to her daughter, quoting Bible verses on the fitness of marriage for women and warning Lucy that she may end up like their "pitiable" spinster neighbor if she rejects Edson. Childishly naive, Lucy listens with "fascinated fear" to her mother's counsel but responds only by whimpering, "I don't like men. I am afraid of them. I want to stay with you" (223). In the end, however, filial obedience compels her to accept Edson's proposal: "Mother says I ought to," she informs him, "and I will" (224).

Lucy's great delight every spring is to make a pilgrimage to the swamp to seek out the arethusa in its first bloom. When Edson offers to pluck her one of the flowers, however, she vehemently resists; she will not allow him to destroy the delicate growth or, in fact, to take any part in her private ritual. The wedding day arrives: the guests are assembled, but Lucy is nowhere to be found. A distraught and sobbing Mrs. Greenleaf now admits, "I don't know but we've made a mistake. . . . I don't know as Lucy ought to have had anybody but her mother" (227). By contrast, Edson reacts with rage, furious that the girl has apparently "set herself against him in a last assertion of her maiden freedom" (227). After a search, Lucy is discovered down at the swamp beside her beloved arethusa. With no resistance, she accompanies them back to the house and is wed. As time goes by and to everyone's surprise, Lucy seems to thrive in her marriage, raising two children and performing her household tasks with skill. But every year without fail she returns alone to the swamp to greet "the rare and anomalous flower with unending comfort and delight" (229).

The excellence of "Arethusa" lies in its provocative lack of resolution concerning the motives for and benefits of marriage. Freeman opposes two women's responses: Mrs. Greenleaf's pragmatic assertion that one should (to quote Sarah Penn from "The Revolt of 'Mother' ") "reckon men in with Providence," unquestioningly taking what is given, and Lucy's trepidation over that which might upset or exert demands on her comfortable, childlike sphere. In addition, Freeman records the male's response to marriage in Edson, who initially decides to court Lucy primarily because she presents a challenge and who persists "because he always seized with a grip . . . upon anything which seemed about to elude him" (221). What is noticeably lacking in each of the three responses is any indication of real love between Edson and Lucy. Though Lucy grows somewhat fond of Edson during their courtship— she at least begins to tolerate his presence—it is Mrs. Greenleaf's practical view of marriage that finally unites the couple. One might expect the worst for Lucy under such conditions: the fragile, spritelike girl paired with the strong-willed, "gripping" man. Paradoxically, as noted, Lucy seems to wax in health and ability in her marriage to Edson. But Freeman's phrasing is carefully ambiguous in the final portion of the story. Though Lucy loves her children, she remains aloof from them, not allowing them or Edson to share in what is still her most intimate experience, the annual visit to the arethusa. She "seems" content, performing her daily duties with precision. Yet the narrator tells us that her life is now but a "little halting verse," punctuated at long intervals by the "fair rhyme" of her annual discovery of the arethusa, an event that has become for her a veritable "refuge from the exigency of life" (229).

Does Lucy benefit by marrying Edson or forfeit her individuality? Freeman leaves the final judgment to her readers. As always for Freeman, human relationships and marriage in particular involve significant compromises for a woman. Certainly the teenaged Lucy exhibits an odd sexual repression and an excessive, childish dependence; Mrs. Greenleaf is justified in worrying about her daughter's future. But marriage and increased responsibility lead to Lucy's growth in these areas: the "babyish" girl evolves into a woman. Moreover, it is greatly to her credit that even as a wife and mother she persists in her solitary annual journey to locate the elusive wild orchid, an emblem of her inviolable self. Though another's by law, "she was forever her own" (229). Nevertheless, an ominous note is sounded throughout the story in the frequent descriptions of Edson that emphasize his egotistic desire "to bend forcibly [Lucy's] will" to his own (227). A man "whose feet were set firmly in the regular tracks of life," Edson has no understanding whatsoever of his wife's finely tuned emotional nature; at one point, for example, he attributes her love for the arethusa to possible mental imbalance, and he finally settles into the notion that it is only a "harmless idiosyncrasy" to be indulged as one would the fancies of a child (227, 229). Marriage for him is mainly the "triumphant possession" of the woman he has desired and attained (229).

Lacking sympathy of heart and mind, Edson and Lucy's marriage, although successful on some level, fails on another, for it merely perpetuates into the next generation Mrs. Greenleaf's own marriage of convenience. In Freeman's time, such a marriage was, of course, a viable option for women who had few choices in life and no means to support themselves. But "Arethusa" invites us to consider what the dreamy and sensitive "flower" of a girl gains or loses by marrying the worldly, forceful, impatient man. Written soon before her own repeatedly delayed wedding to Charles Freeman, this story, along with the similar "The Prism" (1901), may have comprised a type of personal exploration for Freeman, who herself was sometimes described as delicate, dependent, dreamy, and childlike.[68] Freeman's letters around this time express her concern that marriage might "swallow" her identity completely; that it brought with it "unknown quantities" of which she was "afraid" (Kendrick, 243, 256). "Arethusa" may even have had a prophetic edge, for although Charles Freeman, an extrovert with a reputation for fast living and hard drinking, supported his new wife's career, evidence suggests that the emotional sympathy between the temperamentally different partners was tenuous as best. Only seven years after their marriage, Charles commenced the first of several confinements to hospitals and mental institutions when his addiction to alcohol and drugs worsened; the pair legally separated in 1922, a year before his death.

Freeman's most unified collection, *Six Trees* is organized, as Robert Luscher has pointed out, toward a gradual development of theme, from the depiction in "The Elm-Tree" (1903) of "the least encouraging reconciliation of man and nature" to the "completely realized communion with nature" in "The Apple-Tree" (1902).[69] In the former story, elderly David Ransom, on the verge of being displaced from his home by "dogood" neighbors, hides himself in a huge elm. In the latter tale, two contrasting New England lifestyles are opposed in the hardworking, busybody Blakes and the indigent, carefree Maddoxes. Two of the four stories between these frames, "The Balsam Fir" (1901) and "The Great Pine" (1902), are the volume's most skillful. Like "The Parrot," the first examines the inner division a lifetime of resentment, frustration, and repression have produced in a solitary woman and, like Eliot's Prufrock, the mask the woman wears to conceal her real self from public view. Outwardly, Martha Elder "might have been painted as a type of elderly maiden peace and pure serenity by an artist who could see only externals. But," the narrator continues, "it was very different with her from what people thought. Nobody dreamed of the fierce tension of her nerves as she sat at her window sewing ... drawing her monotonous thread in and out of dainty seams; nobody dreamed what revolt that little cottage roof, when it was covered with wintry snows, sometimes sheltered" (*MWFR*, 232). Feeling herself to be like "a caged panther," Martha bitterly rehearses her life's manifold deprivations and confesses her profound loneliness to her neighbor, a feeble deaf woman who is also all alone in the world.

As Christmas approaches, Martha petulantly cries out for at least one holiday celebration, one Christmas tree before she dies. While still speaking, she observes through the window a man poised to chop down one of her fir trees; running outside and grabbing his ax, she threatens to kill him unless he immediately leaves her property. He yields reluctantly. After he is gone, Martha lingers under the balsam fir as a wave of powerful memories suddenly floods over her. She recalls how many dreams of her youth were forged under the tree; as they return to her now, "greeting her like old friends," she "felt suddenly as if the tree were alive. A great, protecting tenderness for it came over her" (235). The moment transforms Martha; she is filled with peace as she realizes that, indeed, her life has contained much joy, that it has been worthwhile. Moreover, her generous act of protecting the tree allows her to move away from crippling self-preoccupation and to perceive, for once, the needy and equally lonely woman at her side. "With the eagerness of one who grasps at a treasure," Martha opens her home to the woman, who weeps in gratitude (236). As in her animal stories, Freeman implies here that for some, caring for the living things of nature can constitute a first step to reintegration into the human family. Martha's transformation is perhaps too rapid to be believable, but it is appropriate to the tale's Christmas theme, which also suggests that divine grace may have been instrumental in producing the life-changing experience that has occurred.

In "The Great Pine," a sailor who has deserted his family many years earlier and is now destitute attempts to navigate a dense forest as he makes his way back to his old home. Losing his path several times and ending up at the same towering pine tree, Dick curses angrily and, in "childish savagery" to "satisfy his own wrath and bitterness of spirit," sets the tree on fire (*MWFR*, 239, 240). But when he sees the rising flames, he just as quickly beats the fire out. Though both actions are impulsive, Dick's saving of the tree from his own destruction works in the ignorant, unimaginative man an unconscious transformation of spirit, "tun[ing] him to a higher place in the scale of things than he had ever held" (241). Resuming his journey, he finally reaches his home. There he discovers that his wife is now dead, and during his long absence she married a neighbor man who now occupies the house. Since the man is bedridden by illness, Dick's young daughter has been forced to run the house and care for the family's new baby. Tension mounts as Dick gruffly questions the sick man about what has passed, and the latter realizes with a shock that the house and property rightfully belong to the returned husband.

The outcome of the awkward situation and the conclusion of the story hinge on Dick's response. Having already effected positive change by reversing the damage he did to the pine tree, Dick now finds the inner strength and will to begin to counteract the mistakes he has made in life. He chooses, in consequence, to assume the role of both mother and father to the ill-assorted family and works tirelessly to feed, clothe, and care for them to the best of his abilities. This story fully reveals the mystical, "intimate connection" of the natural world with the human spirit and exemplifies Emerson's conviction that the "moral influence of nature upon every individual is that amount of truth which it illustrates to him" (Emerson, 39). The truth that Dick gains from his contact with the majestic pine is that of his own power for either good or evil, harm or healing. Like Martha Elder of "The Balsam Fir" and many similar Freeman characters who suffer the harmful effects of exaggerated pride or excessive self-absorption, the sailor is redeemed—freed from the rut of destructive habit—by moving from selfishness to selflessness. The story implies that Dick will endure in his new course of life even when he discovers one day that the great pine to which he owes his transformation has, finally, been burnt to the ground by natural forces.

Although a seeming departure from her early village stories, Freeman's mid-career historical, supernatural, mystery, and symbolic nature stories actually extend the themes of her trademark fiction, broadening and deepening the author's exploration of the elements of the New England character that fascinated her: its manifold repressions, its difficult negotiation in relationships, and the startling "sudden revolt of a spirit that will endure no more."[70] Most importantly, working in these subgenres allowed Freeman to move her work into the realms of the imaginative and mystical without abandoning her essential grounding in realism. She thus fulfilled her stated desire for "more symbolism, more mysticism" in her stories, for fiction that combined "romance and realism . . . more equally than they have ever been" before (Kendrick 382, 110).

Later Stories, 1904–1928:
Continuing Interests, New Moods
and Subjects, Interrelated and
Child-Protagonist Stories

Though Freeman focused on short fiction in various subgenres through-out the middle portion of her career, she continued to pen her signature New England village tales as well. Such stories as "A Stress of Conscience" (1892), "Juliza" (1892), "One Good Time" (1897), and "Hyacinthus" (1904) involve subject matter and situations characteristic of her earliest efforts. Moreover, during this time she continued to produce at least two commissioned holiday tales per year: "An Unlucky Christmas" (1896), "The Pumpkin" (1900), "Susan Jane's Valentine" (1900), and "An Easter-Card" (1901) are some examples. In the last phase of Freeman's writing, from 1904 to 1928, she therefore did not so much return to her typical village stories as cease experimenting with the subgenres that mark the middle period.

There may be several reasons for that decision. Although *The Wind in the Rose-Bush, Understudies,* and *Six Trees* received favorable reviews and sold well, Freeman's publishers and the several literary agents she employed after 1905 evidently did not encourage the author to continue in these directions; they dissuaded her from composing, for example, the series of insect pieces to complement the animal stories of *Understudies* and, later, a series of jewel tales designed to follow "The Jade Bracelet." Though it remained steady, Freeman's popularity around the turn of the century partly resulted from the afterglow of the widespread acclaim her earliest volumes had received. Critically and artistically, however, her reputation had been increasingly jeopardized by her novels. Though each had its loyal following, the 12 novels that appeared after 1894, some running to hundreds of thousands of words, received at best mixed reviews and at worst outright condemnation by critics who lamented that the author persisted in writing ill-wrought, even preposterous novels at the expense of her established forte, the short story. Of the six novels she produced during the last phase of her career, only *The Shoulders of Atlas,* ironically written in just two months for a newspaper contest, is significant in its realistic plot involving a favorite Freeman theme, that of hidden crime and the agonizing deliberations of the morbidly sensitive, guilty conscience. *Shoulders* is also notable in Freeman's oeuvre as the author's most candid exploration of the sexual basis of the New England character's neuroses or obsessions.

Without abandoning her steady stream of short stories and against the advice of her critics, Freeman continued to concentrate her primary energies in the last phase of her career on writing novels. The novel was to her a greater achievement, a "grand opera" as opposed to a "simple little melody," and she ambitiously strove to reach such a lofty artistic goal (Kendrick, 382). In addition, some of her impetus for pursuing other genres besides the short story most likely derived from her desire to ward off the early typecasting that, to her dismay, hounded her throughout her career. Her public not only demanded more of the usual "Mary Wilkins" tales of spinsters in many-turned gowns, poor but proud old folk, and quiet rural villages but even expected the author herself to step out of their pages: as late as 1916, Freeman recorded with thinly veiled scorn how a visiting publisher "seemed really a bit indignant because he did not find me attired in my best black silk and living in New Jersey in these latter days in a little white New England cottage" (Kendrick, 349). But although one can sympathize with Freeman's artistic goals, one can also understand her publishers' wincing each time a new Freeman novel arrived on their desks. Constructive criticism was not welcomed; increasingly peevish as she grew older, Freeman would impetuously "delete whole paragraphs, undoubtedly to the further detriment of the manuscript" if even the slightest suggestion for revision was offered (Kendrick, 280). Yet Freeman persisted in her goal to write longer fiction: at the time of her death from heart failure in 1930, she was considering both an autobiography and a sequel to *Pembroke*.

Freeman's continued focus on novels throughout the last decades of her career no doubt contributed to the marked unevenness of the short stories she also wrote during this time. There are several personal reasons for this unevenness as well. Her worry over not having enough time for her career once married was apparently not borne out in the first few years she lived with Charles; he was sympathetic to his famous wife's endeavors, and he arranged for domestic help so that she could write as much as she pleased. As time went on, however, Freeman became preoccupied with the numerous details involved in the couple's building of an elaborate new home in Metuchen, a showpiece financed with the $20,000 contest money she won for *The Shoulders of Atlas*. The house was completed in 1907, the same year Charles ran for mayor of Metuchen, an election he lost largely because of his growing reputation as an alcoholic; over the next 10 years, his mental and physical health steadily deteriorated. Around the time the couple moved into their new home, Mary Freeman's letters begin to indicate that she was suffering the effects of severe fatigue generated by a long habit of overwork. "I am straining every nerve to write. . . . even my faithful typewriter shows signs of fatigue," she confided to a fellow author (Kendrick, 308). Increasingly, that exhaustion was accompanied by numerous other ailments, including insomnia, headaches, severe bronchial colds, and deafness. Still, though their combined assets rendered the couple quite wealthy, Mary Freeman showed no signs of slackening her strenuous writing pace.

Freeman published 89 short stories for adults between 1904 and 1928 and left at least four others in manuscript form at her death. Approximately half of these were not collected in her lifetime; the other half were reissued by Harper's in five final collections, *The Givers* (1904), *The Fair Lavinia and Others* (1907), *The Winning Lady and Others* (1909), *The Copy-Cat and Other Stories* (1914), and *Edgewater People* (1918). Many of these later stories are holiday tales; both *The Givers* and *The Fair Lavinia* contain a number of them. Others, as Kendrick has noted, are likely reworked versions of earlier manuscripts Freeman had not published but had kept on file (Kendrick, 375). But also among this body of work are a number of pieces that attain the superb depth of theme and quality of execution Freeman achieved more consistently earlier in her career. Most of these pieces reiterate Freeman's primary themes of rebellion against social codes, the quest for authentic spirituality, the mending of family feuds, issues of poverty and pride, and relationships in courtship and marriage.

"The Revolt of Sophia Lane" (1903; later renamed "The Givers") is a first-person narrative told by the title character to well-meaning but thoughtless relatives as an object lesson on the necessity of giving appropriate gifts, a recurrent concern of Freeman's. Motivated by love for her niece Flora, who is about to wed a poor farmer, Sophia relates to the visitors, who have come to congratulate Flora on her engagement, how she mustered the courage the previous Christmas to return every one of the elegant but useless gifts Flora received. Among them were a fancy hair ornament, a precious silk shawl, and a chess set that no one knew how to use ("For the land sake! what's them little dolls and horses for? It looks like Noah's ark without the ark," Sophia exclaimed when she saw it; *MWFR*, 306). The visiting relatives grasp the meaning of

Sophia's parable and tactfully take their impractical engagement gifts—finger bowls and doilies, an "afternoon" tea kettle—back home with them; presumably, more appropriate items will soon follow. Sophia's is the classic Freeman revolt: the sudden eruption of a long-suffering sensibility. This time, however, the situation is as humorous for the reader as it is serious for the protagonist. Like Sarah Penn in "The Revolt of 'Mother' " and numerous other Freeman heroines, Sophia breaks a tacit and seemingly impenetrable social code, in this case the ritual of gracious gift giving and receiving. Also like Sarah Penn, she does so with trepidation and is surprised when she succeeds as well as she does. The comic ending here, in fact, makes for a delightful tale. The humor is Freeman's best: the image of lanky old Sophia trundling fiercely through the snow as she returns the inappropriate presents to their astonished givers evokes a wry irony, at once hilarious and poignant:

> Then I took [back to her] Lizzie Starkwether's bed-shoes, [Sophia relates].
> "Don't they fit?" says she.
> "Fit well 'nough," says I. "We don't want 'em. . . . Because you've given us a pair every Christmas for three years," says I, "and I've told you we never wear bed-shoes; and even if we did wear 'em," says I, "we couldn't have worn out the others to save our lives. When we go to bed, we go to sleep," says I. "We don't travel round to wear out shoes. We've got two pairs apiece laid away," says I, "and I think you'd better give these to somebody that wants 'em—mebbe somebody that you've been givin' mittens to for three years, that don't wear mittens." (311–12)

Another late story of rebellion is also one of Freeman's finest. "The Balking of Christopher" (1912) presents a new rendition of Freeman's frequent theme of an individual's search for spiritual fulfillment in a harsh, demoralizing environment. The story is unique in part because its protagonist is one of Freeman's few believable and well-rounded male characters. An intelligent and sensitive man, Christopher Dodd suddenly "balks" one day at the monotonous, unrelenting labor he has had to perform on the farm every day of his life to eke out a meager living. Without explaining the reason to his wife, Myrtle, he seeks out the town minister and there recites a litany of the hardships that have dogged him throughout his 50 years. "Why did I have to come into the world without any choice?" he demands. "I came into the world whether I would or not; I was forced, and then I was told I was a free agent. I am no free agent. . . . I am a slave—a slave of life" (*MWFR,* 403–4). Wisely, the Reverend Stephen Wheaton listens to the torrent of words without interrupting. When he learns that the revolt Christopher is planning is not as extreme as his bitter words might imply, Stephen agrees to support him in it. Christopher's scheme is to "do just once in my life what I want to do," to abandon the usual spring plowing and planting and, instead, live apart for a while in a cabin on the mountainside so as to "have the spring and the summer, and the fall, too, if I want it . . . to get once, on this earth, my fill of the bread of life" (406–7). He carries out his purpose and, in only a few months, is thoroughly rejuvenated by his rest. Returning down the mountain, he resumes his chores with renewed courage. He has, in addition, gained a new appreciation for the tolerant Myrtle, a woman he wed more out of compassion than out of love but whom he now realizes is exactly the partner most suitable to him.

In "The Balking of Christopher," Freeman combines the Emersonian mysticism that informs some of her mid-career stories with her typical study of rebellion. From the heights of the mountaintop, Christopher gains a spiritual perspective on nature's seasons, as he has the leisure to observe, for the first time in his life, the glory of the trees and flowers in their spring bloom and later in their summer fullness. He now comprehends that, like the ebb and flow of the seasons, his existence is composed of a necessary blending of suffering and pleasure and that both work together for his welfare. His question of "why" to life has been answered through his new perception of the incarnation of spirit: "I have found out that the only way to heaven for the children of men is through the earth," he states finally, a conclusion remarkably similar to that of Robert Frost's birch swinger, who also finds new perspective as a result of his lofty assent (413).[71] As Beth Wynne Fisken has demonstrated in " 'Unusual' People in a 'Usual Place,' " this story likewise involves the more subtle but equally complex rebellions and transformations of the three principal characters besides Christopher.[72] Freeman's usual disdain in her fiction for ineffective or impotent ministers gives way in this story to sympathy in her portrayal of the Reverend Wheaton, who is able to empathize with Christopher's plight because he too "sometimes chafed under the dull necessity of his life" (409). For the first (and only) time in Freeman's world, a clergyman condescends to listen to and learn from one of his flock. Through his vicarious participation in Christopher's quest, Stephen is similarly rejuvenated in spirit; Stephen and Christopher are, in fact, alter egos who achieve a common transformation though they have started from different paths in life. Although she is anxious about her husband, Myrtle, "in her quiet dignity, refuses to condemn what she does not understand; she will not be the nagging wife urged by Christopher's mother and sister" (Fisken 1985, 100). Finally, Christopher's niece Ellen, who takes over the farm during his absence and who eventually marries Stephen Wheaton, is an unusual young woman: she is fearless, strong, and emotionally balanced. It is Ellen, in fact, who comes to represent in the tale the promise of renewal that each succeeding generation—like each cycle of the seasons—carries with it.

Other tales of revolt from Freeman's later group of stories include the skillful "One Good Time" (1897), a story that, like "The Balking of Christopher," concerns a character's onetime rebellion against life's harsh restrictions staged, in this case, by the lavish spending of money; "The Slip of the Leash" (1904), in which a man who abruptly "went wild" deserts his family, only to remain in the vicinity, secretly observing them; "The Strike of Hannah" (1906), a Thanksgiving tale in which an impoverished woman steals a holiday dinner from her wealthy employer "to set the law of equals right"; and the inferior "The Willow-Ware" (1907) and "Dear Annie" (1910), both of which are weakly plotted studies of young women who attempt to resist repressive family circumstances.

In her late fiction, Freeman also pursued her repeated theme of the difficulty of maintaining harmonious relationships and resolving family feuds. In "The Reign of the Doll" (1904), elderly sisters Fidelia and Diantha harbor ill will toward each other that stems from the division of their dead mother's property years before. Though they live in adjacent houses and spy on each other through the curtains, they do not speak or exchange visits and treat each other with the "dignified hostility" that Freeman's obstinate, proud villagers tend to assume (*MWFR*, 319). The mysterious delivery of a doll to one of the sisters begins to act as a balm to their injured sensibilities. Spurred on by memories of their girlhood, the two lonely, childless women are gradually reunited by their care for the doll as they come together to stitch little garments to clothe it:

> As the two women worked, their faces seemed to change. They were tall and bent, with a rigorous bend of muscles not apparently so much from the feebleness and relaxing of age as from defiance to the stresses of life; both sisters' backs had the effect of stern walkers before fierce winds; their hair was sparse and faded, brushed back from

thin temples, with nothing of the grace of childhood, and yet there was something of the immortal child in each as she bent over her doll-clothes. The contour of childhood was evident in their gaunt faces, which suddenly appeared like transparent masks of age; the light of childhood sparkled in their eyes; when they chattered and laughed one would have sworn there were children in the room. And, strangest of all, their rancor and difference seemed to have vanished; they were in the most perfect accord. (325)

This unexpected softening of stubborn spirits through an object as ludicrous and unlikely as a doll is pure Freeman. So is the telling of the story partly through neighborhood gossip, which hints that the doll may have been sent to the sisters as either a mockery of their old-lady, maiden ways or as a well-calculated means to their reconciliation. As in much of her best fiction, Freeman makes fine use here of multiple points of view, indicating both the persistent quality of small-town gossip and the many sides to human relationships. Oblivious to their neighbors' prying eyes and wagging tongues, Fidelia and Diantha sew on in quiet harmony, the enigmatic doll between them "smiling with inscrutable inanity" (332). The final incongruous but winsome image is one of Freeman's most memorable.

Finally, "The Selfishness of Amelia Lamkin" (1908) is also representative of Freeman's most accomplished later short fiction. A hardworking wife and mother in a large household, Amelia Lamkin collapses one day from sheer exhaustion. Near death, she lies prone in bed under doctor's orders for several weeks while her husband, children, and visiting sister try to undertake the numerous chores that Amelia had customarily performed alone. As they struggle to cope, their emotions range from grief and love to "monstrous self-pity" and "unreasoning anger" at Amelia's inability to serve them as she always has (*MWFR*, 389). As time passes, however, each begins to realize the extent of his or her selfishness, which has led to Amelia's illness. Remorse even provokes her daughter Addie to reject her sweetheart and vow to devote the rest of her life to helping her mother.

But the story's examination of selfishness runs deeper than is apparent from this brief sketch of the plot. The doctor, a voice of reason and objectivity amid the clamor and chaos that results from the family's distress, points out to them that the ailing Amelia is equally guilty of selfishness, for "she has worked too hard for everybody else, and not hard enough for herself" (388). Indeed, Amelia epitomizes the domestic ideal, or "true," woman: meek and self-sacrificing, she has even come close to starving herself by eating only the leftover scraps from the others' plates. As the narrator explains, "she had always waited upon [her family] and obliterated herself to that extent that she seemed scarcely to have a foothold at all upon the earth, but to balance timidly upon the extreme edge of existence" (379). Amelia's spinster sister, Jane Strong, has long tried to convince Amelia that her catering to others was not only harming her own health but turning her family members into persons incapable of existing independent of her solicitous care. As Amelia lies exhausted in bed, Jane is now apparently vindicated in her belief. But though professing to be as self-sufficient and hardy as her name implies, Jane Strong collapses into an emotional wreck when confronted with the possibility of her sister's death. When she trips down the cellar steps and lies helpless and alone on the floor with a broken foot, she is able to perceive for the first time that her life has become a sham:

> Jane Strong had kept all the commandments from her youth up. She had always been considered a most exemplary woman by other people, and she had acquiesced in their opinion. Now suddenly she differed with other people and with her own previous estimation of herself. She had blamed her sister Amelia Lamkin for her sweet, subtle selfishness, which possibly loved the happiness of other people rather than their own spiritual gain; she had blamed all the Lamkin family for allowing a martyr to live among them, with no effort to save her from the flame of her own self-sacrifice. Now suddenly she blamed herself. She pictured to herself her easy, unhampered life in her nice little apartment, and was convicted of enormous selfishness in her own righteous person. "Lord!" she said, "what on earth have I been thinking about? I knew Amelia was overworked. What was to hinder my coming here at least half the year and taking some of the burden off her? . . . You've made a nice mess of it, Jane Strong! Instead of snooping around to find the sins of other folks, you'd better have looked at home. Good land!" (392–93)

The haughty self-complacency of the single woman who revels in freedom from all obligations and judges others who don't have that luxury is thus revealed as destructive. The result is that both Jane and Amelia, doubles and mirrors of each other, are indicted for their selfishness. As Martha Cutter explains, "a radical critique of the two most prevalent images [of nineteenth-century women]—the 'Domestic Saint' and the 'New Woman'—exists in 'The Selfishness of Amelia Lamkin,' reflecting Freeman's understanding of the debilitating nature of *all* patriarchal images of femininity. . . . For Freeman, the image of the New Woman is not different from the True Woman; it is just another stereotype."[73] Freeman dissects those two stereotypes and also provides her tale with an "undecidable" open ending. Readers are left to speculate about how both Amelia (who recovers) and Jane will change their behavior given their newfound understanding of themselves. Is a third alternative available for these women—for all women? Freeman, who spent a lifetime exploring the effects of ingrained patterns of behavior, doesn't seem to provide much room for optimism here. Rather, Doctor Emerson's words to the family seem to ring prophetic as, at the story's conclusion, Amelia rises from her bed: "I realize," he has warned them, "how almost impossible it is to prevent self-sacrificing women like your mother from offering themselves up" (388). "Almost impossible," perhaps, but not completely hopeless. Freeman allows her readers the privilege of the final judgment, not only about Amelia and Jane but about the future of women's roles in general as they evolve into a new century.

New Moods and Subjects

As we have seen, many of Freeman's most effective later stories echo the themes and situations of her earliest efforts; the continuity between them is clear. In terms of style, these well-crafted works also retain an emphasis on dialogue in developing plot, although the tightly compressed prose and heavy use of regional dialect from the earlier period is generally absent. Weaker stories from Freeman's late career exhibit the same faults as others scattered throughout her short fiction: contrived or improbable plotting; overly sentimental or conventional endings; and from mid-career on, a tendency toward a verbose, overwritten style. Though Freeman experimented ambitiously, one cannot claim that she developed significantly as a writer over the course of her long career: her best stories from each period resemble each other, as do her poorest.

Some shift in tone from the early to the late stories is apparent, however. The understated yet devastating irony of the early tales gives way in several of Freeman's last pieces to a strident, caustic tone and a frankness of subject matter heretofore unexhibited in the bulk of her short fiction. Alice Glarden Brand recognizes this change in temper, correctly noting that "in [Freeman's] early stories, women, particularly the young, sense the inevitability of their existences as vulnerable to the social order. Society placed a premium on marriage, self-control, and impassiveness.... As Freeman becomes angrier and bolder, her women become angrier and bolder. ... As masculine offenses become more odious, the female defenses become similarly outrageous" (Brand, 84, 96). Thus these seemingly atypical pieces in the author's canon—including "Old Woman Magoun" (1905), "The Secret" (1907), "The Old-Maid Aunt" (1908), "Noblesse" (1913), "The Jester" (1928), and the fragment referred to as "Jane Lennox" (undated)—can be viewed as culminations of issues that Freeman explored time and again, particularly the plight of society's vulnerable or outcast and the social restrictions placed on women, whether married or single.

Both "Noblesse" and "Old Woman Magoun" are tragic tales of women's relative defenselessness in the face of unchecked male power and greed. In each story, a man decides to "sell" a woman to pay a gambling debt. "Noblesse," though not a successful story due to its melodramatic ending, is appalling in its premise. Margaret Lee, an enormously overweight woman, finds herself in late middle age alone in the world and dependent on distant relatives. Sensitive and genteel, she can hardly bear the vulgar young couple with whom she lives, and they in turn are capable of little but crude pity for her. When the husband, Jack, loses on his investments and then gambles away the remainder of his fortune, he forces Margaret to exhibit herself as a circus sideshow freak in order to earn money. Margaret faints when she learns of the plan, but "there was no course open but submission. She knew that from the first."[74] Though Margaret is a religious woman, even her faith in the existence of a better life to come wavers as the horrifying situation is perpetuated: "Daily her absurd unwieldiness was exhibited to crowds screaming with laughter. ... It seemed to her that there was nothing for evermore beyond those staring, jeering faces of silly mirth and delight at sight of her. ... [She] became a horror to herself" (*CC*, 173). Margaret is eventually saved by a noble man, equally overweight, who sacrifices himself by taking her place in the freak show. The narrator's comments on the man's decision summarize Freeman's dark mood in this and other late stories: "There was no romance about it. These were hard, sordid, tragic, ludicrous facts with which he had to deal" (178).

"Old Woman Magoun" is perhaps the most pessimistic of all of Freeman's stories. In this case, the female in peril is a mere child, a naive young girl named Lily, and the degenerate male is her father. The majority of the inhabitants of Barry's Ford are sloven drunkards and halfwits, remnants of the vitiated Barry lineage, of which Lily's father is among the worst. Sheltered after her mother's death by her maternal grandmother, Old Woman Magoun, Lily is kept from contact with her father until she meets him by chance when she is 14 years old. Though Lily is still childlike and clutches a rag doll, Nelson Barry immediately targets her as potential payment to another man for his gambling debt. When Old Woman Magoun becomes aware of Nelson's purpose, her worst fears are realized, for she has long suspected the extent of his depravity. She has no choice, nevertheless, but to turn Lily over to her father. Before doing so, she makes a desperate effort to convince a lawyer from a neighboring town to adopt the girl. When this move fails, she resorts in sheer panic to the only available alternative to Lily's impending rape and exploitation. On the return trip from the lawyer's, Old Woman Magoun allows the unsuspecting Lily to eat poisonous berries. Lily dies in great agony that evening, just before her father arrives to claim her. From that time on, the formerly strong and defiant Old Woman Magoun is considered a "trifle touched"; she is seen walking the village streets, cradling Lily's doll in her arms.

Besides its deeply cynical tone, "Old Woman Magoun" is outstanding among Freeman's short stories for its frankly sexual content. In keeping with her generation, Freeman was fairly reticent about sex, but she was not prudish. The early novel *Pembroke* describes an illegitimate pregnancy and a shotgun wedding, and as noted, thinly veiled references to same-sex relationships can be found in several of her novels and stories. Nevertheless, although the majority of Freeman's tales involve courtship situations, frank discussion of sexuality is largely absent from her short fiction, in part, no doubt, because of the stipulations of the various popular magazines that bought her stories. It is worth noting that when Freeman does dwell on sexuality, it is usually in the context of a threatening or otherwise ominous relationship: for example, Joe Dagget's disturbing presence is symbolized by the chained Caesar in "A New England Nun," and Phoebe Dole jealously murders Maria Wood's male lover in "The Long Arm." In its darkly foreboding subject matter and tone, "Old Woman Magoun" epitomizes Freeman's few but significant stories of sexual strife and plunder.

"The Secret" and "The Old-Maid Aunt" exhibit a fresh boldness about issues of marriage and single life. In the former piece, Catherine Gould becomes incensed when her fiancé, John Gleason, demands that she tell him where she has been when she returns home later than expected one evening. After John angrily stomps out of the house, Catherine's mother and aunt chastise her for not submitting to him, but Catherine insists that she will never marry a man who exerts such jealous control. "John suspected me of going somewhere or doing something I should not," she retorts. "He questioned me like a slave-owner. If he does so before I am married, what will he do after? My life would be a hell. If I see that a door leads into hell, I don't propose to enter it if I can keep out. That's all I have to say."[75] Later, Catherine discusses her now-dwindled prospects for marriage with her worried mother; in the course of their conversation, the generational difference between the two women comes to the forefront:

> "What do I care if I never get married?" [Catherine stated]. "Most of the married women I know would say they wished they were out of it, if they told the truth. . . . Mother," said she—she hesitated a moment, then she continued—"did you never regret that you got married?"
>
> The mother blushed. She regarded her daughter with a curious, dignified, yet shamed expression. "Marriage is a divine institution," said she, and closed her lips tightly.
>
> "Oh, nonsense!" cried Catherine. "Tell the truth, mother, and let the divine institution go. I know father was a fretful invalid two-thirds of the time. . . . [He] never was much of a success as a doctor; he had such a temper and was so miserable himself. And I know you had five children as fast as you could, and they all died except me. Now tell me the truth—if you had it all to live over again, would you marry father?"
>
> The flush faded from Mrs. Gould's face. She was quite pale. "Yes, I would, and thank the Lord for His unspeakable mercy," she said, in a low, oratorical voice, almost as if she were in a pulpit. (*FL*, 200–201)

"The Secret" thus pairs mother and daughter to contrast the attitudes of an older and younger generation of women on the issue of marriage: the theme is one Freeman has examined before, but its handling through the outspoken, liberated Catherine is unique. In addition, the story presents a variation on the author's characteristic study of petty quarrels perpetuated by proud, headstrong individuals. Catherine and John are doubles in this matter, sharing a "terrible similarity of unyielding spirit" (192). After they argue and part ways, Catherine holds out easily enough; she loves John, but she does not need him. In fact, unlike in some Freeman tales, such as "A Patient Waiter" (1886) or "The Witch's Daughter" (1910), here it is not the woman who becomes "love-cracked" over a broken engagement but the man. During the several years they are separated, John grows increasingly ill and morose, whereas Catherine waxes in health, vitality, and beauty. Eventually,

John capitulates and returns to Catherine; even then, Freeman has Catherine deliberate at length, like Esther in "A Conflict Ended," over whether she'd be better off marrying him or remaining single. She finally opts to wed him, but not without regret at forgoing the "peaceful and beautiful and good" aspects of her single life. Ultimately, however, she determines that by never marrying she might "miss the best and sweetest of food for her heart. There was nothing of the nun about her. She was religious, but she was not ascetic" (225).

Catherine Gould is yet another in Freeman's long line of female protagonists who challenge social and familial prohibitions in asserting their freedom in marriage issues. When compared to earlier characters in similar struggles (for instance, Louisa Britton in "Louisa," Louisa Ellis in "A New England Nun," and Lucy Greenleaf in "Arethusa"), it is apparent that Catherine is bolder and more strident. However, although the entrance of an independently minded, fearless young woman like Catherine—truly a "new" woman—is welcome in Freeman's canon, one also recalls that it is precisely the conflict between assertion and repression, between resistance and conformity, that lends Freeman's best short fiction its sharp-edged power and keen psychological insight. Since Catherine experiences little tension of this kind, she remains a relatively flat character and "The Secret" an interesting but not superior story.

"The Old-Maid Aunt" is technically not a short story. Nevertheless, it can be read as one and as such adds considerably to our understanding of the forceful tone detectable in Freeman's later work. Freeman composed the piece as the second chapter for *The Whole Family* (1908), a novel Harper's promoted as a "round-robin" literary gimmick with contributions by 12 popular authors of the day, including Freeman, William Dean Howells, Henry James, Alice Brown, and Elizabeth Stuart Phelps. Each author was to write the first-person narrative of a particular family member; as patriarch of the group, Howells led with the first installment, "The Father," and then forwarded the project to Freeman to continue. Freeman's chapter presents a lively, ironic look at turn-of-the-century expectations for unmarried women past age 30. The "old maid aunt," Lily Talbot, is considered "unfortunate" by family members who patronize her and assume that, because she is a spinster, she cannot possibly be interested in anything but her knitting. Scorning her "brainless" family's lack of sophistication, Lily delights in antagonizing them by, among other things, wearing scandalous pink dresses instead of the drab black more appropriate to her age. She likewise holds in contempt the dowdy, predictable housewives among her circle of acquaintances, especially the dull Mrs. Temple, who even positions the books on her parlor table, as Lily disdainfully relates, "with the large ones under the small ones in perfectly even piles!" "Anything is better," Lily determines, "than the dead level of small books on large ones, and meals on time" (*MWFR*, 347, 358). The sardonic jab is, of course, aimed at Freeman's own famous "A New England Nun," in which the methodical Louisa Ellis hastens to rearrange her books back into their customary order after Joe Dagget has displaced them.

Lily is educated, well traveled, beautiful, and wealthy. Nevertheless, she is reminded daily that she is confined to the limited role of a spinster in others' estimation. To the extent that it is possible, therefore, she uses that role to her advantage. "But I am willing, even anxious, to be quite frank with myself," she states. "Since—well, never mind since what time—I have not cared an iota whether I was considered an old maid or not. The situation has seemed to me rather amusing, inasmuch as it has involved a secret willingness to be what everybody has considered me as very unwilling to be. I have regarded it as a sort of joke upon other people" (345). When the narrative reveals that the young man engaged to Lily's teenaged niece Peggy is actually in love with Lily, Freeman sets up a tantalizing turn of events that purposely distorts Howells's conception of *The Whole Family*'s plot as a homey, nostalgic, and low-keyed one. Howells was dismayed by Freeman's decision and tried to bar her installment. Freeman, however, remained unrepentant (one recalls that she herself married a man seven years her junior), and the chapter stayed. She explained her reasoning at the time to Elizabeth Jordan, editor of *Harper's Bazar* and the project's convener:

> Mr. Howells evidently clings to the old conception of [the spinster]. You and I know that in these days of voluntary celibacy on the part of women an old maid only fifteen years older than a young girl is a sheer impossibility, if she is an educated woman with a fair amount of brains. Moreover, a young man is really more apt to fall in love with her. Why, the whole plot of the novel must be relegated back to Miss Austin [*sic*], and *Godey's Lady's Book* and all that sort of thing, if the old conception holds.... I don't think Mr. Howells realizes this. He is thinking of the time when women of thirty put on caps, and renounced the world. That was because they married at fifteen and sixteen, and at thirty had about a dozen children. Now they simply do not do it. (Kendrick, 313)

Freeman's deliberate twist of plot upset the authors of the subsequent chapters as well as Howells. Though divided on the chapter's merit, the 10 writers followed Freeman's lead in focusing the novel increasingly on family tensions, divisions, and jealousy. Moreover, the story line also came to reflect some of these writers' personal dissensions and artistic rivalries.[76] Though *The Whole Family* intrigued the public because each chapter was issued anonymously in the *Bazar* before being released together as a book, at its conclusion Elizabeth Jordan deemed the entire frustrating project a "mess."

Several of Freeman's later stories concern characters who, like Lily Talbert, chafe at the roles others have assigned them yet use them to their advantage. Her last published story, "The Jester," for example, is a deeply cynical study of a young man who employs his skill at amusing others to mask his lonely soul; tragically, his constant role-playing eventually makes him incapable of authentic human love. The undated fragment "Jane Lennox" may have been written as a type of preliminary sketch for "The Old-Maid Aunt"; the first-person narrative voice is similar, although the mood of "Jane Lennox" is far more bitter. "I am a rebel and what is worse a rebel against the Overgovernment of all creation," states the unmarried protagonist, evidently speaking or writing to herself in a moment of intense self-reflection. "I often wonder," she continues, "if I might not have been very decent, very decent indeed, if I had laid hold on the life so many of my friends lead. If I had only had a real home of my own with a husband and children in it. . . . I am a graft on the tree of human womanhood. I am a hybrid. Sometimes I think I am a monster, and the worst of it is, I certainly take pleasure in it" (Foster, 142–43). The protagonist delights in outwitting those around her in small things, such as lending her unsuspecting neighbor diluted rather than pure vanilla. Thus, although she rages within at the injustice of her single state, the outward manifestation of her rebellion is carefully contained; that she alone knows she is fooling others is part of her secret triumph. She revels in her potential for and not her actual enacting of wholesale revolt: "Here I am, a woman, rather delicately built, of rather delicate tastes, perfectly able to break those commandments, to convert into dust every one of those Divine laws. I shudder before my own power, yet I glory because of it" (Foster, 143). Unfortunately, Freeman broke off this provocative piece at this juncture and never returned to complete it.

Freeman's characteristic theme, that of revolt against stifling social restrictions and the divided self that results from the fray, finds its boldest rendition in these late pieces. As both a single and a married woman, Freeman seems to have experienced such self-division during at least some periods in her life. Her letters testify to the fact that she sometimes felt she possessed two very different sides to her personality; she was also aware of dissonance between how she appeared to others and how she regarded herself. For example, after posing for a photograph in 1892, she remarked to a friend, "I have tried very hard to look cheerful, but I should have enjoyed 'making a face' much more. You think I am modest, but I am not. I am vicious" (Kendrick, 141). Some 20 years later, in 1915, she echoed her character Jane Lennox in telling *Woman's Home Companion* editor Hayden Carruth, "I have a frightful conviction that I look capable of nothing except afternoon teas or breaking all the Commandments and sulking because there are no more" (Kendrick, 347). But the most convincing evidence that the author knew her subject firsthand is her abiding interest in issues of rebellion and self-division throughout her entire career. Some of her final explorations of these issues, in such works as "The Old-Maid Aunt," "The Jester," and "Jane Lennox" indicate Freeman's increasing desire to speak frankly about the ramifications of such inner tension, however dark or disturbing they may be.

When Freeman relocated to New Jersey after her marriage, she assumed she would discover there ample material for her writing. After all, "people are all alike, especially if they happen to be women, whether they live in Massachusetts or Metuchen," she stated optimistically to a newspaper reporter at the time of the move.[77] To her dismay, she proved herself wrong. The upper middle class, staid Metuchen lifestyle bored her and yielded little fruit for her imagination. Consequently, although she continued to write prolifically after her marriage, she rarely employed New Jersey settings or characters. Her few efforts to do so resulted in some of her weakest novels, *The Debtor* (1905), *"Doc" Gordon* (1906), and *The Butterfly House* (1912), works that rankled Metuchenites because of their unflattering portraits of the locale and its inhabitants. Only a handful of the post-1902 stories have New Jersey–like settings. During her years in Metuchen, Freeman relied on her frequent trips back to Randolph and, less occasionally, to Brattleboro for fresh material.

Though her New England settings remain a constant, a number of Freeman's later stories incorporate modern subject matter and reflect the author's new pastimes and concerns. Both Mary and Charles Freeman were avid bridge players in several Metuchen circles, and "The Winning Lady" (1909) satirizes the petty ambitions of card-playing society women. "A Guest in Sodom" (1912), about a man who is driven to distraction by an automobile that perpetually breaks down, is a light-hearted poke at both Freemans, who enjoyed motoring, employed a chauffeur, and owned six automobiles by 1912, one of which, a Stude-baker E.M.F., Mary Freeman dubbed "Every Mechanical Fault" (Kendrick, 339). A handful of stories expresses Freeman's anxiety over the prospect of aging, a fear she mentions several times in her letters. These include "The Travelling Sister" (1908), about a woman who "vacations" by retreating into past memories, and "The Amethyst Comb" (1914) and "Sweet-Flowering Perennial" (1915), both of which concern aging women who, because they are in love with much younger men, desperately attempt to hold on to their youth. Finally, the advent of World War I brought out an ardent patriotic spirit in Freeman, result-ing in "The Liar" (1917), "Both Cheeks" (1917), "The Return" (1921), and several nationalistic poems.

Interrelated and Child-Protagonist Stories

Two final categories of Freeman's stories deserve brief mention. Since her tales of village life and characters often seem closely connected (the name she originally proposed for her first collection was *Among New Eng-land Neighbors*), it is not surprising that Freeman tried her hand at com-posing several series of interrelated pieces over the course of her career. She had precedent in doing so: village sketches united by a first-person narrator who relates her tale with indulgent goodwill and a nostalgic tone were popular throughout the nineteenth century both in Britain and in the United States. These included Mary Russell Mitford's *Our Village* (1824–1832), Elizabeth Gaskell's *Cranford* (1853), and Sarah Orne Jewett's *Country of the Pointed Firs* (1896). Freeman read Gaskell and Jewett and no doubt knew Mitford's work as well. She published her own slender volume of interrelated village sketches, *The People of Our Neighborhood*, in 1898, and the following year produced the short novel *The Jamesons*, which is based on a similar premise. Thereafter, Freeman penned two further series of interrelated pieces: 6 stories about chil-dren written between 1911 and 1914, which subsequently formed the first half of *The Copy-Cat*, and 12 stories written between 1914 and 1918 that, together with a brief preface, make up *Edgewater People*, Freeman's final short-story collection.

Of these interrelated works, only the stories in *People of Our Neighbor-hood* and two or three in the other two collections are significant. The tales in *People of Our Neighborhood* are connected by a garrulous female narrator. As is true with other of Freeman's first-person narratives, such as "Luella Miller," we soon find ourselves less interested in the story being told than in the character of the storyteller. A village insider, the narrator is adept at summarizing the gist of local gossip even as she unapologetically, perhaps even unwittingly, shares in its prejudices. Her first six observations are about various local folk who have been so severely typecast by the community that each has been reduced to little more than an epithet: the unlucky man, the neat woman, the friend of cats, and the like. In her last three tales, the narrator describes the courting activities of some young people at several village events. Although all of her sketches seem innocent on the surface, the fact that the narrator has not only imbibed but thoroughly accepts village biases is disconcerting given Freeman's lifelong empathy for those who vehemently resist such stereotyping. Yet we are provided with little room for further speculation about the speaker: she never fully identifies herself, her position in the village, or her intent in relating her observations. We are, moreover, never made privy to others' conversations with or about her. Consequently, although pleasant reading, the sketches in *People of Our Neighborhood* remain flat and undeveloped. In addition, the volume's organization is loose at best. Freeman wrote the nine sketches for *Ladies' Home Journal* over a two-year period, from December 1895 to December 1897; six were published under the heading "Neighborhood Types" and the remaining three under "Pleasures of Our Neighborhood." Although she evidently strove for some consistency in the tales in narrative voice and in certain individuals who reappear, she made no further revisions to unify the pieces when they were finally collected into one volume. Despite *People*'s flaws, however, it is interesting to note that the book's caricatures were lifelike enough to offend Randolph residents, who murmured that the author "was going too far in writing about her own neighbors, who were just as good as she was" (Foster, 136).

Freeman revisited the genre of interrelated village tales a year later with the novel *The Jamesons*. Here, unlike in *People*, she creates tension and intrigue by establishing a foil to the gossiping insider narrator, Mrs. Sophia Lane, with the arrival of the outsider Mrs. Jameson, a sophisticated city woman bent on improving her "backward" country neighbors. Mrs. Jameson's reforms are, of course, met with skepticism by the villagers, who soon come to tolerate the busybody as just one more type of village eccentric. A broad farce on the "country mouse/city mouse" theme, *The Jamesons* was a popular success, selling more than 8,000 copies in its first month of publication.

Freeman continued writing interrelated works later in her career, although with little distinction. The six stories that feature the same set of children in *The Copy-Cat* ("The Copy-Cat," "The Cock of the Walk," "Johnney-in-the-Woods," "Daniel and Little Dan'l," "Big Sister Solly," "Little Lucy Rose") and two others collected in *The Winning Lady* ("Little-Girl-Afraid-of-a-Dog," "The Joy of Youth") hold little appeal today for most readers, although they were evidently welcomed by their original *Harper's Monthly* audience. As do the other tales with child protagonists scattered throughout Freeman's adult fiction, these concern youthful capers, puppy-love romances, and sentimentalized parent and child relationships. "Little-Girl-Afraid-of-a-Dog" (1906) is the best of this group of stories. Forced to deliver baskets of eggs to a family with a fierce dog, little Emmeline daily undergoes mental and physical anguish over the prospect, yet both embarrassed by her fear and too young to verbalize it, she is unable to convey her terror to her mother. Freeman succeeds in capturing the full extent of Emmeline's inner agony. Always sympathetic to children, Freeman never lost her ability to comprehend the magnified fears and distorted perceptions of a child's world.

Edgewater People was both Freeman's last collection and her final attempt to compose a series of related stories. A brief introduction was inserted in the volume to explain the stories' relationship: purportedly, they demonstrate how the old coastal town of Barr expanded and divided over time into smaller villages, each of which still bears the stamp of its strongly rooted original settlers, especially the Edgewater, Leicester, and Sylvester families. The idea of a fictional study of how certain villages derive their unique characters from their inhabitants is an intriguing one. Unfortunately, this promise is not at all fulfilled in the loosely connected stories that follow. In fact one suspects that Freeman, probably at Harper's bidding, merely tacked on the preface in order to provide some plausible context for uniting the 12 stories, which were originally published in three very different magazines (*Harper's Monthly, Woman's Home Companion, Saturday Evening Post*) over a four-year period. Several of the tales involve Sarah Edgewater, a middle-aged, unmarried, well-off New England woman who acts as a type of family retainer for her various relations. Two of the stories in which she appears present late variations on quintessential Freeman themes. "Sarah Edgewater" (1916) illustrates the ongoing feud between the two Edgewater sisters that originated when, in their youth, Laura "stole" and subsequently married Sarah's beau. The story is convincing in its description of the intense hatred the sisters feel toward each other—Sarah loathes Laura for obvious reasons; Laura's feelings for Sarah are "subtler and more deadly, the hatred of the wrong-doer for the victim of the wrong"—but it falls short in the contrived reconciliation that forms its conclusion.[78] "Value Received" (1916) recalls such early tales as "A Gala Dress" and "Old Lady Pingree" in its portrayal of two impoverished but proud elderly sisters who disdain, but must accept, Sarah Edgewater's charity. To reciprocate, one of the women sews a bonnet for Sarah to wear at her niece's wedding. Though the hat is ridiculously outmoded, Sarah swallows her pride and wears it to the occasion, wisely perceiving "that the one who gives has a duty aside from giving—a sacred duty to the receiver of the gift." "[Sarah] knew that the old sisters had quailed in spirit before her benefits," the narrator explains. "Now it was her turn. She owed it to them to endure the humiliation which she included—whether she would or not—in her weekly gift to the sisters" (*EP,* 98). Indeed, Sarah's wisdom, stability, and serenity make her one of Freeman's strongest female protagonists. Unfortunately, none of the other stories in *Edgewater People* features her in a prominent manner. Moreover, by the middle of this volume, any attempt to unify the stories in any manner has been completely abandoned.

Because of its novel situation, "The Outside of the House" (1914) is the most interesting story among the uneven works in *Edgewater People;* its intimate mixture of pathos and humor also mark it as typical in the author's canon. Retired ship captain Joe Dickson and his taciturn wife, Martha, live quietly in a humble dwelling by the sea. The couple have a clandestine pleasure, however: every year, they eagerly await their wealthy neighbors' departure to Europe so they can dress in their Sunday best and take up daily residence on the gracious home's huge front porch. Freeman reveals the couple's guilty delight gradually, and its utter unexpectedness for two such aged, unassuming people lends the story great charm. As we have seen elsewhere, one of Freeman's unique strengths is her ability to crystallize a story around one sharply drawn picture, to distill, as it were, events and characters into a single, striking image. Candace Whitcomb's screeching out a hymn over her parlor organ in "A Village Singer"; Ann Millet angrily tossing squash out her back door in "An Object of Love"; a parrot pecking a bride's bonnet into shreds in "The Parrot"; Evelina Leonard's midnight pouring of boiling water on a splendid garden in "Evelina's Garden"; two old sisters bent over an inanely smiling doll in "The Reign of a Doll"—these are but a few examples. In "The Outside of the House," the image of Joe, Martha, and the absent neighbors' serving man (who cares for the mansion during the summer and who is in on Joe and Martha's scheme) rocking contentedly in the summer breeze on the well-appointed porch—almost as if they owned the place!—is wonderfully memorable.

As is also characteristic of her most skillful short fiction, Freeman uses nature symbolically in "The Outside of the House." In this story, it serves to complicate the plot as well. The omnipresent sea forever pounding in the background of the tale becomes a type of metaphoric leveling device. Though the home owners possess money and influence, they do not recognize the ocean's power and fail to properly maintain the seawall before they leave for their vacation abroad. Joe and Martha, on the other hand, close to nature and attentive to its rhythms, easily interpret the weather's signs and manage to save the neighbors' property from disaster during a furious nor'easter. Far more important to them than the financial reward they receive for their vigilance is the fact that, because the owners decide to remain overseas for a longer period, they will be able to inhabit the mansion's grand porch undetected for an entire year.

On a recent trip to New York, I made a pilgrimage to the American Academy of Arts and Letters on West 155th Street to view the ornamental doors that in 1938 were dedicated posthumously to Freeman. Inscribed "To the memory of Mary E. Wilkins Freeman and the Women Writers of America," the solid bronze doors stand as a fitting tribute to a writer whose work has ridden the vicissitudes of literary fashion—high popularity in the latter part of the nineteenth century, near obscurity throughout much of the twentieth—and yet has withstood the test of time, having been discovered anew and with delight a century after it first began to appear. Freeman's permanent position in American letters is assured. Grounded in a time and place that have disappeared—late-nineteenth-century rural New England—her short stories exhibit a universality of character that makes them as fully readable and enjoyable today as they were in her own time. The human heart struggling against odds to obtain inner fulfillment, love, and a sense of belonging is the underlying theme of all her fiction. But Freeman's best stories achieve their value through the author's deft and unique handling of this universal theme. With clear and direct vision, Freeman records the myriad, often conflicting forces of personality and society, of individual temperament and cultural norms, that converge to produce the circumstances in which her protagonists find themselves enmeshed. With a carefully balanced tone of empathy and judgment, she quickly cuts through peripheral matters to focus on the characters' secret inner lives as they weigh possibilities and act according to their available options. That their choices are often severely circumscribed is an essential part of Freeman's vision, one that borders on tragicomedy in its understanding of the deep ironies inherent in the human condition.

Moreover, as the inscription on the academy's doors attests, Freeman was at the vanguard of modern professional American women writers in her lifetime. Unapologetically, she made her writing the central fact of her life and forged a career by combining native talent with acquired business acumen. She wrote to express her creative sensibility, and she wrote to sell; she experimented with genre and technique to satisfy her artistic ambition, and she penned hack pieces to maintain the increasingly comfortable lifestyle she craved. That she failed nearly as often as she succeeded—that is, failed by modern critical standards, since nearly all of her work sold well in her lifetime—is not surprising, nor should it be considered a mark against her given the large quantity and variety of her literary output. Finally it is perhaps most important to stress that, though many have attempted it over the years, Freeman's writing simply resists easy categorization. Though the arena in which her characters' struggles are played out is small and largely unchanging, Freeman succeeds in creating a gallery of people in her fiction whose responses to life are as varied as would be those of any sampling of human beings. Freeman's great power comes from her ability to see—really *see*—individual persons and not groups, causes, or agendas. Her stories, therefore, can disturb us with their unshrinking view of reality and entertain us with their poignant humor, but above all, they leave us with sharply etched portraits of memorable characters—Sarah Penn of "The Revolt of 'Mother,' " Martha Elder of "A Balsam Fir," Christopher Dodd of "The Balking of Christopher," Sophia Lane of "The Revolt of Sophia Lane"—characters that, after we are made privy to their tales of rebellion and quiet triumph, we are not soon likely to forget.

Notes to Part 1

1. Edward Foster, *Mary E. Wilkins Freeman* (New York: Hendricks House, 1956), 23; hereafter cited in the text.

2. Brent L. Kendrick, ed., *The Infant Sphinx: Collected Letters of Mary E. Wilkins Freeman* (Metuchen, N.J.: Scarecrow Press, 1985), 410; hereafter cited in the text. Excerpts from many of Freeman's letters cited in part 1 are reprinted in part 2, "The Writer."

3. In Freeman's contribution to *My Maiden Effort: Being the Personal Confessions of Well-Known American Authors As to Their Literary Beginnings* (Garden City, N.Y.: Doubleday, Page and Company, 1921), 265. Reprinted in part 2, "The Writer."

4. "Bazar" was the correct spelling of the magazine's title in its early years.

5. See Freeman's 17 February 1885 letter to Booth (Kendrick, 60–61; reprinted in part 2, "The Writer") for an indication of her eager compliance with Booth's suggestions for revision.

6. Freeman states this in her 21 April 1885 letter to Booth (Kendrick, 62); reprinted in part 2, "The Writer".

7. Like Emily Dickinson, Freeman briefly attended Mount Holyoke Seminary; she left in part because of its emphasis on public confession of faith and its "too strenuous goadings of conscience" (Kendrick, 324).

8. Perry D. Westbrook, *Mary Wilkins Freeman* (Boston: Twayne, rev. ed. 1988), 59; hereafter cited in the text.

9. William Dean Howells, "Editor's Study," *Harper's Monthly* 74 (May 1887): 987, and "Editor's Study," *Harper's Monthly* 73 (September 1886): 641.

10. Howells, "Editor's Study," *Harper's Monthly* 75 (September 1887): 640.

11. Howells, "Editor's Study," *Harper's Monthly* 83 (June 1891): 155–56.

12. Annie Fields, ed., *Letters of Sarah Orne Jewett* (Boston: Houghton Mifflin, 1911), 112.

13. Nathaniel Hawthorne's prefaces remain some of the best sources for a definition of romance as nineteenth-century writers conceived of it. These quotations come from his preface to *The House of Seven Gables* (Columbus: Ohio State University Press, 1965), 1.

14. Minna C. Smith, "Mary Wilkins at Home," *Boston Evening Transcript* (12 June 1890): 4.

15. Freeman to Hamlin Garland, 23 November 1887 (Kendrick, 83), and Freeman, "An Autobiography," in "Who's Who—and Why: Serious and Frivolous Facts about the Great and the Near-Great," *Saturday Evening Post* 190 (8 December 1917): 75; hereafter cited in the text as "Who's Who." Both selections are reprinted in part 2, "The Writer."

16. To an overwhelming degree, Freeman's stories involve female protagonists. Some notable exceptions include "The Great Pine" and "The Balking of Christopher," both discussed at length later in part 1.

17. Freeman, "Good Wits, Pen and Paper," in *What Women Can Earn: Occupations of Women and Their Compensation*, ed. Grace H. Dodge et al. (New York: Frederick A. Stokes, 1899), 29; hereafter cited in the text as "Good Wits." Reprinted in part 2, "The Writer."

18. Charles Miner Thompson, "Miss Wilkins: An Idealist in Masquerade," *Atlantic Monthly* 83 (May 1899): 675; hereafter cited in the text.

19. Leah Blatt Glasser, " 'She Is the One You Call Sister': Discovering Mary Wilkins Freeman," in *Between Women: Biographers, Novelists, Critics, Teachers, and Artists Write about Their Work on Women,* ed. Carol Ascher et al. (Boston: Beacon Press, 1984), 188.

20. Stuart Bradley Shaw, "Mary E. Wilkins Freeman: Realism, Sentimentalism, and Popular Fiction" (Ph.D. diss., University of Illinois at Urbana-Champaign, 1991), 6, 192.

21. Judith Fetterley and Marjorie Pryse cite the following characteristics of women's regionalism in the introduction to their edition of *American Women Regionalists, 1850–1910* (New York: W. W. Norton, 1992), xi–xx: an emphasis on characters' search for identity within a community largely composed of women, the essential relationship of character to place in the process of that self-discovery, and the narrator's empathy for her subjects.

22. See chapter 1, "Toward the Local Colorists: A Theoretical Sketch of Their Sources," in Josephine Donovan, *New England Local Color Literature: A Women's Tradition* (New York: Frederick Ungar, 1983), 11–24.

23. "Notes," *Critic* 14 (23 August 1890): 101.

24. Per Seyersted, *Kate Chopin: A Critical Biography* (Baton Rouge: Louisiana State University Press, 1969), 52.

25. Freeman's influence on Sarah Orne Jewett and Kate Chopin is explored at length in Laurel Vivian Sparks's "Counterparts: The Fiction of Mary Wilkins Freeman, Sarah Orne Jewett, and Kate Chopin" (Ph.D. diss., University of Iowa, 1990). John Getz examines her influence on Sherwood Anderson in "Mary Wilkins Freeman and Sherwood Anderson: Confluence or Influence?" *MidAmerica: Yearbook of the Society for the Study of Midwestern Literature* 19 (1992): 74–86. Barbara White discusses her influence on Edith Wharton in *Edith Wharton: A Study of the Short Fiction* (New York: Twayne, 1991), 29–33, 54–55, 104. Foster states that in 1891 one of Henry James's friends reported that James "has lately been taken with an enormous enthusiasm for [Freeman's] stories. He has been reading them all one after another . . . and has the greatest opinion of them" (Foster, 89). Hamlin Garland followed Freeman's work closely; he corresponded with her, and he mentions her several times in his diaries and in *Roadside Meetings.*

26. Freeman, "The Girl Who Wants to Write: Things to Do and to Avoid," *Harper's Bazar* 47 (June 1913): 272; hereafter cited in the text as "Girl." Reprinted in part 2, "The Writer."

27. Freeman to Fred Lewis Pattee, 25 September 1919 (Kendrick, 385; reprinted in part 2, "The Writer"). Pattee asked Freeman to respond to a series of questions about her art and career as he prepared the introduction to a new edition of *A New England Nun.*

28. Freeman, "Emily Brontë and *Wuthering Heights*," in *The World's Great Woman Novelists*, ed. T. M. Parrott (Philadelphia: The Booklovers Library, 1901), 89, 92–93; hereafter cited in the text as "Brontë." Reprinted in part 2, "The Writer."

29. Amy Kaplan, *The Social Construction of American Realism* (Chicago: University of Chicago Press, 1988), 18.

30. Nearly all of Freeman's stories are set in small New England towns or villages. The few exceptions include "The Happy Day" (1903), set in Paris, and a handful of later stories, such as "The Winning Lady" (1909), set in New Jersey, where Freeman moved in 1902.

31. Jewett could not recall the title of the story, but she remembered its plot well: "Miss Wilkins's story about getting the squashes in one frosty night, and the cats [*sic*] being lost! I can't remember its name though the story is so clear and exquisite to my mind." *Letters of Sarah Orne Jewett*, ed. Annie Fields (Boston: Houghton Mifflin, 1911), 118.

32. Freeman, *A Humble Romance and Other Stories* (New York: Harper and Brothers, 1887), 272; hereafter cited in the text as *HR*.

33. Mary R. Reichardt, ed., *The Uncollected Stories of Mary Wilkins Freeman* (Jackson: University Press of Mississippi, 1992), 25; hereafter cited in the text as *UNC*.

34. Alice Glarden Brand, for example, calls Freeman's work "a taxonomy of disappointments" in "Mary Wilkins Freeman: Misanthropy as Propaganda," *New England Quarterly* 50 (March 1977): 83; hereafter cited in the text. Josephine Donovan concurs by stating, "Something is dying in the fictional world of Mary E. Wilkins Freeman. A way of life—the woman-centered, matriarchal world of the Victorians—is in its last throes." Donovan, "Mary E. Wilkins Freeman and the Tree of Knowledge," in Donovan, *New England Local Color Literature: A Women's Tradition* (New York: Frederick Ungar, 1983), 119.

35. *Critic* 18, n.s. 15 (May 1891): 286.

36. Mary R. Reichardt, ed., *A Mary Wilkins Freeman Reader* (Lincoln: University of Nebraska Press, 1997), 44; hereafter cited in the text as *MWFR*.

37. Elizabeth Meese, "Signs of Undecidability: Reconsidering the Stories of Mary Wilkins Freeman," in Meese, *Crossing the Double-Cross: The Practice of Feminist Criticism* (Chapel Hill: University of North Carolina Press, 1986), 19–38.

38. For example, Henry David Thoreau says about his sojourn at Walden, "But all this is very selfish, I have heard some of my townsmen say. I confess that I have hitherto indulged very little in philanthropic enterprises. . . . As for Doing-good, that is one of the professions which are full. Moreover, I have tried it fairly, and, strange as it may seem, am satisfied that it does not agree with my constitution. . . . [M]ost men, it appears to me, are in a strange uncertainty about [life], whether it is of the devil or of God, and have *somewhat hastily* concluded that it is the chief end of man here to 'glorify God and enjoy him for-

ever.' " *Walden and Civil Disobedience,* ed. Owen Thomas (New York: W. W. Norton, 1966), 49, 61; hereafter cited in the text.

39. Leah Blatt Glasser, "Mary E. Wilkins Freeman: The Stranger in the Mirror," *Massachusetts Review* 25 (Summer, 1984): 330–33.

40. Freeman, "Introductory Sketch" to Biographical Edition of *Pembroke* (New York: Harper and Brothers, 1899), iii. Reprinted in part 2, "The Writer."

41. Grant Overton, "Mary E. Wilkins Freeman," in *The Women Who Make Our Novels* (New York: Moffat, Yard, and Co., 1919), 199.

42. Michele Clark, afterword to *The Revolt of Mother and Other Stories* (New York: Feminist Press, 1974), 194, 195.

43. Marjorie Pryse, "The Humanity of Women in Freeman's 'A Village Singer,' " *Colby Library Quarterly* 19 (June 1983): 74.

44. Huck Finn admires Emmeline Grangerford's doggerel in Mark Twain's *Adventures of Huckleberry Finn* (Berkeley: University of California Press, 1985), 139–40.

45. Westbrook, 48, and Barbara H. Solomon, introduction to *Short Fiction of Sarah Orne Jewett and Mary Wilkins Freeman* (New York: New American Library, 1979), 25.

46. Linda Grasso, " 'Thwarted Life, Mighty Hunger, Unfinished Work': The Legacy of Nineteenth-Century Women Writing in America," *ATQ,* n.s. 8 (June 1994): 105.

47. Freeman, "A Meeting Half-Way," *Harper's Bazar* 24 (11 April 1891): 275.

48. Freeman, *A New England Nun and Other Stories* (New York: Harper and Brothers, 1891), 232; hereafter cited in the text as *NEN.*

49. Freeman et al., "If They Had a Million Dollars: What Nine Famous Women Would Do if a Fortune Were Theirs," *Ladies' Home Journal* 20 (September 1903): 10.

50. Norma Johnsen, "Pieces: Artist and Audience in Three Mary Wilkins Freeman Stories," *Colby Quarterly* 29 (March 1993): 45, 46.

51. Morris Wei-hsin Tien, "The 'Witchcraft Delusion' in Three American Plays," *American Studies* 18 (March 1988): 39.

52. Freeman, *Silence and Other Stories* (New York: Harper and Brothers, 1898), 234; hereafter cited in the text as *S.*

53. For example, see Donovan's chapter and article (on "The Tree of Knowledge" and on "Evelina's Garden") and Getz's article (on "Eglantina") listed in the bibliography.

54. Freeman, *The Love of Parson Lord and Other Stories* (New York: Harper and Brothers, 1900), 136; hereafter cited in the text as *LPL.*

55. Josephine Donovan, "Silence or Capitulation: Prepatriarchal 'Mothers' Gardens' in Jewett and Freeman," *Studies in Short Fiction* 23 (Winter 1986): 45, 47.

56. Ann-Janine Morey, "American Myth and Biblical Interpretation in the Fiction of Harriet Beecher Stowe and Mary E. Wilkins Freeman," *Journal of the American Academy of Religion* 55 (Spring 1987): 757.

57. Fred Lewis Pattee, *The Development of the American Short Story* (New York: Harper and Brothers, 1923), 322.

58. Beth Wynne Fisken, "The 'Faces of Children That Had Never Been': Ghost Stories by Mary Wilkins Freeman," in *Haunting the House of Fiction,* ed. Lynette Carpenter and Wendy K. Kolmar (Knoxville: University of Tennessee Press, 1991), 42.

59. Freeman, "The School-Teacher's Story," *Romance* 13 (February 1894): 14.

60. Alfred Bendixen, afterword to Mary Wilkins Freeman, *The Wind in the Rose-Bush and Other Stories of the Supernatural* (Chicago: Academy Chicago, 1986), 247; hereafter cited in the text as *WRB.*

61. Lillian Faderman, *Surpassing the Love of Men: Romantic Friendship and Love Between Women from the Renaissance to the Present* (New York: William Morrow and Company, 1981), 291.

62. Foster, 135. Foster's 1956 *Mary E. Wilkins Freeman* is a reworking of his unpublished 1930s Harvard dissertation. Writing at that time, he had the benefit of contact with Freeman's surviving relatives, friends, and others who knew her.

63. Mary E. Wilkins [Freeman] et al., *The Long Arm and Other Detective Stories* (London: Chapman and Hall, 1895), 1–2; hereafter cited in the text as *LA.*

64. See Susan Koppelman's "About 'Two Friends' and Mary Eleanor Wilkins Freeman" (listed in the bibliography) for a discussion of the lesbian theme in this story.

65. Ralph Waldo Emerson, "Nature," in *Selections from Ralph Waldo Emerson,* ed. Stephen E. Whicher (Boston: Houghton Mifflin, 1960), 31, 36; hereafter cited in the text.

66. Freeman, "New England, 'Mother of America,' " *Country Life in America* 22 (July 1912): 66–67.

67. Freeman, *Understudies* (New York: Harper and Brothers, 1901), 9; hereafter cited in the text as *U.*

68. Freeman had a very different side to her as well, however; she was a tough-minded, determined businesswoman who thrived in a competitive market by negotiating prices and terms with her publishers and playing one off the other. A 1910 letter to *Harper's Bazar* editor Elizabeth Jordan is typical: "Thank you so much for your invitation to send some stories. . . . I want to, but at the risk of appearing mercenary. Mr. Duneka has agreed to meet my terms [of] $500. per story (I can in reality obtain more elsewhere) and do you want to pay so much? . . . I would love to write stories for the dear old Bazar, for nothing at all, but the money does seem essential in these days of high prices, and I do have many requests, and I am not rich" (Kendrick, 335).

69. Robert M. Luscher, "Seeing the Forest for the Trees: The 'Intimate Connection' of Mary Wilkins Freeman's *Six Trees*," *ATQ*, n.s. 3 (December 1989): 368.

70. F. O. Matthiessen, "New England Stories," in John Macy, ed., *American Writers on American Literature* (New York: Horace Liveright, 1931), 408.

71. I'd like to get away from earth awhile
   And then come back to it and begin over.
   May no fate willfully misunderstand me
   And half grant what I wish and snatch me away
   Not to return. Earth's the right place for love:
   I don't know where it's likely to go better.

Robert Frost, "Birches," in *Robert Frost's Poems*, ed. Louis Untermeyer (New York: Simon and Schuster, 1971), 90.

72. Beth Wynne Fisken, " 'Unusual' People in a 'Usual Place': 'The Balking of Christopher' by Mary Wilkins Freeman," *Colby Library Quarterly* 21 (June 1985): 100; hereafter cited in the text.

73. Martha J. Cutter, "Beyond Stereotypes: Mary Wilkins Freeman's Radical Critique of Nineteenth-Century Cults of Femininity," *Women's Studies* 21 (1992): 383–84.

74. Freeman, *The Copy-Cat and Other Stories* (New York: Harper and Brothers, 1914), 172; hereafter cited in the text as *CC*.

75. Freeman, *The Fair Lavinia and Others* (New York: Harper and Brothers, 1907), 195; hereafter cited in the text as *FL*.

76. For a discussion of the writing of this "corporate" novel, see Alfred Bendixen's introduction to Mary Wilkins Freeman et al., *The Whole Family: A Novel By Twelve Authors* (New York: Frederick Ungar, 1987), xi–li.

77. "Mary E. Wilkins Freeman at Home at Metuchen, N.J.," *New York Herald*, literary section (31 May 1903): 2.

78. Freeman, *Edgewater People* (New York: Harper and Brothers, 1918), 13; hereafter cited in the text as *EP*.

THE WRITER

Introduction

Since Freeman rarely wrote or spoke about her art, her few statements on the subject invite close consideration. In this part of the text, I have assembled every substantial commentary Freeman made on her short-story writing, whether in book preface, magazine article, or personal letter. Until now, much of this material has been all but inaccessible to readers. By grouping these statements for the first time, this section provides rich insight into Freeman's professed artistic goals and techniques as well as into elements of her personality, at times reflective or earnest, at times self-deprecating or wryly humorous.

In the first selection, a brief preface to an 1890 British edition of *A Humble Romance*, Freeman states that one of her aims in her fiction is to preserve the marked traits of a passing generation of New England descendants. In the introduction to a 1899 edition of *Pembroke*, she further elaborates on her many portraits of characters who possess "a deathless cramp of will," a stubbornness so pronounced that it amounts to a kind of spiritual disease. Although written about her novel, this piece is included here because it is Freeman's most detailed nonfiction account of the type of New England character and village that fascinated her, and as such, it throws considerable light on her short stories.

Freeman's advice to budding authors in "Good Wits, Pen and Paper" and "The Girl Who Wants to Write: Things to Do and to Avoid" reveals her own methods and goals. Here, she discusses both practical and theoretical elements of fiction writing, including such matters as the importance of writing only about those subjects one knows best, her organic, or "sequential," approach to plot development, and her ardent support for a distinctly national literature. Her review of Emily Brontë's *Wuthering Heights* is likewise self-reflexive. She is particularly intrigued, for example, by the fact that Brontë wrote fearlessly and knowingly about her subject despite being, like Freeman herself in 1901, unmarried, female, and relatively isolated in a small village. "Perhaps only a maiden woman could portray a scene of such passion and innocence," she comments, describing the torrid love scenes between Heathcliff and Cathy. "Perhaps only a woman could have in her brain the conception of such forces and not make them a part of her own life." Her recognition of the inner, contradictory forces driving Brontë's protagonists points to her own lifelong interest in the powerful psychological factors that determine human behavior. Finally, Freeman responds to reporters' queries about her life and writing in the magazine article "An Autobiography," and in the brief book chapter "My Maiden Effort."

Freeman's letters are equally revealing. The excerpts reprinted here with notes from Brent Kendrick's *The Infant Sphinx: Collected Letters of Mary E. Wilkins Freeman* span her career and disclose in a more personal manner her motives and moods as she took up her daily task of writing. We learn, for instance, of her willingness early in her career to revise her stories according to her editors' suggestions, her paralyzing bouts of anxiety over her work, the "germ" for several stories, such as "A New England Nun," and her typical practice of composing her commissioned holiday stories around a picture. More lengthy comments about her craft are provided in her several letters to Hamlin Garland, Fred Lewis Pattee, and Henry Wysham Lanier. Each of these individuals at differing times posed a series of questions to her about her art and career, Garland for his own interests, Pattee for a 1920 edition of *A New England Nun*, and Lanier for his preface to *The Best Stories of Mary E. Wilkins* (1927).

Note: Except in the case of errors that may distort meaning, the original spelling, punctuation, and style have been retained in the selections that follow.

Author's Preface to the Edinburgh Edition of *A Humble Romance*

These little stories were written about the village people of New England. They are studies of the descendants of the Massachusetts Bay colonists, in whom can still be seen traces of those features of will and conscience, so strong as to be almost exaggerations and deformities, which characterised their ancestors.

These traces are, however, more evident among the older people; among the younger, they are dimmer and more modified. It therefore seems better worth the while to try to preserve in literature still more of this old and probably disappearing type of New England character, although it has been done with the best results by other American authors.

I hope these studies of the serious and self-restrained New England villages may perhaps give the people of Old England a kindly interest in them, and I have accepted with pleasure the proposal of Mr. Douglas to include the *Humble Romance* in his "Series of American Authors."

A Humble Romance and Other Stories (Edinburgh: David Douglas, 1890), v–vi.

Good Wits, Pen and Paper

Of course, it is understood that no girl can become a successful writer of short stories or books unless she has a certain amount of natural ability in that direction. Otherwise all the advice in the world must be of no avail. There must be a spark, however small, of genuine talent in order to have a flame.

When this talent does exist the simplest road to success is the best. There is really little to do except to provide one's self with good pens, good ink and paper, a liberal supply of postage stamps and a more liberal supply of patience, sharpen one's eyes and ears to see and hear everything in the whole creation likely to be of the slightest assistance, and set to work. Then, never cease work for the pure sake of the work, and never write solely for the dollars and fame, while one lives.

A young writer should follow the safe course of writing only about those subjects which she knows thoroughly, and concerning which she trusts her own convictions. Above all, she should write in her own way, with no dependence upon the work of another for aid or suggestion. She should make her own patterns and found her own school.

When it comes to placing stories, books, etc., there is nothing to do but to send them to editors and publishers, with the firm belief that no article really worthy of acceptance will be rejected by them all. Such a result is very unlikely, and it is generally safe to conclude that there is some defect, if not of art, of adaptability, in the article.

The influence of others in placing work is very much overrated. I doubt if many successful authors can attribute their success to anything but their own unaided efforts, and if many can trace the acceptance of first articles to words or letters of recommendation to editors from influential friends.

The keynote of the whole is, as in every undertaking in this world, faithful, hopeful and independent work.

In *What Women Can Earn: Occupations of Women and Their Compensation*, ed. Grace H. Dodge et al. (New York: Frederick A. Stokes, 1899), 28–29.

"Introductory Sketch" to *Pembroke*

Pembroke was originally intended as a study of the human will in several New England characters, in different phases of disease and abnormal development, and to prove, especially in the most marked case, the truth of a theory that its cure depended entirely upon the capacity of the individual for a love which could rise above all considerations of self, as Barnabas Thayer's love for Charlotte Barnard finally did.

While Barnabas Thayer is the most pronounced exemplification of this theory, and while he, being drawn from life, originally suggested the scheme of the study, a number of the other characters, notably Deborah Thayer, Richard Alger, and Cephas Barnard, are instances of the same spiritual disease. Barnabas to me was as much the victim of disease as a man with curvature of the spine; he was incapable of straightening himself to his former stature until he had laid hands upon a more purely unselfish love than he had ever known, through his anxiety for Charlotte, and so raised himself to his own level.

When I make use of the term abnormal, I do not mean unusual in any sense. I am far from any intention to speak disrespectfully or disloyally of those stanch old soldiers of the faith who landed upon our inhospitable shores and laid the foundation, as on a very rock of spirit, for the New England of to-day; but I am not sure, in spite of their godliness, and their noble adherence, in the face of obstacles, to the dictates of their consciences, that their wills were not developed past the reasonable limit of nature. What wonder is it that their descendants inherit this peculiarity, though they may develop it for much less worthy and more trivial causes than the exiling themselves for a question of faith, even the carrying-out of personal and petty aims and quarrels?

There lived in a New England village, at no very remote time, a man who objected to the painting of the kitchen floor, and who quarrelled furiously with his wife concerning the same. When she persisted, in spite of his wishes to the contrary, and the floor was painted, he refused

"Biographical Edition" of *Pembroke* (New York: Harper and Brothers, 1899), iii–vii.

121

to cross it to his dying day, and always, to his great inconvenience, but probably to his soul's satisfaction, walked around it.

A character like this, holding to a veriest trifle with such a deathless cramp of the will, might naturally be regarded as a notable exception to a general rule; but his brethren who sit on church steps during services, who are dumb to those whom they should love, and will not enter familiar doors because of quarrels over matters of apparently no moment, are legion. *Pembroke* is intended to portray a typical New England village of some sixty years ago, as many of the characters flourished at that time, but villages of a similar description have existed in New England at a much later date, and they exist to-day in a very considerable degree. There are at the present time many little towns in New England along whose pleasant elm or maple shaded streets are scattered characters as pronounced as any in Pembroke. A short time since a Boston woman recited in my hearing a list of seventy-five people in the very small Maine village in which she was born and brought up, and every one of the characters which she mentioned had some almost incredibly marked physical or mental characteristic.

However, this state of things—this survival of the more prominent traits of the old stiff-necked ones, albeit their necks were stiffened by their resistance of the adversary—can necessarily be known only to the initiated. The sojourner from cities for the summer months cannot often penetrate in the least, though he may not be aware of it, the reserve and dignified aloofness of the dwellers in the white cottages along the road over which he drives. He often looks upon them from the superior height of a wise and keen student of character; he knows what he thinks of them, but he never knows what they think of him or themselves. Unless he is a man of the broadest and most democratic tendencies, to whom culture and the polish of society is as nothing beside humanity, and unless he returns, as faithfully as the village birds to their nests, to his summer home year after year, he cannot see very far below the surfaces of villages of which Pembroke is typical. Quite naturally, when the surfaces are broken by some unusual revelation of a strongly serrate individuality, and the tale thereof is told at his dinner-table with an accompaniment of laughter and exclamation-points, he takes that case for an isolated and by no means typical one, when, if the truth were told, the village windows are full of them as he passes by.

However, this state of things must necessarily exist, and has existed, in villages which, like Pembroke, have not been brought much in contact with outside influences, and have not been studied or observed at all by people not of their kind by birth or long familiarity. In towns which have increased largely in population, and have become more or less assimilated with a foreign element, these characters do not exist in such a large measure, are more isolated in reality, and have, consequently, less claim to be considered types. But there have been, and are to-day in New England, hundreds of villages like Pembroke, where nearly every house contains one or more characters so marked as to be incredible, though a writer may be prevented, for obvious reasons, from mentioning names and proving facts.

There is often to a mind from the outside world an almost repulsive narrowness and a pitiful sordidness which amounts to tragedy in the lives of such people as those portrayed in *Pembroke*, but quite generally the tragedy exists only in the comprehension of the observer and not at all in that of the observed. The pitied would meet pity with resentment; they would be full of wonder and wrath if told that their lives were narrow, since they have never seen the limit of the breadth of their current of daily life. A singing-school is as much to them as a symphony concert and grand opera to their city brethren, and a sewing church sociable as an afternoon tea. Though the standard of taste of the simple villagers, and their complete satisfaction therewith, may reasonably be lamented, as also their restricted view of life, they are not to be pitied, generally speaking, for their unhappiness in consequence. It may be that the lack of unhappiness constitutes the real tragedy.

Emily Brontë and *Wuthering Heights*

It may possibly be considered as scarcely fair to characterize a writer of only one book as a great novelist, but after all, the proof of the labor lies not in the quantity but in the quality. Perhaps, going even farther, it lies not so much in achievement as in promise. There seems little doubt that had Emily Brontë lived, and had her genius been somewhat toned and crystallized, she might have surpassed her great sister, Charlotte. There are certainly forces at work in *Wuthering Heights* beyond those in *Jane Eyre, The Professor, Villette,* and *Shirley.* While the book is offensive, even repulsive, it has the repulsiveness of power. Charlotte Brontë's books are unmistakably those of a woman—a woman fretting at and scorning the limitations of her sex and her day, yet in a measure yielding to them. But Emily fairly takes the bit between her teeth and overleaps the barriers, and yet with such an innocence of power and necessity as to make one lose sight of the unwontedness.

There is in *Wuthering Heights* the pitilessness of genius, not only toward the sensibilities of the reader, but toward those of the writer. All that Emily Brontë is intent upon is the truth, the exactness of the equations of her characters, not the impression which they make upon her readers or herself. She handles brutality and coarseness as another woman would handle a painted fan. It is enough for her that the thing is so. It is not her business if it comes down like a sledge-hammer upon the nerves of her audience, or even if it casts reflections derogatory to herself. She is an artist after the manner of the creator of the Laocoön. She uses the scalpel as unflinchingly as the brush. She displays naked nerve and muscle unshrinkingly, and has no thought for graceful curves of flesh to conceal them. Had she lived longer she might have become equally acquainted with the truth and power of grace; she might have widened her audience; she might have attracted, instead of repelled; but she could not have written a greater book, as far as the abstract quality of greatness goes. *Wuthering Heights* from first to last is an

In *The World's Great Woman Novelists,* ed. T. M. Parrott (Philadelphia: The Booklovers Library, 1901), 85–93.

unflinching masterpiece. There is evident no quiver of feminine nerves in the mind or hand. The utter fearlessness of the witness of the truth is upon her. She hedges at nothing. She has no thought for her womanly frills. She clears walls at a bound. She mixes her colors not to please and allure, but because of the facts of creation.

Wuthering Heights is almost inconceivable, taken as the work of a woman, still more as the work of a woman living an isolated life in a country parsonage in the midst of barren moorlands. How she ever came to comprehend the primitive brutalities and passions, and the great truth of life which sanctifies them, is a mystery. The knowledge could not have come from any actual experience. The book is not the result of any personal stress. She had given to her a light for the hidden darkness of human nature, irrespective of her own emotions. A lamp was set to her feet in the beginning. If a girl of twenty-eight could write a novel like *Wuthering Heights*, no other conclusion is possible.

Taken as a love story there is nothing in fiction to compare with the savage, irresistible cleaving to one another of Heathcliff and Catherine. It is almost unearthly. Married although Catherine was, and her lover not her husband, one gets a strange sense of guiltiness from this unrestrained might of love. It is made evident as one of the great forces of life; it is beyond earthly consideration; it survives death. It does not deal with the social problem; it is beyond it. It is a fusion of two souls under a law as unchangeable and uncontrovertible as any law of chemistry. While one condemns, one admits the inevitable. One might as well think of questioning the resistless plunge of the rapids toward the brink of Niagara. It is difficult to recall a heroine who, loving a man other than her husband, gives one such a sense of innocence and stern purity. She seems almost to hold a sword against her own heart, even in that wild love scene a few hours before her death. Perhaps this is the principal touch in the book which betrays the woman writer. Perhaps only a maiden woman could portray a scene of such passion and innocence. Perhaps only a woman could have in her brain the conception of such forces and not make them a part of her own life.

We all know the story of those Brontë sisters—the life of those gifted souls in that lonely parsonage in Yorkshire, their spurring one another to further effort—but our wonder as to them never grows less. In these days we say that knowledge of the world, and contact with those who best represent the tendency of the times and its progress, are necessary to success in any work of art. We mention this man or that as coming closely in contact with the true spirit of his day and generation, in most cases seeming to gain his power by unlimited opportunities for knowl-edge. All the gates of humanity have been unbarred to him. In this time of ready transit and contact, there are for a man few obstacles which he cannot overcome in the way of knowledge of his kind; it is still some-what different for a woman. But the Brontës wrote over half a century ago, and they were women hedged about with great spaces of loneliness and insuperable barriers of religion, in an isolated parsonage with more of the dead than the living for neighbors. How did they gain this knowl-edge?

The *how* is very pronounced in the case of both Charlotte and Anne Brontë, perhaps still more in the case of Emily. How this girl knew the truths, the savage but undeniable truths which she had never been taught, the strength of the passions which she had never known and which she would doubtless have held as a shame to her maiden soul, is the question. Who taught her to strike nails on the head as with the hammer of Thor? It seems a case of downright subjective genius, utterly removed from any question of personal experience or outside influence. Even granting that there had come within her observation some such savage and primeval characters as those in *Wuthering Heights,* how did she know how to develop them, and without a flaw in her premises? Her two and two always make four. There is never a slip. We condemn her characters, yet we acknowledge them and their might of personality.

Moreover, all the time we feel that we have to do with them, not with Emily Brontë. The personality of the author is entirely in the back-ground, so entirely that it seems almost an impossibility to dwell upon it, even to think of it without tearing down, as it were, the wall of imperishable work which she has placed before herself. In *Wuthering Heights* we have to deal with Heathcliff and Catherine, and Isabella and Earnshaw, not with the woman who put their histories upon paper. She wrote about them, that was all. She was not in the least responsible for their wild rebellion and revolt against the existing order of things. She saw these souls revolving unto death in a whirlpool of primitive emo-tion, and she depicted them, not omitting one oath or one shade of sav-agery and horror. It is like a great battlefield described by one posted on some calm tower of observation, with a soul so far removed from selfish emotions that it shrinks at nothing. What was it to Emily Brontë if her heroines were beaten, so they *were* beaten? One cannot imagine her weeping over that sad cut in the luckless Isabella's fair neck, though after all she may have wept. It is never safe to judge an artist by his work. He may write with ice or fire, and none but himself know; but

Wuthering Heights gives the impression of impersonality on the part of the author, if ever a book did. It is far different in that respect from Charlotte Brontë's work. There is the nervous throb of a woman's heart through *Jane Eyre* and *Shirley*, but in *Wuthering Heights*, if the throb be there we do not feel it.

Wuthering Heights is the one novel of a woman, dead over half a century, and it is a book which offends and repels, but for all that it is the great work of a great woman novelist.

The Girl Who Wants to Write:
Things to Do and to Avoid

In beginning this article I must admit that, after years of apprentice-ship, I still entertain much doubt of my knowing exactly how to write myself, also a fear lest I may be entirely inadequate as a teacher. It is very easy, of course, to repeat platitudes, but, after all, do they convey much assistance? I may say, never write unless you are sure you have something worth while for a subject. I may say, never write unless you feel that you must. But I really wonder if those rules do apply so gener-ally that the world might not lose much good work were they strictly observed.

Without the slightest doubt, many a writer sits down to her task with-out the faintest idea concerning its ultimate outcome, and does, never-theless, very good work. She is the writer who observes the law of sequence in writing, and there are many like her. Once started, she pro-gresses and reaches good results simply because her mind is of the sequential order—possibly I might even term it the creative order. Within her brain ideas grow and formulate and expand into a full garden. Other writers must of necessity have a full-fledged plot and plan of action. They must study and ponder and weigh before they set pen and ink to paper or the work will not be worth while. These belong to the class who must observe the platitude, "Have something to write about." For them it is really a law. However, writers of the other class have in reality enough subject-matter, but it is evolved after a different fashion.

I therefore, if I had reason to think that a young writer had positive talent, would not dare say, "Be sure that you have something worth while for a subject before you sit down to write," because the writer from her peculiar mentality might not be able to make sure except from the work itself.

The feeling that one "must write" is even a more doubtful proposi-tion. It is, I conclude, supposed to argue such inspiration, such seething

Harper's Bazar 47 (June 1913): 272.

of central fires of genius, that expression or disaster must ensue. In reality a man may write something which will live for the sake of something rather ignoble, and a woman may write something for money with which to buy a French hat. I personally do not believe it matters why the must, as long as it is must. It is never the kind of spur which really signifies, but the speed which results from its prick.

Of course if a boy or a girl has the real creative impulse, that in itself will be enough. No spur of necessity will be required. In fact, when real genius exists I am inclined to believe that less spur better work. Poverty in such cases may hamper. Well-fed and properly cared-for bodies mean brains working with less effort for the few who have the realization that they were born to the work.

I think, first of all, that the writer ought to leave herself out of the whole proposition. Her own emotions and personal experiences are intensely interesting to her and a doting few, but the world at large cares nothing whatever for them. They are looking for the work and not especially for the worker. That may seem untrue to the fêted and petted author, but it is true. The worker passes, but her work lives if it is good work, and that is the only thing which really matters. The successful author's adoring throng all pass with her, but their children's children have the work which may change the course of lives and make history. It seems a bit cruel, but a writer who is a real writer must put her work before everything with one exception. She must sacrifice herself, she must offer up all her own wishes, if need be, for a living sacrifice; but one thing she has no right to offer: that is the best good and happiness of other people. I do not believe that work done at such an expense is ever the best work. Before even the work of genius itself comes the need of humanity. A man or woman may give up fame for the sake of that and be greater than Shakespeare, and in the long run, and the run is past our finite sight, do work which will surpass anything which is now within his or her capacity. Duty to others must come first, then work if the work is to be of the best.

But if a woman be at liberty to write, let her write as if she were running a race in the sight of the world, and the race not for herself, but for the world, and that which will come after the world for her. She must write, above all things, the truth as far as she can see the truth, as clearly as she can see it, and even the truth must be held back unless it is of a nature to benefit and not poison. But one must write with courage, being once convinced of the truth of that which she writes. She must not write to please an editor or a public incapable of being pleased with the best, because in that very long run of the world she will by so doing defeat her own ends. She will end by not pleasing, although she be hailed with acclamations at first. The applause will die and her audience be gone.

I do not tell young women to write on one side of the paper, to send typed copies, to study the needs of individual journals, to send again and again, because all that has been written a thousand times. It is the A B C of writing and I assume the A B C already learned. It is the very earnest and vital *how* which I am endeavoring to explain. There are, however, some details of technique which I may not observe as strictly as I ought, but which nevertheless I think should be observed. Above all things, in the matter of style strive for clarity. Write even about difficult themes in such a way that a child can understand to some extent as far as his little experience goes. The mystic style is never the best style. It proves a mind in a mist which can only produce words in a mist of meaning. It proves, moreover, a certain cowardice. The writer who has really something to write does not need to hesitate about writing it clearly, throwing the full light upon it, confident that no defects of logic, imagination, or sense can be discovered. Often a writer covers his lack of these essentials by a flood of unintelligible words which sound to the passing reader like wisdom of the profoundest order, whereas in reality it is simply a flimsy concealing of ignorance by a shower as of tinsel. If you lack complete mastery of the language, use short sentences and simple words. Later on you can, if you choose, coin, and use that which is out of fashionable currency and use, and coin toward the wealth of the language. But go slowly at first. All great speed is preceded by slowness and wariness of first effort.

Write about the things which interest you or you will be in great danger of not interesting others, but never make interesting others the chief incentive to work. The essential worth of the work must come first, but of course its quality of interest is necessary to make it well and widely known. Avoid imitation, which is often unconscious and has to be detected by your own sense. Never emulate style, plot, or subtlety of meaning, however you may admire another author. Better to go your own gait, although you may toddle and limp, than to go the gait of another.

Once started, once sure that you can write, that you want to write, never become discouraged. An editor is only human. He may be mistaken in his estimate of your work. Try to estimate your own work as unsparingly as you would the work of another and then stand by your guns. It is not conceited nor egotistical to believe in the merit of one's work after it has been subjected, and honestly, to the severest tests which you can use. It is egotistical and conceited to think highly of one's self because one has done the work, but it is simply just to think highly of the work if it is good.

It is a great mistake to listen too much to individual criticisms of literary efforts and to be swayed by them. The consequence is often an entire lack of originality and a subservience of style to a thousand different rules resulting in no style. You must learn to be your own mentor. In writing, as in everything, it is every one for himself if anything is to be accomplished that is individually accomplished. The old adage, "Too many cooks spoil the broth," is a very good one for the young writer.

There is another point upon which I wish to write, and write tentatively, since I am well aware that my views may not coincide with those of others, and that is criticism and the wisdom or folly of trying to profit by it. Speaking for myself, while I am always very glad to listen to and learn from highly established authority, I do think that a young author is in danger if she places much stress upon the opinions of others. She must remember that a reviewer is paid for reviewing and that it is always possible that her own estimate of her work may be the correct one. She may, under the influence of the reviewer, either overrate or underrate her story.

This is liable to hinder progress either by self-satisfaction, which leads her to stop climbing, or by discouragement, which does exactly the same thing. The woman who is paid to review her story may herself not only be incapable of writing one as good, but may be over-enthusiastic in praise or over-carping in criticism. The girl who has real talent is very apt to have a sensitive nature too easily influenced by the opinion of another. She is often raised to the undesirable skies of self-conceit or plunged into the equally disastrous valley of humiliation by a printed estimate of her work which may be thoroughly fallacious. For that reason I consider it often very unwise for a writer who is timidly trying her wings of first flight to read reviews of her work. Often it may be profitable and lead to advance, oftener perhaps not.

After a writer has established herself, it is for her to judge whether it is for her benefit or injury to read everything which is written about her work. When she has herself so well in hand that she is not in danger of writing the way Tom wishes or the way Dick wishes or the way Harry wishes and losing all originality, it may easily be a very good thing for her to read all opinions and glean advice where she can.

Part 2

As I said before, this is all really tentative, and I emphasize it simply because I realize the undesirable heights and undesirable depths possible to any very highly strung sensitive creature doubtful of her power. She must not allow herself to be influenced by divers opinions and be led astray by every wind of doctrine when it may be that her own little way is the one and only way for her.

I have had letters innumerable from young writers who sent specimens of their work for my opinion. Even when the work was undeniably bad I have hesitated to pronounce a verdict. I have also hesitated to praise, because the girl may have struck just her one little sweet note which she could never repeat and the result in either case would be pitiful. I think I should prefer to be a surgeon rather than a critic. The task of both is practically the same, but the surgeon has a good light for his task and often the critic must do his in darkness as far as any actual knowledge of his patient is concerned. Still, critics are necessary as surgeons are necessary. The question is simply, when necessary.

The old saying, "The pen is mightier than the sword," might be changed to, *The pen is deadlier than the sword*. I doubt if all critics realize this as does the writer who has felt the undeserved lash and caught the undeserved laurel and seen the result in the degeneracy of her work. I think this must have happened at least once, speaking conservatively, to every author. A writer is not a member of an orchestra and the leader is not of the same importance to her as to an orchestra. It is *better* that one does not play in time and tune with all the others.

I now wish to speak of something very near my heart, and that is the great importance of a distinctly national literature. America is young, pitifully so compared with many other nations who have made their indelible mark for all time in literature. If a writer is American she should carry her patriotism into her work. She should make it essentially of her own country. America has so much to do before she can march abreast with the great seers of other countries, and every young artist, whether in literature or anything else, should strive for her honor and hold it very dear. We should have our great musicians, our great painters, our great sculptors, our great writers, who are of America and only America. We have some; we must have more; and the more is for the young. The old perhaps have labored under greater difficulties; the young may see many of those difficulties overcome and the way broader and plainer for swift and eager minds.

The literary future of one's own country is a very high goal toward which to strive, not for one's own sake, but for the sake of the nation.

Everybody should love and revere his country, but the talented ones more than others because they can do more for her. They can set her in her high place. So, above all else, if you are an American writer write as if your pen were the American flag to be held high above your own head and above your own good for the sake of the place of America among the nations. It is not necessary, in order to achieve this end, to lay always the scene of one's story in America, but look upon the scene with American eyes and write from American viewpoints.

An Autobiography

I am assuming that the various details relating to my life have appeared often enough already, and that it is unnecessary to repeat them. Bald facts are not especially interesting, and one cannot offer much besides bald facts unless one happens to be of the Mary MacLane type of writer.

It occurs to me that I have never read a severe criticism of an author's own work by the author, and that it may be an innovation. I am therefore proceeding to criticize the story by which I consider myself lamentably best known, and that is The Revolt of Mother. It was in an evil day I wrote that tale. It exposed me to much of which I could not dream. This very morning I have a letter concerning that story. Somebody wishes to use it in a book. I fear I am mostly known by The Revolt of Mother. My revolt against the case is perfectly useless. People go right on with almost Prussian dogmatism, insisting that The Revolt of Mother is my one and only work. It is most emphatically not. Were I not so truthful, having been born so near Plymouth Rock, I would deny I ever wrote that story. I would foist it upon somebody else. It would leave me with a sense of freedom I have not known since that woman moved into her husband's barn in print.

In the first place all fiction ought to be true, and The Revolt of Mother is not in the least true. When I wrote that little tale I threw my New England traditions to the winds and trampled on my New England conscience. Well, I have had and still have retribution. It is not a good thing to produce fiction which is not true, although that sounds paradoxical. The back bone of the best fiction is essential truth, and The Revolt of Mother is perfectly spineless. I know it, because I am of New England and have lived there. I had written many true things about that cluster of stainless states and for a change I lied.

In "Who's Who—and Why: Serious and Frivolous Facts about the Great and the Near-Great," *Saturday Evening Post* 190 (8 December 1917): 25, 75.

Sometimes incessant truth gets on one's nerves. It did on mine. There never was in New England a woman like Mother. If there had been she most certainly would not have moved into the palatial barn which her husband had erected next the mean little cottage she had occupied during her married life. She simply would have lacked the nerve. She would also have lacked the imagination. New England women of that period coincided with their husbands in thinking that sources of wealth should be better housed than consumers. That Mother would never have dreamed of putting herself ahead of Jersey cows which meant good money. Mother would have been to the full as thrifty as Father. If Mother had lived all those years in that little cottage she would have continued to live there. Moving into the new barn would have been a cataclysm. New England women seldom bring cataclysms about their shoulders.

If Mother had not been Mother, Father would never have been able to erect that barn. Instead there would have been bay-windows on the cottage, which would have ceased to be a cottage. Ambitious New England women do not like cottages. They wish for square rooms on the second floor. Women capable of moving into that barn would have had the cottage roof raised to insure good bedrooms. There would have been wide piazzas added to the house, and Father would simply not have dared mention that great barn to Mother. Father would have adored Mother, but have held her in wholesome respect. She would have fixed his black tie on straightly of a Sunday morning and brushed his coat and fed him well, but she would have held the household reins. As a rule women in New England villages do hold the household reins, and with good reason. They really can drive better. Very little shying or balking when Mother drives. Father is self-distrustful, and with facts to back him, when it comes to managing the household.

Mother usually buys Father's clothes for him. He knows he would be cheated were he to attempt it. Besides, he is shy of chewing an end of fabric to test the color. Mother is valiant.

It is a dreadful confession, but that woman called "Mother" in The Revolt of Mother is impossible. I sacrificed truth when I wrote the story, and at this day I do not know exactly what my price was. I am inclined to think gold of the realm. It could not have been fame of the sort I have gained by it. If so I have had my punishment. Not a story since but somebody asks "Why not another Revolt of Mother?" My literary career has been halted by the success of the big fib in that story. Too late I admit it. The harm is done. But I can at least warn other writers. When you write a short story stick to the truth. If there is not a story in the truth knit until truth happens which does contain a story. Knit, if you can do no better at that than I, who drop more stitches than any airplane in Europe can drop bombs. You can at least pull out the knitting, but a story printed and rampant is a dreadful thing, never to be undone.

My Maiden Effort

In reality I suppose my "maiden effort" was poetry. I suppose that is nearly everybody's maiden effort, if they own up, but since no sane person can possibly call me a success in poetry, I begin with prose.

It was a prize story. I do not own a copy. The one and only was loaned and never returned and is somewhere, with unreturned umbrellas, in limbo.

It is a pity I haven't it, because as I remember it, it was quite passable as an imitation of Charles Dickens. The title was "A Shadow Family."

The story won a prize of fifty dollars and when I went with a friend to claim it the Prize Committee thought the friend must have written the story because I did not look as if I knew enough. She could easily have secured my prize, but she had a New England conscience. That fifty dollars still looms up as larger than all the billions of debt consequent upon the World War. Lucky for Europe that she does not have to pay *that* fifty dollars. It has the market value of the Solar System.

The first step I took upon receiving it was to invest cautiously a small portion in souvenirs bought in ten cent stores, then in their sweet infancy. Then I gave away the rest.

I hope nobody will think me too good for earth because of that. I gave joyfully and it is the one and only instance where my bread has been returned to me manyfold.

I immediately left poetry as a result of that story and sent "Two Old Lovers" to *Harper's Bazaar*. It was accepted after being nearly turned down because the editor at first glance at my handwriting thought it was the infantile effort of a child, not worth reading.

When I got the check for that out of the post-office box I nearly collapsed with pure pride and delight.

I put one dollar of that into an envelope and sent it to an impecunious woman whom I did not know. I bought a souvenir for my father, one for my mother, and oil paints for myself. Then I painted some pan-

In *My Maiden Effort: Being the Personal Confessions of Well-Known American Authors As to Their Literary Beginnings* (Garden City, N.Y.: Doubleday, Page and Company, 1921), 265–267.

sies from life on a little piece of Academy board. That piece of art is in the same limbo with the umbrellas and the prize story.

Then—after my father died—my assets were four dollars in hand and a mortgaged half of a building,—I sold my first story to *Harper's Magazine,* and received a check for seventy-five dollars.

I fear my altruism and love for art were at that time in abeyance for I know only too well what I did with that sum. I gave away a tenth, as an old man might carry a chestnut in the pocket as a charm against rheumatism; but I was wearing shabby black. I bought at once a fine gown, trimmed with black fur, and a fur-trimmed silk coat, and sailed down Main Street in a certain village, disgracefully more elated over my appearance than possible literary success.

However, I give myself the tardy credit of being perfectly conscious, whether or not I have succeeded, in caring more in my heart for the art of my work than for anything else.

Excerpts from Letters

To Edward Everett Hale, 2 September 1875

I thank you very much for your kindness in writing to me and advising me as you have done. I dont think I shall ever forget it. The letter coming as it did and from whom it did was like a cup of cold water to a thirsty soul, not that I wish to add my voice to the wail, that arises so generally from young authors, concerning a lack of appreciation of their dawning genius. I truly believe that I have met so far with all the appreciation I have merited. There has never been anything to appreciate until very recently, and very little now, But I cannot help loving a few words of praise and encouragement and being very grateful for them when they come.

I dont mean to be irreverent, but it seems as if God gave me sugarplums sometimes, just as mamma used to, when I was a little girl, for being good. I dont know how it may be with me in after years, but now, when I read over a poem of my own, after being laid by for six months, it gives me a sort of intellectual nausea, and I do not work over it and polish it, because the metal seems to me, too poor to bear it. I have never yet said of a limping line or of any line that "it is good enough;" when I do, it will be time for me to lay by my pen. You know much and I almost nothing about such matters and I want to believe everything you say when you advise me so kindly, but however it may be with others it does not seem to me that I am "the best critic of my own art." I think, in order to be a good critic, one must neither love nor hate. And I find it impossible not to do the one or the other, in judging my own works. Myself is an object of such intense, vital interest to myself, that I can no more pronounce impartially concerning them than a mother can, concerning her own children. I need the caution you gave me about writing too much. I am sensible that my work during last winter was

Excerpted, with notes renumbered, from *The Infant Sphinx: Collected Letters of Mary E. Wilkins Freeman,* ed. Brent L. Kendrick (Metuchen, N.J.: Scarecrow Press, 1985), 57–64, 66, 69, 73, 82–84, 93, 95, 97, 99, 195, 309–310, 381–385, 401–2, 410–411. Reprinted by permission.

more remarkable for quantity than for quality. At the same time the caution is one that I shall take great pleasure in heeding, for setting aside the fact that I am constitutionally lazy, it is never from anything but a sense of duty that I commence to write. All the pleasure for me lies in the first knowledge of the conception, it is torture to touch it, to handle it, as I am obliged to do in order to express it, if I could only let the *Beauty* lie in my heart and not look at it, only feel that it was there, I should be happy, but to take it in my hand and put [it] into a rhythmical frame is like handling a butterfly. I rub all the gloss off and it is never what it was at first to me. But there is all eternity to work in and if one can only make patience immortal some time my fingers may grow so supple and gentle that they can touch Beauty without harming her and show her unspotted to people to make them happier.

To Eliza Anna Farman Pratt, Summer 1884

I am glad you like the colonial stories.[1] How soon do you want the others? I think, in order to do them, I shall have to have the M.S. in your hands, for a short time. I cant remember enough to keep the connections, not even the character's names. . . . I called on Mrs. Kate Upson Clark,[2] who is summering in Charlemont, the day before I left Shelburne Falls.[3] . . . She said my Tin Pedlar story[4] had made a great hit, and people noticed it a good deal. I am glad if it has, but I can hardly believe it. Mr. Alden[5] has just taken another story, and Miss Booth[6] repeats that I must send all my stories there first. Yes, the way looks clearer to me than it has ever done, but it is odd how my own distrust of every story I write grows. I never was very self-confident, but I am worse and worse. I am actually miserable over every one of these little stories and I make my friends miserable, too. One of these days, I shall have to pay them a percentage of the profits, for enduring my company. I accept people's praises for one story complacently, but I dont have the least faith in another, but I shall try to overcome it.

To Mary Louise Booth, 17 February 1885

I received your kind letter Saturday. Thank you very much for it. I think I do like criticism, and am grateful for it, when I can truly feel that it is a just one, and one from which I can get practical help, and I know that it is in this case. Why, I went straight to work, and altered every sentence in my Wayfairers, which ended with a preposition, and there were ever so many of them: two on the first page, I read. I have been very careless. I think sometimes that it is impossible for me to put to any practical use, the precepts in books. I have a Rhetoric on my table.

I will certainly try to polish my style, as you advise. I shall be very careful in this story, which I am writing now, and you see please, if it has not fewer mistakes.

The matter of detail, I feel a more difficult matter for me to remedy, than the mere polishing up of sentences. I dont know just how, though I understand that it ought to be done. I think I shall have to do it slowly, but I shall bring it about, I hope in time.

I suppose the trouble is, the uncomfortable feeling, I have, that I am not telling things exactly as they are, and making everything clear, if I dont mention everything. The more I write, the more I see that there is a great deal to writing. A story seems to me now, more of an undertaking than it did, and the feeling will grow on me. I think of Longfellow's "Art is long."[7] I suppose it looks so near at first, and then, as one goes on, One sees that it is not; for it seems to stretch out forever. But if Art be fixed, and One is immortal, I suppose the distance between must lessen.

I wish, if it is not too much trouble, that you would mention to me, any like mistakes, of which I may be guilty. I think I can learn the best, that way, by someone's telling me.

I am glad that you like my Cat story.[8] It was really my Cat, and I am gladder, because I was so fond of him. He was a striped and white cat, and he was extravagantly fond of squash. . . . I am on another story with an old woman in it; I only hope people wont tire of my old women. I wonder if there is such a thing, as working a vein so long, that the gold ceases to be gold. But there is no use in worrying, for another vein might open. Thank you again, and I am truly more and more thankful that I know you, and more anxious to do you credit.

To Mary Louise Booth, 21 April 1885
[Freeman tells of a sickly neighbor woman.]

The poor thing has probably overworked, and overworked, when she was far from well. No body knows how some of these country women, with large families, and small purses do work. O they are the ones I would help, if I were rich.[9] Nothing, hardly, touches me so much. . . . I begin to see that there is one beautiful thing which comes from this kind of work, and the thing I have the most need of, I think. One is going to find friends because of it; and when one has no one of their very own, one does need a good many of these, who come next.

Part 2

I am writing a story, which I hope will prove worth something. I am wishing more than I have done, to undertake some larger work, and have an uneasy feeling because of it. Lately the conviction grows on me, of heights and heights, and depths, and depths, which I have never dreamed of, and I doubt more and more my own proportion with regard to them. I do not want to undertake any work for which I am unequal, and if waiting can make me equal to it, I want to wait. I have a feeling that with anything of this sort, it is more a question of natural growth, than of deliberate effort, though I suppose that is against all the rules and precepts.

To Mary Louise Booth and Anna W. Wright, 17 March 1886

I have been writing to day, and just counting up with great disgust, the few pages I have written, copying at that. I am copying all this story. I never worked so hard over one, but I much fear it is no better than the others. I have so many characters in it, and it is now work for me to manage them. But it is a love story, and my heroine is a young girl, whom I am trying very hard not to make horrid.

To Mary Louise Booth, 31 March 1886

I was sorry the story I sent was so long. To day I have written a little tale, concluding with a neat allusion to church, for the Congregationalist.[10] I wouldn't write these if I did not like the money. However it only takes a very little while. But it does not seem to me just right, to write things of that sort on purpose to get money, and please an editor.

To Mary Louise Booth, 28 April 1886

Monday afternoon, I went a-hunting material too: We went to an old lady's birthday-party. But all I saw worth writing about there was a poor old dog, who had been chained thirteen years, because he bit a man once, in his puppy-hood.[11] I have felt like crying every time I have thought of him. He wagged his tail, and looked so pitiful, he is half blind too.

To Mary Louise Booth, 8 September 1886

I am going to send a story to you.[12] I suppose it is so tragic, with the heroine frozen stiff, that no body will want it, but I have it done, and so will send it. It was in my head long, and I thought I might as well write it; and have it over.

To Mary Louise Booth, 5 November 1887

I have seen some of the notices about my book and thought them very kind. I was delighted with Mr. Howells' in the magazine,[13] only I felt as if I did not deserve it. It is some weeks now since I have touched my long story. Sometimes I think I ought to drop it and begin another. I fear the subject may be one that I do not yet quite know how to handle, still I dislike to give it up, it seems so vacillating. I think I will keep on a little longer. I read some where that all the way Alphonse Daudet[14] could write a book was never to look back, and read it over, if he did, he would give it up in disgust. Sometimes I think that is all the way I can do, still I am positive that the book would be dreadful if I did. I begin to see very plainly that there are rocks ahead in my literary course, that I may split upon; though I cannot just define their nature to myself. One of these days if I can find out my own rocks, I think I may acquire more decision of motion, but I shall have to find them out myself.

To Hamlin Garland, 23 November 1887

I shall be very happy to answer your questions as far as I am able. You ask me whether I am trying to depict characters and incidents of the present time or of any particular region, or whether I wish to deal with the past New England life. Well, I suppose I do not know, I have a fancy that I can myself, discover my own aims, better from my own work, than in any other way. I have never thought of it before, but I suppose I should as soon write about one time and one class of people as another, provided they appealed to my artistic sense, and I knew enough about them. So far I have written about the things of which I know the most, if I should ever be equally conversant with other subjects I do not see why I should not write about them. So much for your first question.

Next you ask me if the idea of being true is always present with me. I can answer quite positively to that, and I think it is possibly the only question concerning which I could be quite positive. Yes, I do think more of making my characters *true* and having them say and do just the things they *would* say and do, than of anything else, and that is the only aim in literature of which I have been really conscious myself. Not that I am always successful in pursuing it, one cant always tell what *true* is.

To Hamlin Garland, 8 December 1887

Yes I do consider that I am writing about the New England of the present day, and the dialect is that which is daily in my ears. I have however a fancy that my characters belong to a present that is rapidly becoming *past,* and that a few generations will cause them to disappear. Still this may be only a fancy.

Part 2

To Hamlin Garland, 1 March 1889

I think you are right in assuming that realism is not a fashion. I do not think I could be realistic because it is fashionable. I do not think I knew it was fashionable when I began. I have sometimes wondered what I should have done had I lived a while ago in the romantic age of litera-ture. I wonder if I *would* have written like the rest. I dont believe it. But I suppose no one fully measures or understands the strength of the ten-dencies of the times, they are like waves that we have not even a Moon for. I may be realistic in spite of myself because I am in a realistic age. A few centuries or half a century ago I might have been romantic for the same reason. But I do certainly not believe that realism is due to a delib-erate following of the fashion, in any genuine author. One does not look into new novels as one looks into milliners windows.

To Kate Upson Clark, circa 5 March 1889

I have just received a compliment which surpasses anything that I ever have had before, and I think, anything that you have ever had. I met a theosophist, in an old gold plush wrap, a cinnamon brown dress, and a green bonnet, who said that I did write such beautiful stories that she thought I must have passed through many incarnations, and must be—a very old soul.

I felt a little indignant, not knowing rightly whether it was a compli-ment or not to be told that I was several thousand years old. But now I have come to the conclusion that age in the soul means eternal youth, and I am awfully set up and expect that respect and veneration which is due me. I dare say that Mr. James Russell Lowell is a mere baby com-pared to me if the truth were known! That theosophist would be so beautiful in a story it does seem a pity to waste her!

To Sarah Orne Jewett, 12 August 1889

You dont know how glad I am that you do like my Gentle Ghost, for I have felt somewhat uncertain as to how it would be liked. It is in some respects a departure from my usual vein, and I have made a little lapse into the mystical and romantic one for which I have a strong inclination, but do not generally yield to. Mr. Alden liked the story very much, Miss Booth, not so very well. And I believe I rather laugh at myself for writ-ing it, but that forlorn little girl had been in my head a matter of a dozen years, and I had put her in a poem with poor success once. I felt that she must be disposed of, so about two years ago, I put her in the Gentle Ghost.

Dear Miss Jewett, you are lovely to write to me so about my stories, but I never wrote any story equal to your "White Heron."[15] I dont think I ever read a short story, unless I except Tolstoi's "Two Deaths,"[16] that so appealed to me. I would not have given up that bird any more than you would, if he had come first.

To Sarah Orne Jewett, 10 December 1889

You are lovely to like my Ann Lizy,[17] and tell me so. These realistic children's stories are rather a new field for me, and I am delighted to have anyone say I do well in it. Really when I was a little girl, my father found a nice little parcel of patchwork squares, and brought them to me to put in my quilt. I think that put the story in to my head. I suppose it seems to you as it does to me that everything you have heard, seen, or done, since you opened your eyes on the world, is coming back to you sooner or later, to go into stories, and things. And I never knew it at the time, and I think there is something rather awful about it, as if I had been scudding all the time before, a high wind, instead of walking at my own gait, as I thought. But I dont believe I am making you know what I mean.

To Henry Loomis Nelson, 31 August 1897

I am a little doubtful about stating definitely the subject of the story, for I am rather experimenting, and am not quite sure as to results. I have thought, that I might write something entirely different if I did not like this. The story which I have begun, is called—A Brotherhood of Three[18]—and is a story of three way-farers. I am not quite sure, myself, as to whither they will fare, except into some sort of a Christmas situation. I am sorry not to give you anything more definite, but I never know much about a story, myself, at this stage, and if I try to force the knowledge, and abide by it, I fear I shall spoil it all.

To Hayden Carruth, 11 July 1906

Yes, Five hundred dollars for a Thanksgiving story[19] to be delivered for the first of August, unless you can give me a few days grace, is the understanding. It will be a New England story. . . . I think I can give you already a title (although I may change the name of the woman) The Strike of Hannah Jennings. I will suggest, although I may be exceeding my province, for a first illustration a well dressed, prosperous family, grandparents, parents, aunt with beau, little girls, and boy, standing with bewildered and ag[h]ast faces, at an entirely empty table, in a well furnished dining-room; for a second illustration the same people with hastily adjusted wraps standing before a miserable little shanty, in the open door of which stands defiantly a tall, angular, strong-faced, poor woman. In the background, a miserable interior swarming with children, and a table loaded with a Thanksgiving dinner. If an artist cares, or you think advisable for him to follow out these suggestions, I will suit the story to the pictures.[20] If you wish for fewer figures, I will write for them. I have not the story fully in mind, but shall have soon. It gives me pleasure to write it for you, and I shall endeavor to make it suitable for your Magazine.

To Fred Lewis Pattee, 5 September 1919

Certainly here are the "Few leading Facts."[21] Born in Massachusetts:[22] straight American, with a legend of French lineage generations back. My family moved to Vermont when I was still of tender age, and naturally I went too. We lived in Brattleboro. Vt.[23] Sometimes I wonder if the marvelous beauty of that locality was not largely instrumental in making me try to achieve anything. I lived there until my parents and only sister died, when I was little more than a girl. Then I returned to Randolph, Mass, and made my home with friends.[24] I was forced to work for my mere living, and of course continued writing which I had already begun, although when my father, the last of my family died, I had earned very little. I had written only three stories, that is real stories for adults. One was a prize story, $50, the others were accepted by Harper & Brothers.[25] I wrote and stories were accepted. I wrote novels, with fair success. I never wrote a "best seller," but I am entirely satisfied without that. Most of my work has been done in Randolph, Mass. and here where I came to live when I married Dr. Charles M. Freeman of Metuchen. N.J.[26] I still write.

In answer to your question concerning any influence of other writers which may [have] formed my style, it may seem egotistical but there was none. I did, however strange it may seem, stand entirely alone. As a matter of fact, I would read nothing which I thought might influence me. I had not read the French short stories. I had not read Miss Jewett's stories. I had read Poe.[27] I read a great deal, but very little fiction except the Classics. Of course I read Dickens[28] and Thackeray[29], and Poe, and some translations of heavy German novels, and translations of Goethe.[30] I also read translations from the Greek, I remember being delighted at a very early age, with some of the Greek Philosophers, I can not remember which. I was on very intimate terms with mythological people. I read Ossian,[31] I read a lot of poetry. But it is quite true that I read nothing which could be said even remotely to influence me. If I had been influenced I should have written very differently because most of my own work, is not really the kind I myself like. I want more symbolism, more mysticism. I left that out, because it struck me people did not want it, and I was forced to consider selling qualities. Of course I tried to make my work good along its own lines. I would not have written for money alone.

You ask "What directed you toward the short story?"

I think the answer is very simple. The short story did not take so long to write, it was easier, and of course I was not *sure* of my own ability to write even the short story, much less a novel.

I do consider the art of the novel as a very different affair from that of the short story. The latter can be a simple little melody, the other can be a grand opera.

I am very glad that the Revolt of Mother has succeeded. I thank you very much for the honor you do me in including me in your Century Readings,[32] and I congratulate you upon the success of the work ... I will add, that although I have repeatedly heard that I was founded on Jane Austin,[33] I have never read one of her books.

To Fred Lewis Pattee, 25 September 1919

On another page I answer your questions as best I am able. It is as difficult for me to reply truthfully to some, as if they did not concern me at all. If I have attempted self-analysis, and of course I must have occasionally, like most people, I have met problems, half remembered powers, half remembered achiev[e]ments, which might not be even real, but just mythical for we all can invent myths, if they are myths, that I have given up.

As I wrote, I am convinced that the form of expression I have used, is not the best for me, but it was forced upon me by my New England conscience, which is about all of New England I own.

Circumstances seemed to make it imperative for me to do that one thing, and no other. I did not at the time think much about the choice. I think more now. As I wrote, it is too late to consider another choice. I may have years of life left for the purpose, but I am not strong enough for very hard work, have had too many severe colds. Writing is very hard work, as you know, although nobody among the laboring ranks, or the resting ranks, thinks authors labor. I thank you for writing me as you did. I need encouragement as much as when I began. I doubt always results although I never doubt power if rightly used. So you cheer me very much, make me feel quite somebody. You may not believe this. It is true.

[Pattee sent Freeman eight questions. Here are two of them (italicized), followed by Freeman's answers:]

6. *I have long admired your five or six* vers de societe *lyrics in the Bric-a-Brac column of the Century in the early [1880s.] I wish you had done more of them. Aside from those and the lyric in the 1890 Harpers "Now is the Cherry in Blossom," and the collection of child verse published by Lothrop, have you written other verse? I hope so. The lyric gods certainly were good to you and I hope you have not disappointed them.*

I wrote no more *vers de societe*.[34] No more Cherries in Blossom.[35] My dear Sir, do you remember I wrote you that I had to earn my living? I did not write this, but I also had an Aunt to support. How could I have accomplished these absolutely necessary feats on poetry.

7. *I think you were caught in the realistic rush of the 80s and early 90s with its fierce demand for the concrete, the localized unusual, the Kipling rush and freshness, the short unit of measure, and were swept along in spite of yourself. Had you been born a generation earlier you would have been either a lyrist with intense notes or a Hawthorne working problems with the deeper materials of the human heart. You are in soul more akin to Hawthorne than to anyone else. Am I right in my conjecture? I shall not make these remarks in my criticism of you unless you agree.*

No "realistic rush"—"no Kipling freshness," swept me along in spite of myself. Pen and ink and paper involved slight capital, and were most obviously at hand. I sat down and wrote my little stories about the types I knew, they sold. That is really all. Very simple.

You may be right. Given perfect freedom of choice, which I was not given, I might have been a lyrist, but the notes would certainly have been "intense." I do not know if I am "akin to Hawthorne." I do not care for him as I care for Tolstoi, Scheinkewitz, and Hardy.[36] You understand. I have never bothered to analyze myself, and fear I cannot. I will, however, state one thing. I do know, and have always known, my accomplished work is not the best work of which I am capable, but it is too late now.

To Jean O'Brien, 27 February 1926

I have read your poem. It has a certain charm for me, but I fear no editor will take it.

I wish I could help you, for the path of a writer is hard to-day, but I think no harder than that of a painter-artist. Everything is different since the War[37] and since even the pre-war days for I think the change antedated the War.

As nearly as I can understand the situation, there is in arts and letters a sort of frantic impulse for something erratic, out of the common. Sometimes in order to secure desired effects, they go back, without I think, even realizing it, to old, even ancient writers like Smollett[38] and Fielding[39] and imitate with what seems to me poor success.

Of course the things in the highest price magazines are not flawless. I do not wish to be quoted, for I might be accused of ulterior reasons, but it is simply impossible to even understand much that appears. I think the cheap magazines are far better. The Evening Post has good stuff, so has The Ladies Home Journal, The Womans Home Companion, Liberty and a lot of others.

The Saturday Evening Post pays well, and is well edited.

I have not myself any more pull or influence than you have. I wonder if it will console you a bit if I tell you that after my success and with my measure of international fame, I am none too sure of a market for my own wares.

I simply cannot sell my nice poetry. I can give some away to Contemporary Verse[40] which does not pay but is well edited, and I do think it is good advertising.

I am about as bewildered by the whole situation as you are. I doubt if the authors are deliberately treated unfairly. The editors are not especially interested in them, they are out for money. They try to supply what they consider the popular taste. I do think they often err in judgment as what that taste is, because I hear so much criticism from people and know of so many who stop subscriptions, also because I fail to believe that the public is so foolish as to really like some of the fare offered it.

You see I cannot help you at all. I see nothing for you [to do] but to stick to it if you care enough, and when the things come back be as much of a soldier as you can and realize that you are in the same boat with many others.

I surely hope that you will yet have success. I know how awful it is not to.

To Henry Wysham Lanier, circa October 1926

I did not want to write at all. I wanted to be an artist. But for lack of paint, etc., and sufficiency of pens, ink, and paper, I wrote.

I started with poems, religious. I took myself quite seriously then, also my Work. I showed these pious efforts to a Vermont clergyman,[41] and he told me I was a genius, or to that effect. I thought he knew. Fortunately, I never offered those early poems for publication, and they are nonexistent.

Then I wrote children's verses for a little Fall River magazine. It did not pay, but the editor was extremely kind: she wrote me encouraging letters which really meant more than dollars, though the family purse was very lean.

Next I wrote verses and stories for the defunct *Wide Awake*, for $10 per. They were later collected in book form. The verses today sell better, comparatively, than any of my books. I do not know about the collection of stories, *The Pot of Gold*, for I never had royalty for that. I assume it circulates, from the number of letters which I have received about it, from both this country and abroad.

I wrote my first adult story, a fifty-dollar-prize tale, for a Boston paper. It was called "A Shadow Family," and was a poor imitation of Dickens. I loaned that and it was never returned, and no copy exists.

Then I wrote "Two Old Lovers," and Miss Booth accepted it for *Harper's Bazar,* and sent me a check for $25.

She accepted it by the merest chance, for she thought at first sight it was written by a child—the writing was so unformed; she nearly tossed it away, but something arrested her attention: she read it and accepted it.

After that very little was returned. "A Humble Romance" was taken by Mr. Alden for *Harper's;* afterward he published my first novel, *Jane Field*, as a serial.

I could not readily abandon my desire to be an artist. With a portion of that twenty-five dollars I bought paints, and started in to paint. I found I could mix colors, but could not paint, and had sense enough to relinquish art.

Notes to Part 2

1. Four colonial stories published in *Wide Awake:* "The Bound Girl," 21 (August 1885), 191–96; "Deacon Thomas Wales' Will," 21 (September 1885), 223–27; "The Adopted Daughter," 21 (October 1885), 311–16; and "The 'Horse House Deed,' " 22 (March 1886), 228–33. The stories were collected and published by D. Lothrop and Company in 1886 under the title *The Adventures of Ann: Stories of Colonial Times.*

2. Mrs. Kate Upson Clark (1851–1935), writer and editor. She contributed fiction for children and adults to the Harper periodicals, *Wide Awake*, and *Atlantic Monthly*. She was editor of *Good Cheer* (1882 to 1887) and of *Romance* (1892 to 1894). She was also active in the community and civic life of Brooklyn, N.Y., where she lived. In 1884 she was summering at Charlemont, Massachusetts, on the Deerfield River.

3. Shelburne Falls, Massachusetts. Freeman spent the early part of 1884 there in the home of Dr. and Mrs. Charles Severance.

4. "A Humble Romance," *Harper's*, 69 (June 1884), 22–30.

5. Henry Mills Alden (1836–1919), editor of *Harper's Weekly* (1864 to 1869) and of *Harper's Monthly* (1869 to 1919). The story mentioned could be "An Honest Soul," *Harper's* 69 (July 1884), 302–6, or, more probably, "A Gatherer of Simples," *Harper's*, 69 (October 1884), 787–93.

6. Mary Louise Booth (1831–1889), author, translator, and editor of *Harper's Bazar* from 1867 until the time of her death.

7. Henry Wadsworth Longfellow (1807–1882), American poet.

8. "An Object of Love," *Harper's Bazar*, 18 (February 14, 1885), 112–14.

9. Throughout her life Freeman sympathized with the poor. See, for example, her contribution to "If They Had a Million Dollars," *Ladies' Home Journal*, 20 (September 1903), 10.

10. "An Old Selfishness," *Congregationalist*, 38 (June 3, 1886), 190.

11. Freeman used the chained dog episode in her "A New England Nun," *Harper's Bazar*, 20 (May 7, 1887), 333–34.

12. Probably "A Patient Waiter," *Harper's Bazar*, 19 (November 6, 1886), 730–31.

13. William Dean Howells, "Editor's Study," *Harper's*, 75 (September 1887), 640.

14. Alphonse Daudet (1840–1897), French novelist and short story writer.

15. *A White Heron and Other Stories* (Boston: Houghton, Mifflin, 1886).

16. Freeman must have in mind Tolstoi's "Three Deaths."

17. "Ann Lizy's Patchwork," *St. Nicholas*, 17 (November 1889), 44–49.

18. "A Brotherhood of Three," *Harper's Weekly*, 41 (December 18, 1897), 1248–50.

19. "The Strike of Hannah," *Woman's Home Companion*, 33 (November 1906), 9–10, 50–52.

20. It is worth noting here that Freeman has returned to her earliest writing technique: the use of pictures as springboards for her poetry and/or short stories.

21. Pattee was editing for Harper's Modern Classics series Freeman's *A New England Nun and Other Stories* (New York and London: c. 1920) and had written to Freeman to obtain factual information for the volume's biographical and critical introduction.

22. Freeman was born in the house at 68 South Main Street, Randolph, Massachusetts, on 31 October, 1852.

23. In 1867 Freeman and her family moved to Brattleboro, Vermont, where her father and Orin Slate operated a dry goods store.

24. Freeman's sister, Anna Holbrook Wilkins, died May 27, 1876; her mother Eleanor Lothrop Wilkins, died December 9, 1880; and her father, Warren Edwards Wilkins, died April 10, 1883. After the death of her father, Freeman returned to Randolph and made her home with the family of her childhood schoolmate, Mary Elizabeth Wales.

25. The prize story was "The Shadow Family," *Boston Sunday Budget,* January 1, 1882. The next two Freeman adult stories to be published were "Two Old Lovers," *Harper's Bazar* 16 (March 31, 1883), 198–99; and "The Bar Light-House," *Harper's Bazar,* 16 (April 28, 1883), 267.

26. Freeman was married in Metuchen, N.J., on January 1, 1902.

27. Edgar Allan Poe (1809–1849).

28. Charles Dickens (1812–1870).

29. William Makepeace Thackeray (1811–1863).

30. Johann Wolfgang von Goethe (1749–1832).

31. Ossian was the Scottish Gaelic name for Oisin, the legendary warrior-poet of the Fenian cycle of hero tales about Finn and his war band. In 1762 the Scottish poet James Macpherson "discovered" the poems of Oisin and published *Fingal* (1762) and *Temora* (1763), supposedly translations from 3rd century Gaelic originals, but in fact the works were largely Gaelic translations of Macpherson's own compositions.

32. *Century Readings for a Course in American Literature* (New York: Century Company, 1919) included Freeman's "The Revolt of 'Mother.' "

33. Jane Austen (1775–1817).

34. These verses appeared in the "Bric-a-Brac" column of *Century:* "Sweet Phyllis," 24 (September 1882), 799; "Boy's-Love," 26 (October 1883), 959; "It was a Lass," 26 (April 1884), 959; "Love in the Willow," 28 (June 1884), 318; "Her Bonnet," 28 (August 1884), 640; "A Maiden Lady," 30 (August 1885), 654.

35. *Harper's,* 80 (May 1890), 881. Freeman, of course, had written other verse (particularly children's poetry), notably *Decorative Plaques* (Boston: D. Lothrop, 1883) and *Once Upon a Time and Other Child Verses* (Boston: Lothrop, 1897). Additionally, there were other uncollected poems that had appeared in *Wide Awake* and *St. Nicholas.* Other Freeman poems written up to the time of Pattee's query—and the list is by no means comprehensive—include: "The Mandolin," *Our Continent,* 1 (May 17, 1882), 218; "Love and the Witches," *Century,* 40 (June 1891), 286; "Pastels in Prose," *Harper's,* 86 (December 1892), 147–48; "Cyrano de Bergerac," *Harper's* 99 (June 1899), 37; "The Lode Star," *Scribner's,* 27 (May 1900), 572; "Nonsense Verses," *Harper's,* 111 (August 1905), 483; "Wake Up, America!" in Louis Raemaker's *America in the War* (New York: Century, 1918), p. 34. After Pattee's query, Freeman published "Morning Light,"

Harper's, 142 (December 1920), 17; "The Prisoner," *Contemporary Verse*, 14 (July 1922), 12; "The Vase," *Contemporary Verse*, 14 (July 1922), 13. Additionally, according to Edward Foster's *Mary E. Wilkins Freeman* (New York: Hendricks House, 1956), Freeman left at the time of her death a "sheaf of unpublished verse" written mainly after 1910 (p. 215).

36. Henryk Sienkiewicz (1846–1916), Polish novelist, especially known for his *Quo Vadis?*

37. World War I (1914–1918).

38. Tobias George Smollett (1721–1771).

39. Henry Fielding (1704–1754).

40. "The Prisoner," *Contemporary Verse*, 14 (July 1922), 12; "The Vase," *Contemporary Verse*, 14 (July 1922), 13.

41. Possibly Reverend George Leon Walker of the Centre Congregational Church in Brattleboro. In addition to his theological pursuits, he was particularly interested in Colonial Literature.

Part 3

The Critics

Introduction: Four Perspectives on "A New England Nun"

Criticism of Freeman's short stories has increased dramatically over the last few decades. Although feminist scholars have led the way in redis-covering Freeman, as they have with many neglected American women authors, other methods of inquiry, including formalist, psychoanalytic, and revisionist criticism, have been applied to a number of Freeman's stories, further illuminating the author's artistry. Most criticism has focused on a handful of Freeman's best early tales, such as "A New England Nun," "The Revolt of 'Mother,' " and "A Village Singer," although recent scholarship shows signs of broadening the range of examined sto-ries, for instance, the supernatural and symbolic stories as well as such later works as "The Balking of Christopher" and "The Selfishness of Amelia Lamkin." Several recent books, including a collection of letters, a literary biography, and a new edition of short stories, are testimony to the growing Freeman revival.

In making the selections for this part of the text, I had two options: to bring together unrelated articles on three or four stories or to group several articles that present different perspectives on a single story. The choice was not an easy one, as many fine critical works exist. I opted, finally, for the latter route as the more cohesive and, I hope, instructive one for the student of Freeman's short fiction. Since its earliest publica-tion, "A New England Nun" has been controversial. Moreover, as noted in part 1, Freeman fought the implications of the stereotype the story engendered all her life; she was continually bemused by those who assumed the plot was autobiographical. Along with "The Revolt of 'Mother,' " "A New England Nun" defined the typical Mary Wilkins Freeman story in her day as much as it does in our own. And rightly so: it is a skillful and provocative variation on Freeman's lifelong exploration of women's decision making in the face of manifold social restrictions on their behavior, particularly in courtship and marriage.

The debate over Louisa Ellis's choice not to marry her longtime fiancé, Joe Dagget, continues today. Is Louisa, as Marjorie Pryse argues

in "An Uncloistered 'New England Nun,' " "heroic, active, wise, ambitious, and even transcendent," a visionary and an artist who, in refusing
Joe, makes a conscious decision to establish "an alternative pattern of
living for a woman"? Or is she, as Aliki Barnstone maintains in "Houses
within Houses: Emily Dickinson and Mary Wilkins Freeman's 'A New
England Nun,' " an oddly unemotional woman who sleepwalks through
life, fearful of the loss of control any change might induce? The story
invites both readings, making it one of the most intriguing of the many
purposely ambiguous stories in Freeman's oeuvre. Other aspects of "A
New England Nun" are explored in the final two essays in this section.
In "Mary E. Wilkins Freeman's 'Soft Diurnal Commotion': Women's
Work and Strategies of Containment," Lorne Fienberg examines the
story's opposition between men's and women's work, the former
depicted as "depersonalized, unfulfilling," and monotonous, and the latter, as performed by Louisa, varied, individualized, and satisfying.
Martha J. Cutter's "Mary E. Wilkins Freeman's Two New England
Nuns" pairs the tale with the lesser-known "Louisa" and notes that the
stories' protagonists can be conceived as doubles, one successfully negotiating between the needs of self and others and the other failing to
achieve the necessary but delicate balance between these competing
claims.

Marjorie Pryse

In his biography of Mary Wilkins Freeman, Edward Foster writes that
" 'A New England Nun' . . . has been considered Miss Wilkins' definitive
study of the New England spinster."[1] Yet because the spinster has traditionally carried such negative connotations, critics and historians have
either phrased their praise of Freeman as apologies for her "local" or
"narrow" subject matter, or deemed her depiction of Louisa Ellis in "A
New England Nun" as ironic. Jay Martin views her as "an affectionately
pathetic but heroic symbol of the rage for passivity." He judges that protagonists like her "have no purpose worthy of commitment. . . . Lacking
a heroic society, Mary Wilkins' heroes are debased; noble in being, they
are foolish in action."[2] Foster concludes that "it is precisely the absence
of desire and striving which is the story's grimly ironic point."[3] Pathetic,
passive, debased, foolish, lacking in desire or ambition: such a portrait,
they imply, invites the reader to shun Louisa Ellis. Definitive study
though she may be, we are not to admire or emulate her.

When Louisa Ellis reconsiders marriage to Joe Dagget, she aligns herself against the values he represents. Her resulting unconventionality
makes it understandably difficult for historians, themselves the intellectual and emotional products of a society which has long enshrined these
values, to view her either perceptively or sympathetically. For Louisa
Ellis rejects the concept of manifest destiny and her own mission within
it; she establishes her own home as the limits of her world, embracing
rather than fleeing domesticity, discovering in the process that she can
retain her autonomy; and she expands her vision by preserving her virginity, an action which can only appear if not "foolish" at least threatening to her biographers and critics, most of whom have been men.

In analyzing "A New England Nun" without bias against solitary
women, the reader discovers that within the world Louisa inhabits, she
becomes heroic, active, wise, ambitious, and even transcendent, hardly
the woman Freeman's critics and biographers have depicted. In choosing

"An Uncloistered 'New England Nun,' " *Studies in Short Fiction* 20 (Fall 1983): 289–95.
Reprinted by permission of *Studies in Short Fiction*. Copyright 1983 by Newberry College.

solitude, Louisa creates an alternative pattern of living for a woman who possesses, like her, "the enthusiasm of an artist" (p. 9).[4] If she must sacrifice heterosexual fulfillment (a concept current in our own century rather than in hers) she does so with full recognition that she joins what William Taylor and Christopher Lasch have termed "a sisterhood of sensibility."[5] For all of her apparent sexual repression, her "sublimated fears of defloration,"[6] she discovers that in a world in which sexuality and sensibility mutually exclude each other for women, becoming a hermit like her dog Caesar is the price she must pay for vision. "A New England Nun" dramatizes change in Louisa Ellis. A situation she has long accepted now becomes one she rejects. The story focuses on what she stands to lose, and on what she gains by her rejection.

Although Louisa's emotion when Joe Dagget comes home is "consternation," she does not at first admit it to herself. "Fifteen years ago she had been in love with him—at least she considered herself to be. Just at that time, gently acquiescing with and falling into the natural drift of girlhood, she had seen marriage ahead as a reasonable feature and a probable desirability of life. She had listened with calm docility to her mother's views upon the subject. . . . She talked wisely to her daughter when Joe Dagget presented himself, and Louisa accepted him with no hesitation" (p. 7). Wilkins implies in this passage that the "natural drift of girlhood" involving eventual marriage does require gentle acquiescence as well as wise talk from her mother, and that in taking Joe Dagget as her lover, Louisa has demonstrated "calm docility"—as if she has agreed to accept a condition beyond her control. When Joe Dagget announces his determination to seek his fortune in Australia before returning to marry Louisa, she assents "with the sweet serenity which never failed her" (p. 6); and during the fourteen years of his absence, "she had never dreamed of the possibility of marrying any one else." Even though "she had never felt discontented nor impatient over her lover's absence, still she had always looked forward to his return and their marriage as the inevitable conclusion of things" (p. 7). Conventional in her expectations as in her acquiescence to inevitability, however, she has yet placed eventual marriage "so far in the future that it was almost equal to placing it over the boundaries of another life" (pp. 7–8). Therefore when Joe Dagget returns unexpectedly, she is "as much surprised and taken aback as if she had never thought of it" (p. 8).

Given the nature of Joe Dagget's departure, and that of other men of the region after the Civil War who went West or moved to the cities, individually enacting the male population's sense of manifest destiny,

Louisa Ellis chose a positive course of action in making her solitude a source of happiness. For Joe Dagget would have stayed in Australia until he made his fortune. "He would have stayed fifty years if it had taken so long, and come home feeble and tottering, or never come home at all, to marry Louisa." Her place in such an engagement, in which "they had seldom exchanged letters" (p. 6), was to wait and to change as little as possible. Joe Dagget might return or he might not; and either way, Louisa must not regret the passing of years. Within such a narrow prescription for socially acceptable behavior, "much had happened" even though Joe Dagget, when he returns, finds Louisa "changed but little" (p. 8). "Greatest happening of all—a subtle happening which both were too simple to understand—Louisa's feet had turned into a path, smooth maybe under a calm, serene sky, but so straight and unswerving that it could only meet a check at her grave, and so narrow that there was no room for any one at her side" (p. 7). In appearing to accept her long wait, she has actually made a turn away from the "old winds of romance" which had "never more than murmured" for her anyway (p. 8). Now, when she sews wedding clothes, she listens with "half-wistful attention" to the stillness which she must soon leave behind.

For she has no doubt that she will lose, not gain, in marrying Joe Dagget. She knows, first, that she must lose her own house. "Joe could not desert his mother, who refused to leave her old home. . . . Every morning, rising and going about among her neat maidenly possessions, she felt as one looking her last upon the faces of dear friends. It was true that in a measure she could take them with her, but, robbed of their old environments, they would appear in such new guises that they would almost cease to be themselves" (p. 8). Marriage will force her to relinquish "some peculiar features of her happy solitary life." She knows that "there would be a large house to care for; there would be company to entertain; there would be Joe's rigorous and feeble old mother to wait upon" (p. 9). Forced to leave her house, she will symbolically have to yield her world as well as her ability to exert control within it.

She will also lose the freedom to express herself in her own art. She possesses a still with which she extracts "the sweet and aromatic essences from roses and peppermint and spearmint. By-and-by her still must be laid away" (p. 9). In Perry Westbrook's view, this still symbolizes "what her passivity has done to her." In distilling essences "for no foreseeable use," she "has done no less than permit herself to become unfitted for life."[7] Such an interpretation misses the artistic value, for Louisa, of her achievement in managing to extract the very "essences" from life itself—not unlike her fellow regionalist's [Robert Frost's] apple-picker ("Essence of winter sleep is on the night / The scent of apples . . ."). Her art expresses itself in various ways. "Louisa dearly loved to sew a linen seam, not always for use, but for the simple, mild pleasure which she took in it" (p. 9). Even in her table-setting, she achieves artistic perfection. Unlike her neighbors, Louisa uses her best china instead of "common crockery" every day—not as a mark of ostentation, but as an action which enables her to live "with as much grace as if she had been a veritable guest to her own self" (p. 2). Yet she knows that Joe's mother and Joe himself will "laugh and frown down all these pretty but senseless old maiden ways" (p. 9).

She seems to fear that the loss of her art will make her dangerous, just as she retains "great faith" in the ferocity of her dog Caesar, who has "lived at the end of a chain, all alone in a little hut, for fourteen years" (p. 10) because he once bit a neighbor. Louisa keeps him chained because "she pictured to herself Caesar on the rampage . . . she saw innocent children bleeding in his path . . ." (p. 12). In spite of the fact that he looks docile, and Joe Dagget claims, " 'There ain't a better-natured dog in town' " (p. 11), Louisa believes in his "youthful spirits," just as she continues to believe in her own. Louisa fears that Joe Dagget will unchain Caesar—" 'Some day I'm going to take him out' " (p. 11), he asserts. Should he do so, Louisa fears losing her vision rather than her virginity. Caesar, to Louisa, is a dog with a vision which, as long as he is chained, he retains, at least in his reputation: "Caesar at large might have seemed a very ordinary dog, and excited no comment whatsoever; chained, his reputation overshadowed him, so that he lost his own proper outlines and looked darkly vague and enormous" (p. 11). Only Louisa senses that setting the dog free would turn him into a "very ordinary dog," just as emerging from her own "hut" after fourteen years and marrying Joe Dagget would transform her, as well, into a "very ordinary" woman—yet a woman whose inner life would be in danger. Louisa "looked at the old dog munching his simple fare, and thought of her approaching marriage and trembled" (p. 12).

In addition, because the name Caesar evokes an historical period in which men dominated women, in keeping Caesar chained Louisa exerts her own control over masculine forces which threaten her autonomy. David Hirsch reads "A New England Nun" as Louisa's "suppression of the Dionysian" in herself, a Jungian conflict between order and disorder, sterility and fertility. He concludes that Caesar's continuing imprisonment "can be viewed as a symbolic castration," apparently of Louisa herself.[8] To a point, the story appears to justify Hirsch's assertions, for Caesar's first entrance in the story visually evokes phallic power: "There was a little rush, and the clank of a chain, and a large yellow-and-white dog appeared at the door of his tiny hut, which was half hidden among the tall grasses and flowers" (p. 2). Yet Caesar emerges from his hut because Louisa has brought him food. If the image involves castration, it portrays Louisa intact and only masculine dominance in jeopardy.

Ambiguous images of sexuality abound in this story, sedate as Louisa's life appears to be. When she finishes feeding Caesar and returns inside her house, she removes a "green gingham apron, disclosing a shorter one of pink and white print." Shortly she hears Joe Dagget on the front walk, removes the pink and white apron, and "under that was still another—white linen with a little cambric edging on the bottom" (p. 3). She wears not one but three aprons, each one suggesting symbolic if not actual defense of her own virginity. When Dagget visits, "he felt as if surrounded by a hedge of lace. He was afraid to stir lest he should put a clumsy foot or hand through the fairy web, and he had always the consciousness that Louisa was watching fearfully lest he should" (p. 6). The visual image of clumsy hand breaking the "fairy web" of lace like the cambric edging on Louisa's company apron suggests once again that Louisa's real fear is Joe's dominance rather than her own sexuality. Joe, when he leaves, "felt much as an innocent and perfectly well-intentioned bear might after his exit from a china shop." Louisa "felt much as the kind-hearted, long-suffering owner of the china shop might have done after the exit of the bear" (p. 5). In Joe's absence she replaces the additional two aprons, as if to protect herself from his disturbing presence, and sweeps up the dust he has tracked in. When she imagines marrying Joe, she has visions of "coarse masculine belongings strewn about in endless litter; of dust and disorder arising necessarily from a coarse masculine presence in the midst of all this delicate harmony" (p. 10).

Taylor and Lasch discuss the nineteenth-century myth of the purity of women in a way which explains some of Louisa's rejection of Joe Dagget and marriage itself.

> The myth itself was yet another product of social disintegration, of the disintegration of the family in particular. It represented a desperate effort to find in the sanctity of women, the sanctity of motherhood and the Home, the principle which would hold not only the family but society together.

When Louisa waits patiently during fourteen years for a man who may or may not ever return, she is outwardly acceding to the principle by which women in New England provided their society with a semblance of integration. However, as Taylor and Lasch continue,

> the cult of women and the Home contained contradictions that tended to undermine the very things they were supposed to safeguard. Implicit in the myth was a repudiation not only of heterosexuality but of domesticity itself. It was her purity, contrasted with the coarseness of men, that made woman the head of the Home (although not of the family) and the guardian of public morality. But that same purity made intercourse between men and women at last almost literally impossible and drove women to retreat almost exclusively into the society of their own sex, to abandon the very Home which it was their appointed mission to preserve.[9]

Louisa Ellis certainly repudiates masculine coarseness along with domesticity—for while within her own home she maintains order with the "enthusiasm of an artist," in Joe Dagget's house, supervised by a mother-in-law, she would find "sterner tasks" than her own "graceful but half-needless ones" (p. 9). In rejecting Joe Dagget, then, in the phrasing of Taylor and Lasch, she abandons her appointed mission.

Freeman goes farther than Taylor and Lasch, however, in demonstrating that Louisa Ellis also has a tangible sense of personal loss in anticipating her marriage. One evening about a week before her wedding, Louisa takes a walk under the full moon and sits down on a wall. "Tall shrubs of blueberry vines and meadow-sweet, all woven together and tangled with blackberry vines and horsebriers, shut her in on either side. She had a little clear space between them. Opposite her, on the other side of the road, was a spreading tree; the moon shone between its boughs, and the leaves twinkled like silver. The road was bespread with a beautiful shifting dapple of silver and shadow; the air was full of mysterious sweetness" (pp. 12–13). As she sits on the wall "shut in" by the tangle of sweet shrubs mixed with vines and briers, with her own "little clear space between them," she herself becomes an image of inviolate female sexuality. However, what she looks at "with mildly sorrowful reflectiveness" is not physical but imaginative mystery. Within the protection of the woven briers, Louisa's ability to transform perception into vision remains intact. What might be described as embattled virginity from a masculine point of view becomes Louisa's expression of her autonomous sensibility.

Therefore when she overhears Joe Dagget talking with Lily Dyer, "a girl full of a calm rustic strength and bloom, with a masterful way which might have beseemed a princess" (p. 13), and realizes that they are infatuated with each other, she feels free at last to break off her engagement, "like a queen who, after fearing lest her domain be wrested away from her, sees it firmly insured in her possession" (p. 16). Freeman writes, "If Louisa Ellis had sold her birthright she did not know it, the taste of the pottage was so delicious, and had been her sole satisfaction for so long" (p. 17). In rejecting marriage to Joe Dagget, Louisa feels "fairly steeped in peace" (p. 16). She gains a transcendent self-hood, an identity which earns her membership in a "sisterhood of sensibility."

In the story's final moment, she sees "a long reach of future days strung together like pearls in a rosary, . . . and her heart went up in thankfulness." Like Caesar on his chain, she remains on her own, as the rosary's "long reach" becomes an apotheosis of the dog's leash. Outside her window, the summer air is "filled with the sounds of the busy harvest of men and birds and bees" from which she has apparently cut herself off; yet inside, "Louisa sat, prayerfully numbering her days, like an uncloistered nun" (p. 17). Freeman's choice of concluding image—that Louisa is both nun-like in her solitude yet "uncloistered" by her decision not to marry Joe Dagget—documents the author's perception that in marriage Louisa would have sacrificed more than she would have gained. If the ending of "A New England Nun" is ironic, it is only so in the sense that Louisa, in choosing to keep herself chained to her hut, has thrown off society's fetters. The enthusiasm with which Louisa has transformed "graceful" if "half-needless" activity into vision and with which she now "numbers" her days—with an aural pun on poetic meter by which Freeman metaphorically expands Louisa's art—would have been proscribed for her after her marriage. Such vision is more than compensatory for Louisa's celibacy. Louisa's choice of solitude, her new "long reach," leaves her ironically "uncloistered"—and imaginatively freer, in her society, than she would otherwise have been.

In looking exclusively to masculine themes like manifest destiny or the flight from domesticity of our literature's Rip Van Winkle, Natty Bumppo, and Huckleberry Finn, literary critics and historians have overlooked alternative paradigms for American experience. The very chaos which the challenge of the frontier for American men brought to the lives of American women also paradoxically led these women, in nineteenth-century New England, to make their own worlds and to find them in many ways, as Louisa Ellis does, better than the one the men had left. The world Louisa found herself inhabiting, after the departure of Joe Dagget for Australia, allowed her to develop a vision stripped of its masculine point of view which goes unnoticed—both in her own world, where Joe returns to find her "little changed," and in literary history, which too quickly terms her and her contemporaries sterile spinsters. Yet Louisa Ellis achieves the visionary stature of a "New England nun," a woman who defends her power to ward off chaos just as strongly as nineteenth-century men defended their own desires to "light out for the territories." The "New England nun," together with her counterpart in another Freeman story, "The Revolt of 'Mother,' " establishes a paradigm for American experience which makes the lives of nineteenth-century women finally just as manifest as those of the men whose conquests fill the pages of our literary history.

Notes

1. Edward Foster, *Mary E. Wilkins Freeman* (New York: Hendricks House, 1956), p. 105.

2. Jay Martin, *Harvests of Change: American Literature, 1865–1914* (Englewood Cliffs, N.J.: Prentice-Hall, 1967), pp. 150–51.

3. Foster, p. 106.

4. Mary Wilkins Freeman, "A New England Nun," in *A New England Nun and Other Stories* (New York: Harper & Bros., 1891). Page numbers are included in parentheses in the text.

5. William R. Taylor and Christopher Lasch, "Two 'Kindred Spirits': Sorority and Family in New England, 1839–1846," *New England Quarterly,* 36 (1963), 34.

6. David H. Hirsch, "Subdued Meaning in 'A New England Nun,' " *Studies in Short Fiction,* 2 (1965), 131.

7. Perry Westbrook, *Mary Wilkins Freeman* (New York: Twayne Publishers, 1967), pp. 58–59.

8. Hirsch, pp. 133, 131.

9. Taylor and Lasch, p. 35.

Aliki Barnstone

Louisa Ellis lives between the walls of a solidly built house; her house-keeping is meticulously clean and ordered. She has devised a methodology for the achievement of peace of mind: the maintaining of an absolutely chaste life. Her occupation of doing traditional woman's work has become her preoccupation:

> She had been peacefully sewing at her sitting-room window all the afternoon. Now she quilted her needle carefully into her work, which she folded precisely, and laid in a basket with her thimble and thread and scissors. Louisa Ellis could not remember that ever in her life she had mislaid one of these little feminine appurtenances, which had become, from long use and constant association, a very part of her personality.[1]

The choice of the word "appurtenance" to refer to Louisa's needle is revealing, for the word means not only an appendage (in law, the buildings, and improvements belonging to a house), but a privilege or right. Louisa has exercised the privilege to design the pattern of her life and, with her needle, she has stitched it up.

Louisa has been engaged to be married for fourteen years and in those years her fiancé has been absent:

> In that length of time much had happened. Louisa's mother and brother had died, and she was all alone in the world. But greatest happening of all—a subtle happening which both were too simple to understand—Louisa's feet had turned into a path, smooth maybe under a calm, serene sky, but so straight and unswerving that it could only meet a check at her grave, and so narrow that there was no room for any one at her side.[2]

Excerpted, with notes renumbered, from "Houses within Houses: Emily Dickinson and Mary Wilkins Freeman's 'A New England Nun,' " *Centennial Review* 28 (Spring 1984): 129–45. Reprinted by permission of *Centennial Review*.

To face the deaths of all one's family and to be left "all alone" cannot be regarded as a painless experience. Louisa, in her formality, seems to have experienced what Dickinson describes in her famous poem, "After great pain, a formal feeling comes."[3] The poem reads, "The Feet, mechanical, go round." On her "straight and unswerving path" Louisa's movements, like her house, are impeccably ordered and "formal." As if she were sleepwalking the peaceful rooms of a house in a recurrent dream, her thoughts follow the same order; as, for example, her thoughts about her lover, Joe Dagget, do. As an absent lover Joe brought her no pain, no upheaval; rather, the thought of him is a safe room, a reassurance:

> She had been faithful to him all these years. . . . Her life, especially for the last seven years, had been full of a pleasant peace, she had never felt discontented nor impatient over her lover's absence; still she had always looked forward to his return and their marriage as the inevitable conclusion of things. However, she had fallen into a way of placing it so far in the future that it was almost equal to placing it over the boundaries of another life.[4]

Yet how peaceful has Louisa's solitude been? The language of the narrations of the deaths of Louisa's mother and brother and of Louisa's faithfulness to Joe in his absence are remarkably free of emotion. No grief over the deaths is noted; nor feelings of abandonment, loss, or anger over Joe's absence. Her life of "pleasant peace" has been exclusionary: she "never dreamed" of another; she "never felt discontented nor impatient." It is curious that the peacefulness has been "especially in the last seven years." If she "never felt discontented," why does the peace occur "especially in the last seven years"? Did the death and the loneliness put Louisa's feet on the path to never-never land?—that double-negative land where one neither dreams nor is discontented, where there is neither ecstasy nor woe?

Louisa's passions, "the old winds of romance,"[5] have died: "the wind had never more than murmured; now it had gone down, and everything was still."[6] Now that Joe has returned Louisa cannot unchain her passion which, like her dog, Caesar (punished for having bitten a neighbor), has "lived at the end of a chain, all alone in a little hut, for fourteen years."[7] She cannot allow Caesar to assume the place of king in her life. Like the bitten neighbor, "who was choleric and smarting with the pain of his wound" and who "demanded either Caesar's death or complete ostracism,"[8] Louisa fears the pain of his bite: for her, the bite of pain, of sexuality, of longing. If we think for a moment that the repetition of the fourteen years is fortuitous, the narrator quickly assures us that it is not: "it was now fourteen years since, in a flood of youthful spirits, he had inflicted that memorable bite, and with the exception of short excursions, always at the end of the chain ... the old dog had remained a close prisoner."[9] Seeing the dog deprived "of all innocent canine joys," Joe says, " 'it's downright cruel to keep him tied up there. Some day I'm going to take him out.' "[10] Louisa sees "innocent children bleeding in his path."[11]

For Louisa the "memorable bite" of Joe's love has been transferred to Caesar; it has, in effect, become not memorable, but suppressed. It is not so much that Louisa has transferred her love for Joe to the dog, but rather, that the dog embodies the disturbances which she has diligently been purifying from her life. The loss of control over Caesar represents not only the chaos she fears Joe may bring to her life—"[the] dust and disorder arising necessarily from a coarse masculine presence in the midst of all this delicate harmony"[12]—but the chaos she fears may be unleashed within herself. When Joe enters again:

> He seemed to fill up the whole room. A little yellow canary that had been asleep in his green cage at the south window woke up and fluttered wildly, beating his little yellow wings against the wires. He always did so when Joe Dagget came into the room.[13]

Louisa herself is being aroused, beating her wings against the cage she has set up for herself, and crossing over the "boundaries of another life."[14] This freedom, paradoxically, robs her of her "appurtenance": she becomes subject to the parts of her soul which she has made formal, like the china she uses every day: "Louisa was slow and still in her movements; it took her a long time to prepare her tea; but when it was ready it was set forth with as much grace as if she had been a veritable guest to her own self."[15] This, then, is Louisa's "appurtenance": to serve herself; neither to serve anyone else nor to be served. She is free of those impurities of human contact: anger, loss, sexuality, guilt, desire.

Joe's return puts Louisa in a double bind. Like Penelope, she has been "patiently and unquestioningly waiting."[16] Now, though he brings disorder to her life, "it was not for her, whatever came to pass, to prove untrue and break his heart."[17] That "untrue" gesture would bring guilt and sully her unquestionable purity. Significantly, like Penelope, a part of Louisa's chastity is her nonproductivity:

> Louisa dearly loved to sew a linen seam, not always for use, but for the simple, mild pleasure which she took in it. She would have been loath to confess how more than once she had ripped a seam for the mere delight of sewing it together again. Sitting at her window during long sweet afternoons, drawing her needle gently through the dainty fabric, she was peace itself.[18]

Penelope weaves in day and unweaves at night, not only to deceive her suitors, but to avoid revealing herself in her art. "Louisa had almost the enthusiasm of an artist over the mere order and cleanliness of her solitary home."[19] The word "almost" is important, for Louisa is not an artist. Louisa has no inspiration, she is "almost enthusiastic" and her activity produces "mere order."

Her other activity, aside from sewing and cleaning, is the distilling of the essences of "rose and peppermint and spearmint."[20] The process of distillation removes the organic quality from the plant. The sweet smell has been removed from its body and from the natural cycles of growth and decay. "She gloated gently over her orderly bureau-drawers, with their exquisitely folded contents redolent with lavender and sweet clover and very purity. Could she be sure of the endurance of even this?"[21] If we consider the other meaning of the word "drawers" it would seem that "their contents redolent" are, in effect, both hidden and embalmed. The organic quality of her life, too, is distilled. Her "very purity" is a kind of endurance and an exclusion of the effects of time. Thus, her still provides her with "stillness": and she distills for the "mere pleasure of it"[22] (just as she tidies for the "mere order" of it and sews for the "mere delight" of it).

In marriage, "Sterner tasks than these graceful but half-needless ones would probably devolve upon her."[23] Louisa is, therefore, relieved when she sees her way out; when she discovers that Joe is in love with Lily and that to break the engagement would involve neither breaking his heart nor proving "untrue."

After telling Joe "she shrank from making a change"[24] she feels almost nothing. The episode is like a forgotten nightmare: one wakes half-conscious of a disturbance and as the day progresses all traces of the dream are gone.

Louisa, all alone by herself that night, wept a little, she hardly knew why; but the next morning, on waking, she felt like a queen who, after fearing lest her domain be wrested away from her, sees it firmly insured in her possession.[25]

As this paragraph reveals, it is Louisa's blocking of knowledge that makes her feel like a queen. The adjectives describing her speak of her "pretty but senseless old maiden ways,"[26] her "foolish comfort."[27] She has ordered her house of consciousness so as to be senseless—without senses—and foolish—without thought. She does not know why she weeps; she knows only that the endurance of precisely her method of endurance is assured:

> If Louisa Ellis had sold her birthright she did not know it, the taste of the pottage was so delicious, and had been her sole satisfaction for so long. Serenity and placid narrowness had become to her as the birthright itself. She gazed ahead through a long reach of future days strung together like pearls in a rosary, every one like the others, and all smooth and flawless and innocent, and her heart went up in thankfulness. Outside was the fervid summer afternoon; the air was filled with the sounds of the busy harvest of men and birds and bees; there were halloos, metallic clatterings, sweet calls, and long hummings. Louisa sat, prayerfully numbering her days, like an uncloistered nun.[28]

In these last sentences we return to Louisa's paradoxical "appurtenance." The same blind faith that led her to devise her peaceful method of waiting for her man has led her to renounce what in the nineteenth century was unquestioningly regarded as a woman's role, the role of wife and mother. Louisa is innocent and chaste, yet "like an uncloistered nun." She is free because she is imprisoned in a secular religion of cleanliness. The outside is in the heat of a "fervid summer" that includes "men and birds and bees." Her birthright is a compulsive renunciation of all that is divided, fecund, changing. She has gone to a stillness, to an unearthly, private and unknowing heaven.

Notes

1. Mary Wilkins Freeman, "A New England Nun," in *Short Fiction of Sarah Orne Jewett and Mary Wilkins Freeman*, ed. Barbara H. Solomon (New York: Signet–New American Library, 1979), p. 349.

2. Freeman, p. 353.

3. Emily Dickinson, Poem 341, *The Complete Poems of Emily Dickinson,* ed. Thomas J. Johnson (Boston: Little, Brown, 1980), p. 162.

4. Freeman, p. 353.

5. Freeman, p. 354.

6. Freeman, p. 354.

7. Freeman, p. 355.

8. Freeman, p. 355.

9. Freeman, pp. 355–356.

10. Freeman, p. 356.

11. Freeman, p. 356.

12. Freeman, p. 355.

13. Freeman, p. 350.

14. Freeman, p. 353.

15. Freeman, p. 349.

16. Freeman, p. 352.

17. Freeman, p. 356.

18. Freeman, pp. 354–355.

19. Freeman, p. 355.

20. Freeman, p. 354.

21. Freeman, p. 355.

22. Freeman, p. 354.

23. Freeman, p. 354.

24. Freeman, p. 359.

25. Freeman, p. 359.

26. Freeman, p. 355.

27. Freeman, p. 355.

28. Freeman, p. 360.

Lorne Fienberg

Much of the passionate intensity of Mary E. Wilkins Freeman's fiction subsists in the shadows. In the shadows, private domestic spaces and obscure garden plots, Freeman's women toil for their daily bread, for their dignity and self-esteem, and also for their autonomy as human beings. Theirs are the quotidian tasks of domestic housekeeping, reserved almost exclusively for women, so routine and essential as to be accorded no financial value in a capitalist economy. When Freeman's women emerge from the shadows to claim recognition for their activities, their fellow New England villagers are stunned by the vigor of their appeal. Eccentricity, obstinacy, even revolt are deemed the motivations underlying the demand to acknowledge the importance of women's work. The gentle shock Freeman's stories can, even yet, deliver is an indication that we have still not settled this pressing question: how is women's work to be valued in the marketplace?[1] Indeed, as we ponder the issue, Freeman's fiction is well worth considering anew.

As the workday draws to a close in the opening paragraphs of "A New England Nun," Freeman inscribes the social and economic conditions that inform many of her short stories. The setting and principal action of this story are established in a series of contrasts or oppositions, as the reader observes Louisa Ellis's domestic enclosure and the spacious landscape that she views through her sitting-room window. The window serves both as a threshold, the boundary between two distinct spheres, and as a frame, a means for Louisa to appropriate and to control potentially threatening forces which that landscape represents.

The tranquillity of the scene is deceptive, and the most significant feature of the landscape is deliberately embedded in a catalogue of rural details:

> Somewhere in the distance cows were lowing and a little bell was tin-
> kling; now and then a farm-wagon tilted by, and the dust flew; *some*

Excerpted, with notes renumbered, from "Mary E. Wilkins Freeman's 'Soft Diurnal Commotion': Women's Work and Strategies of Containment," *New England Quarterly* 62 (December 1989): 483–504. Reprinted by permission of *New England Quarterly*.

blue-shirted laborers with shovels over their shoulders plodded past; little
swarms of flies were dancing up and down before the people's faces in
the soft air.[2]

The passage does not specify the kind of work the laborers perform,
but certain inferences can be made about the silences. Whether the
work is industrial or agricultural, the men clearly must journey to some
remote site, where they earn wages in service to others. Their shovels,
which they obviously must provide, suggest that their toil is hard and
their employer ungenerous. Like their return journey, their work is
communal, performed in a synchronized, perhaps mechanized, fashion.
Their plodding gait indicates exhaustion, the dulled motions of animals,
and also the alienation from labor that is both repetitious and controlled
by forces external to the rhythms of the task. Freeman's compound sentence finally effects the dehumanization of the laborers by juxtaposing
them against a herd of cows and a swarm of flies.

While the waning of the light brings an end to the toil of the "blue-
shirted laborers," Louisa Ellis's "soft diurnal commotion" persists in a
variety of domestic chores. Her solitary sewing has been meticulous,
precise, and highly individualized:

> Now she quilted her needle carefully into her work, which she folded
> precisely, and laid in a basket with her thimble and thread and scissors.
> Louisa Ellis could not remember that ever in her life she had mislaid
> one of these little feminine appurtenances, which had become, from
> long use and constant association, a very part of her personality.
> ("NEN," p. 1)

Louisa has translated the work process into a ritual that manifests her
self-mastery and her mastery of her environment. Her diminutive tools
are rendered in marked contrast to the men's shovels, for they are
expressions of an autonomy and human personality that the laborers
lack.

Also in marked contrast to the drudging sameness of the laborers'
work is the variety of Louisa's. In the single page following the opening,
Louisa harvests currants for her tea; she cleans her produce and feeds
the stems to the hens; she sets the table and prepares her solitary tea.
Her meal consists of the currants, a plate of cakes and biscuits which
she has baked, and a salad of lettuce "which she raised to perfection in
her little garden" ("NEN," p. 2). After her meal, she feeds the dog; she

cleans up after tea and polishes the china; she returns once more to her sewing.

Judged by the standards of the marketplace, Louisa's work is trivial and unrelated to society's economy. She offers neither her labor nor its fruits for sale, and so her work may be characterized as nonproductive and without value. And yet her domestic economy provides her not only with an ample subsistence (a self-sufficiency that the gospel of progress frequently derogates) but with a means to self-fulfillment. Louisa's determination to preserve the value of her domestic ritual when her betrothed, Joe Dagget, unexpectedly reappears after a fourteen-year absence exemplifies the dilemma many of Freeman's women face as they attempt to define themselves through their work.

Dagget's "heavy step on the walk" immediately establishes his link to the plodding blue-shirted laborers. That he has fled to Australia "to make his fortune" ("NEN," p. 6) may be a mark of masculine energy and manifest destiny, but his departure just as forcefully signals that no fortunes were to be made in the rural New England of the late nineteenth century, where the wave of farm foreclosures and the flourishing of the factory system deprived men of their economic independence. Work for men like Joe Dagget has little value in the doing; its primary purpose is to accumulate a sufficient display of material riches to secure one's esteem in the community. After fourteen years of accumulating, however, Joe returns only to perform the back-breaking work of "haying all day."

The threat that Joe Dagget poses upon his invasion of Louisa's domestic sphere has usually been interpreted as no more than the fulfillment of a normative sexuality. By this standard, Louisa's final renunciation of Joe has been viewed as a case of "total atrophy or passivity of the volition."[3] Joe's dust, which settles upon Louisa's housekeeping, also introduces a larger threat, however, for it brings inside her home the alien economy of the exterior landscape. This economy of depersonalized, unfulfilling toil and dubious "fortunes" is in danger of demolishing the domain of well-ordered self-sufficiency that Louisa strives to preserve. In asserting her independence from male volition, she consciously chooses an "alternative pattern of living": she happily returns to the shadows to reap the satisfactions that are denied New England men in their work.[4]

The body of "A New England Nun" provides repeated instances of Louisa's religion of domesticity. She distills the aromatic essences of flowers and herbs "for the mere pleasure of it" ("NEN," p. 9). In acts of devotion she polishes the window panes "until they sh[i]ne like jewels" and orders her "bureau-drawers, with their exquisitely folded contents redolent with lavender and sweet clover and very purity" ("NEN," pp. 9–10). It is less the objects she reveres, however, than the act of caring for them. "Louisa had almost the enthusiasm of an artist over the mere order and cleanliness" of her home. Moreover,

> Louisa dearly loved to sew a linen seam, not always for use, but for the simple, mild pleasure which she took in it. She would have been loath to confess how more than once she had ripped a seam for the mere delight of sewing it together again. Sitting at her window during long sweet afternoons, drawing her needle gently through the dainty fabric, she was peace itself. ("NEN," p. 9)

No accumulation or monetary value but artistry, pleasure, delight, sweetness, and the ability to translate her own person into "peace itself": these are the values that Louisa Ellis's self-absorption and her work affirm.

Louisa's domestic strategies of containment, her efforts to hold the outside world at bay, are both delicate and powerful. Upon his visits Joe "felt as if surrounded by a hedge of lace. He was afraid to stir lest he should put a clumsy foot or hand through the fairy web" ("NEN," p. 6). Finally, when Louisa sets Joe free to marry Lily Dyer, her self-sacrifice is simultaneously an act of self-fulfillment. The narrator's evaluation of Louisa's return to her work and to her window stresses the ambiguity of her choice for readers who inhabit the exterior landscape. But there is no uncertainty for Louisa:

> If Louisa Ellis had sold her birthright she did not know it, the taste of the pottage was so delicious, and had been her sole satisfaction for so long. Serenity and placid narrowness had become to her as the birthright itself. She gazed ahead through a long reach of future days strung together like pearls in a rosary, every one like the others, and all smooth and flawless and innocent, and her heart went up in thankfulness. ("NEN," p. 17)

Women's work serves, then, as a central action in Mary E. Wilkins Freeman's fiction, from her earliest collections of short stories, and also as a primary metaphor for the self-definition and personal fulfillment of her characters. Freeman confines her women to the domestic sphere and considers the strategies they employ to preserve autonomy and to assure that their work can be performed to their personal satisfaction.[5] In several stories, such as "A Humble Romance," "A Gatherer of Simples," and "A Taste of Honey," female characters emerge from their homes to test the value of their entrepreneurship and their goods publicly in the marketplace, but in each case they return to the domestic sphere to enact alternative personal economies.

Today's readers should not be frustrated by that retreat, however, nor alienated by the satisfactions Freeman's women are able to achieve in their "soft diurnal commotion." These are contingent values created by the double bind. From the perspective of a society that continues to struggle nearly a century later to reconcile the claims of the domestic and political economies, and to produce for both men and women opportunities for fulfilling work, Freeman's fictive exploration of this fundamental conflict is a heroic one.

Notes

1. The growing body of literature on domestic work in the United States follows a long period of neglect. The works I have found valuable in shaping my understanding of housework include: Carl N. Degler, *At Odds: Women and the Family in America from the Revolution to the Present* (New York: Oxford University Press, 1981); Nona Glazer-Malbin, "Housework: A Review Essay," *Signs* 1 (Summer 1976): 905–22; Heidi I. Hartmann, "The Family as the Locus of Gender, Class and Political Struggle: The Example of Housework," *Signs* 6 (Spring 1981): 366–94; Sheila Rothman, *Woman's Proper Place: A History of Changing Ideals and Practices, 1870 to the Present* (New York: Basic Books, 1978); Kathryn Kish Sklar, *Catherine Beecher: A Study in American Domesticity* (New Haven: Yale University Press, 1973); Carroll Smith-Rosenberg, *Disorderly Conduct: Visions of Gender in Victorian America* (New York: Alfred A. Knopf, 1985); Susan Strasser, *Never Done: A History of American Housework* (New York: Pantheon, 1982); and Eli Zaretsky, *Capitalism, the Family and Personal Life,* revised ed. (New York: Harper and Row, 1986).

2. Mary E. Wilkins Freeman, "A New England Nun," *A New England Nun and Other Stories* (New York: Harper and Brothers, 1891), p. 1; italics mine. All further references to "A New England Nun" are from this edition and will appear in the text preceded by "NEN."

3. Perry D. Westbrook, *Mary Wilkins Freeman* (New York: Twayne, 1967), p. 57.

4. Marjorie Pryse, "An Uncloistered 'New England Nun,' " *Studies in Short Fiction* 20 (Fall 1983): 289.

5. Of course, not all students of culture or literature would agree that the domestic sphere can offer such possibilities. For an exploration of the deleterious effects of the cult of domesticity, see Carol Holly's excellent article on Elizabeth Stuart Phelps, "Shaming the Self in 'The Angel Over the Right Shoulder,' " *American Literature* 60 (March 1988): 42–60.

Martha J. Cutter

Over the past thirty years, no other short story by Mary E. Wilkins Freeman has fueled as much controversy as her "A New England Nun." The controversy centers on the title character's decision not to marry her estranged fiancé: should we interpret Louisa Ellis's decision as a rejection of life or as a valid, self-affirming choice of autonomy?[1] What many critics seem to have overlooked, however, is that within the volume *A New England Nun and Other Stories* (1891) there are actually *two* Louisas who decide not to marry; indeed, there are actually *two* New England nuns. Louisa Ellis, of course, of the short story titled "A New England Nun" must decide whether to marry her fiancé of fourteen years, Joe Dagget. She willingly and happily allows Joe to marry another woman, and in doing so she maintains her lifestyle. Similarly Louisa Britton, the protagonist of the short story titled simply "Louisa," must decide whether to marry a wealthy suitor, Jonathan Nye. Like Louisa Ellis, Louisa Britton happily allows her suitor to marry another woman, thereby retaining her autonomous lifestyle and her dreams. Thus both Louisas choose to remain single in order to protect the integrity and needs of the self.

By using feminist psychological and historical theories about women's self-definition and by placing these two stories in the context of Freeman's life and work as a whole, I will suggest an alternative way of reading Freeman's fictions.[2] Like many of Freeman's female characters, Louisa Ellis and Louisa Britton find themselves enmeshed in a "web" of relationships; their actions affect not only themselves but the people who surround them. For these women successful self-definition seems to entail achieving a balance between the selflessness prescribed by the 19th-century Cult of True Womanhood and their need for autonomy. When Freeman's characters resolve this conflict between their responsibilities to others and the needs of the self, the text affirms their actions

"Mary E. Wilkins Freeman's Two New England Nuns," *Colby Quarterly* 26 (December 1990): 213–25. Reprinted by permission of *Colby Quarterly*, Colby College, Waterville, Maine.

and decisions with supportive language, imagery, and plot resolution. But when they fail to achieve a balance between self and other, the language and imagery surrounding the central female character are contradictory. Therefore, when we contrast these two New England nuns, we can see Freeman's depiction of a paradigm for feminine psychological self-definition. For Mary Wilkins Freeman there seem to be more ways than one to reject marriage, and some versions of this decision represent an active choice of freedom rather than a passive reaction to external forces and circumstances. Although these two characters—Louisa Ellis and Louisa Britton—are very different, the moral dilemma they must resolve is similar. Both women are clearly oriented toward the relational, toward the maintenance of what psychologist Carol Gilligan has called a web of relationship, and this orientation influences their marital decision. Neither of these women actually desires to marry her suitor, yet both Louisas consider marriage because they believe that individuals other than themselves would be harmed by their refusal to marry. Louisa Ellis, for example, believes that she would hurt Joe Dagget if she were to break her "troth" to him. Louisa Britton feels pressure of a different sort; poor, she is urged by family and friends to marry her wealthy suitor in order to save her family from starvation.[3] Not surprisingly, historians who have studied this time period have found such an orientation to a web of relationship to be quite common. Nancy Cott, Barbara Welter, and Carroll Smith-Rosenberg have all concluded that during this time period women were encouraged to be subservient, selfless, domestic, and pious. As Cott argues, the Cult of Domesticity, of True Womanhood, "prescribed women's appropriate attitude to be selflessness. The conventional cliché 'that women were to live for others' was substantially correct, wrote the author of *Woman's Mission*. . . ."[4] Women, then, were encouraged to orient themselves entirely toward the needs of other individuals, to be subservient and self-denying to the last.

Given this historical psychological profile of feminine selflessness, it is no wonder that women of this time period—including Mary Wilkins Freeman—had an ambivalent attitude toward marriage. Love, marriage, and family meant a loss of self, a total submersion of identity in the role of "wife" and "mother." Consequently, as Annis Pratt notes, women's writing frequently depicts an "either-or" attitude toward selfhood and marriage; there is a "conviction that one cannot develop fully as a woman in a love relationship and also develop as a human being. . . ."[5] Freeman herself manifested this "either-or" attitude toward selfhood and marriage, delaying her own marriage for nine years because she was fearful that it might interfere with her work. She also feared the loss of identity which she associated with marriage; writing to a female friend who was soon to be married, Freeman remarks: "I know how you feel. . . . I am to be married myself before long. . . . If *you* don't see the old *me*, I shall run and run until I find her. And as for you, no man shall ever swallow you up entirely. . . ."[6] Ultimately, when Freeman did marry in 1902 (at the age of fifty), she felt that she lost both her ability to write and her identity. Her writing suffered because she had to leave her own locale and move to New Jersey where, Freeman said, "I have not a blessed thing to write about." And as Leah Blatt Glasser suggests, Freeman's marriage did force her to part with the "old me"; she lost the sense of control over her writing and her life which she had always maintained.[7]

In her own life, then, Freeman acutely felt the conflict between marriage and identity, between individual autonomy and the selflessness prescribed for women by the cult of marital domesticity. Her fiction explores this conflict through numerous portraits of women inside and outside of marriage. The title character of "The Selfishness of Amelia Lamkin" (1909), for example, demonstrates the total loss of identity that can occur in "traditional" marriage; Amelia Lamkin, the perfect domestic saint, is so self-effacing that she even forgets to nourish herself, and she nearly dies of starvation and exhaustion caused by her extensive catering to her large and demanding family. Similarly, Sarah Penn of "The Revolt of 'Mother' " (1891) is a perfect domestic saint, a masterful keeper of "her box of a house" who has never spoken up to her husband; one day, however, she revolts, moving her family into a new barn in order to provide them with a more spacious home. Stories such as these explore the various alternatives possible within marriage but are ambivalent about whether women can maintain their identities, given the patriarchal structure of marriage.[8]

Yet another series of Freeman's stories explores the conflict between autonomy and love through a female character's decision to remain single, and these portraits help to contextualize the controversy surrounding "A New England Nun." A number of Freeman's women are given the option to marry yet do not. Jane Strong, Amelia's sister in "The Selfishness of Amelia Lamkin," is attractive and has had opportunities to marry but remains single in order to preserve her autonomy. Evelina, of "Evelina's Garden" (1898), is also attractive but does not pursue marriage; instead she remains single all her life, investing her creativity and energy in her garden. On the other hand, Eunice Fairweather of "A

Moral Exigency" (1887) and Inez Moore of "A Taste of Honey" (1887) both refuse to marry because of personal obligations and principles; as Barbara Johns says, "Aware of their sexuality and alive to the possibility of romance, these women regard personal integrity as an essential value that marriage ought not to violate."[9]

It is certainly not true, then, as Perry Westbrook states, that all Freeman's young women "have one main goal in life: to find a husband in a scarce market."[10] Many of Freeman's female characters demonstrate a desire and an ability to resist strong social pressures which replicate the institution of marriage and motherhood. Yet these women do so with varying degrees of consciousness, with varying awareness of what they are gaining and losing. As Emily Toth notes, the choice of celibacy by a female character can be either a repressive renunciation or "a strong, authentic choice leading to Freedom," "a fulfillment of greater desires."[11] Similarly, in a study of the spinster in New England literature, Barbara Johns argues that some of Freeman's characters choose spinsterhood as an act of moral heroism because they "regard personal integrity as an essential value that marriage ought not to violate." Yet there is another set of female characters whose spinsterhood is not "a clear-cut choice made on their own behalves" but rather a negative reaction to the pressure of circumstances.[12] In other words, certain of Freeman's characters opt to remain single as a reaction to forces *outside* themselves: coincidences, rejections, the demands of others. But another group of Freeman's characters opt to remain single as a reaction to forces *within* themselves; determined to heed their inner voices, they actively choose celibacy and autonomy.

The recent descriptions of feminine development provided by the self-in-relation school of psychology may offer insight into how 19th-century women like Louisa Ellis and Louisa Britton could heed their inner voices and actively choose freedom and self-definition.[13] Relational psychologists like Carol Gilligan argue that women view the world from a framework of connectivity, in terms of a web of relationship.[14] For women, the pressure to marry, to continue to expand one's network of connectivity, and to heed the demands of others is particularly strong. Women's psychological development, therefore, involves moving from a "conventional" phase where responsiveness to others is the sole concern to a "post-conventional" phase where responsiveness to others, as well as to the self, is balanced; women must learn to include themselves "in an expanding network of connection."[15] With Louisa Ellis, Freeman portrays a woman who is unable to move beyond the selflessness and subservience to others prescribed by the cult of femininity; Louisa Ellis remains trapped in the "conventional" stage of subordinating the needs of the self to the needs of others. With Louisa Britton, on the other hand, Freeman portrays a character who operates from a "post-conventional" moral paradigm that incorporates the self into the weighing and balancing of needs. Rather than subscribing to a cult of true womanhood, Louisa Britton validates the needs of the individual self, apart from this constricting image, and actively chooses to remain single because she knows that this decision is right for herself.

As the story "A New England Nun" opens, we learn that "It was late in the afternoon, and the light was waning" (1).[16] This opening statement about the time of day is one of the many metaphors in the story which illustrate Louisa's state and which hint at a certain ambiguity in her portrayal. Although Louisa was engaged when she was just a young girl, she has awaited the return of her fiancé for fourteen years. During these years, Louisa has grown accustomed to being alone: "Louisa's feet had turned into a path, smooth maybe under a calm, serene sky, but so straight and unswerving that it could only meet a check at her grave, and so narrow that there was no room for any one at her side" (7). However, after fourteen years of earning his fortune in Australia, Louisa's fiancé Joe Dagget does return, and the couple go forward with their wedding plans, although neither Joe nor Louisa really wishes to be married and although neither one is very comfortable in the other's presence.

Both Louisa and Joe are willing to honor their fourteen-year-old pledges to each other, although both have much to lose in doing so. Joe is in love with another woman—Lily Dyer—and, by marrying Louisa, Joe will lose something that he clearly values—his relationship with Lily. Yet Louisa's losses from the marriage are much greater and, indeed, in many ways, they are the focus of the story. Joe may feel like a clumsy intruder in Louisa's house, but it is not in Louisa's house that Joe will live: "Joe had made some extensive and quite magnificent alterations in his house. It was the old homestead; the newly-married couple would live there, for Joe could not desert his mother, who refused to leave her old home. So Louisa must leave hers" (8). And over the past fourteen years, Louisa has grown accustomed to her home, to her "neat maidenly possessions" (8) and to her "senseless old maiden ways" of distilling essences and sewing her linen seams, over and over (9).

Indeed, these activities and possessions constitute, for Louisa, a genuine lifestyle.[17] Through her home, Louisa defines herself as a domestic artist and achieves a source of fulfillment:

Louisa had almost the enthusiasm of an artist over the mere order and cleanliness of her solitary home. She had throbs of genuine triumph at the sight of the window-panes which she had polished until they shone like jewels. She gloated gently over her orderly bureau-drawers, with their exquisitely folded contents redolent with lavender and sweet clover and very purity. Could she be sure of the endurance of even this? (9–10)

In fact, Louisa knows that in marriage she will have to give up her "ways": "Joe's mother, domineering, shrewd old matron that she was . . . and very likely even Joe himself . . . would laugh and frown down all these pretty but senseless old maiden ways" (9). Louisa thus fears the loss of her domestic art, of her very lifestyle, in a marriage to Joe: "She had visions, so startling that she half repudiated them as indelicate, of coarse masculine belongings strewn about in endless litter; of dust and disorder arising necessarily from a coarse masculine presence in the midst of all this delicate harmony" (10).

Louisa has defined a lifestyle for herself, a "delicate harmony," an autonomous and fulfilling existence. Yet Louisa is willing to give up this harmony in order not to hurt Joe: she thinks "of her approaching marriage and tremble[s]" but honors her pledge none the less:

Still no anticipation of disorder and confusion in lieu of sweet peace and harmony, no forebodings of Caesar on the rampage, no wild fluttering of her little yellow canary, were sufficient to turn her a hair's-breadth. Joe Dagget had been fond of her and working for her all these years. It was not for her, whatever came to pass, to prove untrue and break his heart. (12)

Louisa may be obsessive, she may be repressed, but in a certain clear way she is also amazingly brave, for her sacrifice is extreme.[18] In faintly veiled hints, the text suggests that Louisa may not survive such an uprooting. For example, Louisa associates her marriage with "the boundaries of another life" (8) so that "going about among her neat maidenly possessions, she felt as one looking her last upon the faces of dear friends" (8).[19] The vision she has of mangled "innocent children" (12) may well be her vision of herself after her marriage to Joe. Of course, it has been argued that the bloody imagery suggests Louisa's fear of the loss of her virginity, but in a much larger sense Louisa fears the loss of herself when she and Joe's "interests and possessions should be more completely fused in one" (11). Louisa fears that in this fusion she will lose not only the essences she distills but the "essence" of herself; the delicate harmony she has achieved over the years. Her personality and lifestyle—and perhaps her life itself—will be erased.

Fortunately Louisa discovers that Joe is in love with Lily and ends her engagement. But Louisa is only able to take a self-preserving act *after* she has been assured that her actions will not harm anyone else; it is only *after* she overhears a conversation and learns of Joe's love for Lily that she feels free to end her engagement. Not coincidentally, it is at this point that the text becomes particularly ambivalent. Louisa feels "like a queen" (16)—surely an image which suggests feminine empowerment. Yet the following images suggest passivity, futility, even death:

> Now the tall weeds and grasses might cluster around Caesar's little hermit hut, the snow might fall on its roof year in and year out. . . . Now the little canary might turn itself into a peaceful yellow ball night after night. . . . Louisa could sew linen seams, and distill roses, and dust and polish and fold away in lavender, as long as she listed. . . . (16)

These images, in and of themselves, gently hint that Louisa has folded herself away, locked herself into a repetitive and meaningless existence, but the following images suggest Louisa's isolation even more strongly: "Outside was the fervid summer afternoon; the air was filled with the sounds of the busy harvest of men and birds and bees; there were halloos, metallic clatterings, sweet calls, and long hummings. Louisa sat, prayerfully numbering her days, like an uncloistered nun" (17). Louisa has resisted the "compulsory heterosexuality" (to use Adrienne Rich's phrase) of the world around her; she has refused to become a part of the world of men and birds and bees.[20] But hers is a passive resistance; rather than heeding her inner voice, Louisa has allowed chance, circumstances, coincidences, and the needs of others to dictate her fate.

Furthermore, after carefully going to great lengths to establish that Louisa will lose a great part of herself in a marriage to Joe Dagget (Joe Dagger?), Freeman undercuts Louisa's choice of spinsterhood by suggesting that Louisa is not fully conscious of what she has chosen. The story ends in a series of complicated, unresolvable paradoxes and of sentences that hinge on conditional, contorted allusions: "*If* Louisa Ellis had sold her birthright she did not know it, the taste of the pottage was so delicious, and had been her sole satisfaction for so long. Serenity and placid narrowness had become to her as the birthright itself" (17, emphasis mine). The text suggests a blocking of consciousness wherein "placid narrowness" becomes Louisa's birthright. As Barnstone has pointed out, Louisa does not know what she has chosen; she does not know if she has sold her birthright; she does not know why she weeps; she is, in a very real way, senseless.[21] The underlying biblical metaphor—the story of Jacob and Esau—further suggests Louisa's short-sightedness. Like Esau, Louisa only sees a small part of the picture: she can only be relieved that her lifestyle has been preserved. But she cannot see the larger picture in which she might have actively chosen to preserve her lifestyle; in which she herself might have chosen to make celibacy and freedom—rather than "placid narrowness"—her birthright.

Louisa is satisfied with the outcome of events, with her "placid narrowness"—but is Freeman? Louisa has only acted in a way that validates the needs of the self when they do not conflict with the needs of others. She has reached Gilligan's "conventional" stage of moral development in which the demands of the self are subordinated to the demands of others, but she cannot reach Gilligan's post-conventional level in which she would realize, like Gilligan's subject Sarah, that she must make "a choice to include herself, not to rule herself out from consideration but to consider her own needs as well as those of others in deciding what was the best thing to do."[22] Rather than heeding her inner voice, Louisa ignores the needs of the self: "Louisa . . . thought of her approaching marriage and trembled. Still no anticipation of disorder and confusion in lieu of sweet peace and harmony . . . were sufficient to turn her a hair's-breadth" (12). Louisa has achieved an autonomous lifestyle, but she is willing to sacrifice it for the sake of others. Fortunately, Louisa's lifestyle is preserved; chance and an overheard conversation intervene. But fortune is not always so kind, and Freeman seeks to indicate that women must be more active participants in their own self-construction.[23]

Although few critics have analyzed Freeman's short story "Louisa," it does provide an example of how women can be active participants in their self-constructions, despite the limits imposed by a patriarchal society.[24] Like Louisa Ellis, Louisa Britton chooses not to marry, not to subscribe to "The Cult of True Womanhood" and become a domestic saint. But Louisa Britton chooses celibacy actively, because it is right for herself. Although she does care for others, she is not willing to sacrifice her "essence," the essential part of herself, for others. Like Louisa Ellis, she chooses to remain a New England nun, but she chooses rationally and actively, and the text affirms her decision emphatically.

The conflict of "Louisa" centers on the protagonist's attempt to support her family through means other than marriage. Louisa Britton is the sole breadwinner for a very poor family that consists of her ailing mother and her senile old grandfather. Louisa once had a job as a school-teacher through which she supported her family, but she lost this job to the daughter of a more influential family. Still, Louisa is selfless in her attempts to feed her family—working in the fields, hiring herself out to other farmers for pay—doing anything just to obtain food for her family. The one thing Louisa is unwilling to do for her family, however, is to marry Jonathan Nye, her wealthy suitor.

Although both Louisas are considered attractive and indeed mar-riageable, a number of economic and social differences set these two characters apart; where Louisa Ellis is economically independent, for Louisa Britton marriage seems an economic necessity. Furthermore, there are also important chronological or developmental differences. Louisa Ellis's personality and character are already formed; she has a placid serenity and mild sweetness that rarely fail her. Louisa Britton, on the other hand, is much less placid; her demeanor and appearance are variable, her personality still evolving, still malleable: "Louisa was very pretty when pleased and animated, at other times she had a look like a closed flower. One could see no prettiness in her" (392). Louisa Ellis has learned, in T. S. Eliot's phrase, to "prepare a face to meet the faces that you meet," and this face never changes. Louisa Britton has yet to define what this face will be. It is integral to our understanding of the story to see that Louisa Britton (and Freeman herself) holds out for the right to be self-defined; women should not be forced to define themselves solely through marriage, solely through patriarchal inscrip-tions of the proper role of a "True Woman."

In terms of personality formation and class, then, these two stories portray their central characters in very different ways. I am not claiming that these two Louisas are the same character, although they may be doubles.[25] What I am claiming, however, is that these two very different women must deal with a very similar issue. In fact, the "marriage plots" of both stories are remarkably similar. In both stories marriage is less an issue of true emotion and more an issue of social propriety, of subscrib-ing to a cult-like notion of femininity in which "The true woman's place was unquestionably by her own fireside—as daughter, sister, but most of all as wife and mother."[26] The idea that marriage is women's only true fulfillment is apparent in Louisa Ellis's recollection of Joe Dagget's courtship: "Fifteen years ago she had been in love with him—at least she considered herself to be. Just at that time, gently acquiescing with and falling into the natural drift of girlhood, she had seen marriage ahead as a reasonable feature and a probable desirability of life" (7).

187

What impels Louisa to marry Joe is a combination of social and familial pressure, and Freeman points out that Louisa had to be talked into marriage: "She had listened with calm docility to her mother's views upon the subject. Her mother was remarkable for her cool sense and sweet, even temperament. She talked wisely to her daughter when Joe Dagget presented himself, and Louisa accepted him with no hesitation" (7). Louisa's mother, it seems, was a domestic saint, remarkable for her "cool sense and sweet, even temperament," and she pressured her daughter to take on this role. Her daughter did not resist.

A similar pattern of social and familial pressure seems to be at work in "Louisa"; Louisa Britton's mother pressures Louisa to marry Jonathan Nye, just as Louisa Ellis's mother pressured Louisa to accept Joe. Although the Brittons are very poor, Mrs. Britton's attraction to the marriage seems, at first, less a matter of economic necessity and more a matter of social pride and distinction. Mrs. Britton covets Jonathan Nye's social status and believes it will be hers if Louisa marries him: "The projected marriage with Jonathan Nye was like a royal alliance for the good of the state. Jonathan Nye . . . was the largest land-owner; he had the best house . . . [Mrs. Britton] saw herself installed in that large white house as reigning dowager" (394–95). But the marriage to Jonathan Nye is actually necessary for the family's physical survival. When Louisa refuses to respond to any of Jonathan's romantic overtures, Mrs. Britton informs Louisa: " 'Then me an' your grandfather'll starve . . . that's all there is about it. We can't neither of us stan' it much longer' " (400).

Marriage, then, in both plots, is a social and economic institution replicated through mothers who have been conditioned to believe that it is the only alternative for "true" women. It is small wonder, then, that Louisa Britton's mother cannot understand Louisa's refusal to marry Jonathan Nye: "All the obstacle was Louisa's obstinacy, which her mother could not understand. . . . There was no more sense, to her mind, in Louisa's refusing him than there would have been in a princess refusing the fairy prince and spoiling the story" (395). But Louisa does "spoil" the story; she refuses to marry Jonathan, and he marries Ida Mosely instead. The fairy tale ending—in which the "princess" marries her "prince" and lives happily ever after—is ruined; yet another more realistic ending concludes this "tale." Jonathan's runner-up choice for a spouse, Ida Mosely, is the schoolteacher who has taken Louisa's job away from her. When it seems that Jonathan will propose to Ida, the townspeople ask Louisa to return to her job. So the story concludes with

Jonathan's prospective marriage to another woman, just as "A New England Nun" ends with Joe's prospective marriage to Lily Dyer.

These stories' endings, therefore, both contain an unexpected reversal of the traditional marriage plot, an unexpected inversion which involves the "prince" marrying someone else and the "princess" going back to her own life. Even specific actions within the final descriptions of these two inversions recur. At the end of "A New England Nun," Louisa sits with her needlework at her window, feeling fairly "steeped in peace" (16). She sees Lily Dyer go by but is not disturbed: "Lily Dyer, tall and erect and blooming, went past; but she felt no qualm. . . . She gazed ahead through a long reach of future days . . . and her heart went up in thankfulness" (16–17). At the end of "Louisa," Louisa Britton, similarly, sits looking outside and sees someone go by—someone who represents the loss of marriage: "Louisa . . . opened the front door and sat down on the step. . . . Some one passed—a man carrying a basket. Louisa glanced at him, and recognized Jonathan Nye by his gait." But Louisa Britton, like Louisa Ellis, feels no qualms: "[Jonathan] kept on down the road toward the Moselys', and Louisa turned again from him to her sweet, mysterious, girlish dreams" (406). Louisa Britton, like Louisa Ellis, returns prayerfully to her own dreams.

Despite this similarity of action, the conclusions of these stories are interpreted very differently by Freeman. As I have mentioned, there is a great deal of ambiguity in the imagery surrounding Louisa Ellis at the end of "A New England Nun," and Louisa Ellis is cut off from "the fervid summer afternoon; the air . . . filled with the sounds of the busy harvest of men and birds and bees" (17). Louisa Britton, on the other hand, sits on the steps of her house—literally and symbolically on the threshold. She has not cut herself off from the outside world; she has merely chosen to bide her time and to maintain her own dreams:

> Louisa . . . crept into the sitting-room. It was warm and close there, so she opened the front door and sat down on the step. The twilight was deep, but there was a clear yellow glow in the west. One great star had come out in the midst of it. A dewy coolness was spreading over everything. The air was full of bird calls and children's voices. Now and then there was a shout of laughter. (406)

Louisa is a part of this scene, but she is also apart. In fact, she is (a)part: both inside and outside, on the border between the world of marriage and of children's voices, and of the "close" atmosphere of her self-supported home. She has retained her right to choose between these two realms—the realm of autonomous, self-supporting existence and the realm of marriage, fertility, and heterosexual love. And the text validates her right to choose by portraying her as being at peace with her environment and by providing an environmental symbol of her blessing in the "clear yellow glow in the west" and the "one great star" which has come out in the midst of it.

Unlike the conclusion of "A New England Nun," then, the setting which concludes "Louisa" portrays a heroine at peace with the natural setting. In fact, the descriptions of natural settings which conclude Freeman's stories often contain crucial clues about the story's interpretation as a whole. This is particularly true of the volume *A New England Nun and Other Stories*. "The Revolt of 'Mother,' " for example, concludes with a setting which suggests the possibility of peaceful coexistence between man and woman: "The twilight was deepening. There was a clear green glow in the sky. Before them stretched the smooth level of field; in the distance was a cluster of hay-stacks like the huts of a village; the air was very cool and calm and sweet. The landscape might have been an ideal one of peace" (468). Similarly, at the conclusion of "Christmas Jenny"—another tale from this collection—Freeman blesses her female character with a peaceful setting and a rising star.[27] Louisa Britton, Jenny Wrayne, and Sarah Penn have all taken active steps to control their destinies and have all—in one way or another—revolted against the patriarchal structures which confine them. It is no coincidence that Freeman blesses each of these characters with environmental harmony and portrays them as being at peace with their settings.

Louisa Britton has other resemblances to strong female characters depicted by Freeman. Louisa appears to be fully conscious of her own needs and desires like Jane Strong of "The Selfishness of Amelia Lamkin" and Eunice Fairweather of "A Moral Exigency." Also, like Jenny Wrayne of "Christmas Jenny," Louisa seems willing to question her society's gender restrictions. Louisa is strong enough to rake hay like a man, and she is also somewhat androgynous in appearance; working in the fields all summer, her "face grew as sunburnt as a boy's, her hands were hard and brown" (396). Louisa Britton seems to exhibit a psychological profile described by Sarah Sherman: she is "Woman before the Fall, before the consciousness of her weakness was imposed on her. . . ."[28]

Characters such as Louisa Britton, Jenny Wrayne, and Jane Strong may be moving toward the profile of the "New Woman" which began to appear in the 1890s; "New Women" were more autonomous—both professionally and personally—than "True Women." Yet even "New Women" like Louisa Britton still retain vestiges of the domestic saint's mentality. Louisa Britton, like Louisa Ellis, sees the world as a web of relationship; she struggles to support her family, even traveling fourteen miles to beg for food from a stingy uncle. The Herculean effort of this task is clear, but Louisa's resolution does not waver: "Her head was swimming, but she kept on. Her resolution was as immovable under the power of the sun as a rock. . . . It was like a pilgrimage, and the Mecca at the end of the burning, desert-like road was her own maiden independence" (404–05). Louisa genuinely cares for her family, and she will toil endlessly for them. She will give up anything—except the essential, herself, her maiden independence.

Louisa Britton, therefore, exhibits Gilligan's "post-conventional" stage of moral reasoning. She sees and acknowledges a web of connectivity between individuals, but she also allows herself to be a valid part of the picture. Against the demands of her mother and her grandfather, she balances the demands of her self and chooses not to marry. And the story validates her decision, both through its imagery and its plot resolution. Upon returning from her heroic pilgrimage, Louisa learns that her suitor has decided to marry Ida Mosely and that she will therefore get her job back. Furthermore, while Louisa's mother and all of their neighbors have assumed that by marrying Jonathan, Louisa could have provided her family with a more secure existence, upon her return Louisa learns that Jonathan had no intention of providing for her family. As Louisa's mother tells her daughter at the end of the story: " 'if Jonathan had you, he wa'n't goin' to have me an' father hitched on to him; he'd look out for that' " (405–06). In the end Louisa's mother and friends approve of her decision not to marry Jonathan. But, unlike Louisa Ellis, Louisa Britton makes the right decision for her own self, because it is the right decision for herself—not for others. That it turns out to be the right decision for her family is important and not coincidental in terms of Freeman's overall aims. Louisa Britton has validated her right to her dreams, to her soul; she has retained the right to define her still malleable personality, and Freeman approves most strongly of Louisa's self-creation.

"Strong, indeed, is the girl who can decide within herself where duty lies, and follow that decision against the combined forces which hold her back. She must claim the right of every individual soul to its own path in life, its own true line of work and growth," states Charlotte Perkins Gilman in *The Home: Its Work and Influence* (1903).[29] A developmental framework such as Gilligan's clarifies the unique psychological and moral dilemma which is clearly present in Freeman's depiction of 19th-century women, as well as indicating how women can claim "the right of every individual soul to its own path in life." With Louisa Ellis, Freeman portrays a woman who cannot mediate the conflict between self and other; she portrays a woman who will not actively "decide within herself where duty lies." With Louisa Britton, on the other hand, Freeman portrays a woman who not only decides "within herself where duty lies" but also follows "that decision against the combined forces which hold her back." Therefore, when these two stories are read together and placed in the context of Freeman's other marital fictions, we can see Freeman theorizing a way that women of this time period can achieve self-definition. When women are active participants in their self-construction rather than the passive victims of external circumstances and the demands of others, the choice of celibacy and autonomy can be construed positively and unambiguously. And when women heed their inner voices rather than merely reacting to external forces, they may be freed from choosing between the equally limited and limiting alternatives offered by a patriarchal society to women of this time period. Woman's birthright, after all, is not marriage, per se, but the right to understand and define her own options.

Notes

1. Negative readings of Louisa Ellis's decision not to marry Joe Dagget can be found in David Hirsch's "Subdued Meaning in 'A New England Nun,' " *Studies in Short Fiction,* 2 (Winter 1965): 124–36, and Aliki Barnstone's "Houses within Houses: Emily Dickinson and Mary Wilkins Freeman's 'A New England Nun,' " *Centennial Review,* 28 (Spring 1984): 129–45. More positive interpretations are argued by Susan Allen Toth in "Defiant Light: A Positive View of Mary Wilkins Freeman," *New England Quarterly,* 46 (March 1973): 82–93, and by Marjorie Pryse in "An Uncloistered 'New England Nun,' " *Studies in Short Fiction,* 20 (Fall 1983): 289–95.

2. Before the last ten years, of course, Freeman was seen by most critics as a chronicler of New England Puritanism in its decline or as a local colorist. It is only recently that the tools of feminism and feminist psychology have been applied to Freeman's work. See, for example, Leah Blatt Glasser's "Mary E. Wilkins Freeman; The Stranger in the Mirror," *Massachusetts Review,* 25 (Summer 1984): 323–39, or Josephine Donovan's "Silence or Capitulation: Prepatriarchal 'Mothers' Gardens' in Jewett and Freeman," *Studies in Short Fiction,* 23 (Winter 1986): 43–48. Neither Donovan nor Glasser, however, have analyzed either of the texts I will discuss from a feminist historical and psychological viewpoint.

3. A number of critics have noted that women in Freeman's stories tend to be oriented toward the relational. See, for example, Victoria Aarons, "A Community of Women: Surviving Marriage in the Wilderness," *Portraits of Marriage in Literature* (Macomb: Western Illinois Univ. Press, 1984), 141, 144; or Julia Bader, "The Dissolving Vision: Realism in Jewett, Freeman, and Gilman," in *American Realism: New Essays*, ed. Eric J. Sundquist (Baltimore: Johns Hopkins Univ. Press, 1982), 177.

4. Nancy Cott, *The Bonds of Womanhood: "Woman's Sphere" in New England, 1780–1835* (New Haven: Yale Univ. Press, 1977), 71. See also Carroll Smith-Rosenberg, *Disorderly Conduct: Visions of Gender in Victorian America* (New York: Oxford Univ. Press, 1985), and Barbara Welter, "The Cult of True Womanhood: 1820–1860," *American Quarterly*, 18 (Summer 1966): 151–74.

5. See "Women and Nature in Modern Fiction," *Contemporary Literature*, 13 (Autumn 1972): 490.

6. *The Infant Sphinx: Collected Letters of Mary E. Wilkins Freeman*, ed. Brent L. Kendrick (Metuchen, N.J.: The Scarecrow Press, 1985), 243. Mary Reichardt discusses these letters in her dissertation " 'A Web of Relationship': Women in the Short Stories of Mary Wilkins Freeman," Univ. of Wisconsin–Madison, 1987, 131–32. For more about the connection between Freeman's marital fiction and her own marital relations, see Glasser, "The Stranger in the Mirror," 323–24.

7. See Glasser's "Legacy Profile: Mary E. Wilkins Freeman," *Legacy*, 4 (Spring 1987): 40.

8. See "The Prism" (1901) and "Arethusa" (1901) for other stories which indicate Freeman's concern that marriage damages women's individuality. Stories such as "A Tragedy from the Trivial" (1901) and "Sour Sweetings" (1918) further depict "the emotional cruelty married life can bring to women after . . . marriage," as Mary Reichardt explains (" 'A Web of Relationship,' " 166). Particularly toward the end of Freeman's marriage, the view of marital relations presented in her fiction seems to have become increasingly bitter. Although at first Freeman's marriage seems to have been relatively happy, Charles Freeman eventually became a violent drug addict and alcoholic; Mary had to institutionalize him in 1921, and when he died his will left Mary only one dollar.

9. "Some Reflections on the Spinster in New England Literature," *Regionalism and the Female Imagination: A Collection of Essays*, ed. Emily Toth (New York: Human Sciences, 1985), 36.

10. See *Mary Wilkins Freeman* (New York: Twayne, 1967), 51.

11. Emily Toth, "The Independent Woman and 'Free' Love," *The Massachusetts Review*, 16 (Autumn 1975): 656 and 657.

12. Johns, "Some Reflections," 36.

13. Sandra Zagarell has suggested that the theories of Carol Gilligan may have special relevance to 19th-century women since Gilligan articulates, perhaps unconsciously, "values that were prominent in nineteenth-century women's culture. . . ." See "Narrative of Community: The Identification of a

Genre," *Signs*, 13 (Spring 1988): 508. Gilligan's findings have not gone unchallenged; Judy Auerbach, Linda Blum, Vicki Smith, and Christine Williams's "Commentary on Gilligan's *In a Different Voice*," *Feminist Studies*, 11 (Spring 1985): 149–61, for example, fault Gilligan for being ahistoric and essentialistic and for promulgating a highly idealized conception of "woman." However, I believe that a limited use of Gilligan's findings can help us understand the psychology of 19th-century women since Gilligan describes a developmental framework which is geared toward understanding female selflessness. Nonetheless, I do not see this essay's conclusion as being based on Gilligan's theories; rather, Gilligan's theories merely help to clarify the psychological profile and development which is already present in Freeman's fiction.

14. Carol Gilligan, *In a Different Voice: Psychological Theory and Women's Development* (Cambridge: Harvard Univ. Press, 1982). "A web of relationship" is Gilligan's phrase; but it is also the title of Mary Reichardt's 1987 dissertation. However, Reichardt does not apply Gilligan's theories to "Louisa" or "A New England Nun," nor does she see these stories as warranting a feminist interpretation.

15. *In a Different Voice*, 39.

16. Mary E. Wilkins, *A New England Nun and Other Stories* (New York: Harper, 1891). All page references to Freeman's stories are from this edition and will be cited parenthetically within the text.

17. A recent article by Lorne Fienberg analyzes women's work in Freeman's fiction and argues that Louisa Ellis "has translated the work process into a ritual that manifests her self-mastery and her mastery of her environment." See *The New England Quarterly*, 62 (1989): 485. It is true that through her work Louisa has found an "alternative pattern of living," but once Joe returns she is willing to sacrifice it. Louisa therefore allows chance and coincidence to determine her course of action rather than acting assertively to preserve her self-mastery.

18. Marjorie Pryse has also a positive reading of Louisa Ellis's bravery; see "An Uncloistered 'New England Nun,' " 289.

19. Not coincidentally, in Freeman's short stories marriage is often associated, literally, with the death of fragile female characters. See, for example, "Old Woman Magoun" (1909) or "The Selfishness of Amelia Lamkin" (1909).

20. Adrienne Rich, "Compulsory Heterosexuality and Lesbian Existence," *Powers of Desire: The Politics of Sexuality*, ed. Ann Snitow, Christine Stansell, and Sharon Thompson (New York: Monthly Review Press, 1983), 177–205.

21. According to Barnstone, it is Louisa's "blocking of knowledge that makes her feel like a queen. . . . She has ordered her house of consciousness so as to be senseless—without senses—and foolish—without thought" ("Houses within Houses," 134).

22. *In a Different Voice*, 122.

23. I would note a similarity between Louisa Ellis's choice of celibacy and Evelina's in "Evelina's Garden." Evelina refuses to acknowledge the glance of a young man who is attracted to her, and he marries someone else. As with Louisa Ellis, it is not clear whether Evelina understands what she has chosen and what she has renounced. Josephine Donovan also notes the similarity between these two stories; see "Silence or Capitulation," 46.

24. Although "Louisa" has been frequently anthologized and admired, to my knowledge no extended critical analysis of it exists. Barbara Johns does comment on Louisa Britton's unwillingness to compromise herself but sees this as a decision to "hold out for romantic love" ("Some Reflections," 35).

25. Glasser has suggested that Freeman's fiction often expresses the conflict between repression and rebellion through the use of doubles. Thus Freeman's "rebellious heroines are shadowed by passive, socially acceptable characters . . ." ("Stranger in the Mirror," 323). Louisa Ellis could be the "passive, socially acceptable" double for the rebel, Louisa Britton.

26. Barbara Welter, "The Cult of True Womanhood: 1820–1860," 162.

27. See Sarah Sherman's article "The Great Goddess in New England: Mary Wilkins Freeman's 'Christmas Jenny,' " *Studies in Short Fiction*, 17 (Spring 1980): 157–64. Of course, the rising star at the end of "Christmas Jenny" is much more overtly religious in its symbolism.

28. "The Great Goddess in New England," 160.

29. *The Home: Its Work and Influence* (Urbana: Univ. of Illinois Press, 1903), 268.

Chronology

1852	Born Mary Ella Wilkins on 31 October in Randolph, Massachusetts, the second child of Warren Wilkins and Eleanor Lothrop Wilkins.
1867	Moves with family to Brattleboro, Vermont, where Warren Wilkins runs a dry goods store. Enters Brattleboro High School.
1870	Graduates from high school and enters Mount Holyoke Seminary.
1871	Leaves Mount Holyoke because of ill health.
1876	Anna Wilkins, Mary's only surviving sibling, dies.
1877–1880	Publishes first children's verses, without pay, in *Good Times* (Boston).
1880	Eleanor Wilkins dies.
1881–1882	Publishes children's verses in *Wide Awake* and *St. Nicholas*.
1882	Receives $50 from the *Boston Sunday Budget* for first adult story, "The Shadow Family."
1883	Warren Wilkins dies. Returns to Randolph to live with the Wales family. *Decorative Plaques* (first collection of children's literature) published. *Harper's Bazar* accepts "Two Old Lovers" for publication. Five more stories follow in *Harper's Bazar* this year.
1884	*The Cow with the Golden Horns and Other Stories.*
1886	*The Adventures of Ann: Stories of Colonial Times.*
1887	*A Humble Romance and Other Stories,* first collection of adult short stories.
1891	*A New England Nun and Other Stories.*
1892	*Red Robin, a New England Drama,* first play. *The Pot of Gold and Other Stories. Young Lucretia and Other Stories.*

197

1893   *Jane Field,* first novel. *Giles Corey, Yeoman: A Play.*

1894   *Pembroke.*

1895   Collaborates with Joseph Edgar Chamberlin on "The Long Arm." *Comfort Pease and Her Gold Ring.*

1896   *Madelon.*

1897   *Jerome, a Poor Man. Once Upon a Time and Other Child Verses.* Becomes engaged to Dr. Charles Manning Freeman.

1898   *Silence and Other Stories. The People of Our Neighborhood.*

1899   *The Jamesons.*

1900   *The Love of Parson Lord and Other Stories. The Heart's Highway.*

1901   *Understudies. The Portion of Labor.*

1902   Marries Charles Freeman on 1 January and moves to Metuchen, New Jersey.

1903   *Six Trees. The Wind in the Rose-Bush and Other Stories of the Supernatural.*

1904   *The Givers.*

1905   *The Debtor.*

1906   *"Doc" Gordon.*

1907   *The Fair Lavinia and Others. By the Light of the Soul.*

1908   *The Shoulders of Atlas,* winner of the *New York Herald's* novel-writing contest. "The Old-Maid Aunt," chapter in *The Whole Family: A Novel by Twelve Authors.*

1909   *The Winning Lady and Others.*

1912   *The Yates Pride: A Romance. The Butterfly House.*

1914   *The Copy-Cat and Other Stories.*

1915   Collaborates with William Dinwiddie on motion picture adaptation of *Pilgrim's Progress.*

1917   Collaborates with Florence Morse Kingsley on *An Alabaster Box,* which is also made into a motion picture.

1918   *Edgewater People.*

1919 Production of *False Evidence,* a motion picture based on *Madelon.*

1921 After years of alcohol and drug abuse, Charles Freeman is committed by Mary to the New Jersey State Hospital for the Insane at Trenton. Released the same year, he lives apart from his wife.

1922 Mary is legally separated from Charles Freeman.

1923 Charles Freeman dies, having disinherited his wife. Mary and Charles's four sisters successfully contest the will.

1926 Receives the William Dean Howells Gold Medal for distinguished work in fiction from the American Academy of Arts and Letters. Along with Edith Wharton, is one of the first women elected to membership in the Department of Literature, the National Institute of Arts and Letters.

1927 *The Best Stories of Mary E. Wilkins,* edited by Henry Wysham Lanier.

1930 Having ailed in her later years from deafness, headaches, bronchial afflictions, and insomnia, Mary Wilkins Freeman dies of a heart attack on 13 March.

1938 Ornamental doors installed at the American Academy of Arts and Letters in New York are dedicated "To the Memory of Mary E. Wilkins Freeman and the Women Writers of America."

Selected Bibliography

Primary Works

Adult Short Story Collections

The Best Stories of Mary E. Wilkins. Ed. and intro. Henry Wysham Lanier. New York: Harper and Brothers, 1927. "A Humble Romance," "The Revolt of 'Mother,' " "Little-Girl-Afraid-of-a-Dog," "A New England Nun," "One Good Time," "The Last Gift," "A New England Prophet," "A Village Singer," "Old Woman Magoun," "The Joy of Youth," "Billy and Susy," "The Butterfly," "Both Cheeks," "A Solitary," "Two Old Lovers," "Gentian," "The Wind in the Rose-Bush," "A Conflict Ended," "A Conquest of Humility," "The Apple-Tree," "Noblesse," "The Outside of the House," "Coronation," "The Gold," "The Gospel According to Joan."

The Copy-Cat and Other Stories. New York: Harper and Brothers, 1914. "The Copy-Cat," "The Cock of the Walk," "Johnny-in-the-Woods," "Daniel and Little Dan'l," "Big Sister Solly," "Little Lucy Rose," "Noblesse," "Coronation," "The Amethyst Comb," "The Umbrella Man," "The Balking of Christopher," "Dear Annie."

Edgewater People. New York: Harper and Brothers, 1918. "Sarah Edgewater," "The Old Man of the Field," "The Voice of the Clock," "Value Received," "The Flowering Bush," "The Outside of the House," "The Liar," "Sour Sweetings," "Both Cheeks," "The Soldier Man," "The Ring with the Green Stone," " 'A Retreat to the Goal.' "

The Fair Lavinia and Others. New York: Harper and Brothers, 1907. "The Fair Lavinia," "Amarina's Roses," "Eglantina," "The Pink Shawls," "The Willow-Ware," "The Secret," "The Gold," "The Underling."

The Givers. New York: Harper and Brothers, 1904. "The Givers," "Lucy," "Eglantina," "Joy," "The Reign of the Doll," "The Chance of Araminta," "The Butterfly," "The Last Gift."

A Humble Romance and Other Stories. New York: Harper and Brothers, 1887. "A Humble Romance," "Two Old Lovers," "A Symphony in Lavender," "A Tardy Thanksgiving," "A Modern Dragon," "An Honest Soul," "A Taste of Honey," "Brakes and White Vi'lets," "Robins and Hammers," "On the

Walpole Road," "Old Lady Pingree," "Cinnamon Roses," "The Bar Light-House," "A Lover of Flowers," "A Far-Away Melody," "A Moral Exigency," "A Mistaken Charity," "Gentian," "An Object of Love," "A Gatherer of Simples," "An Independent Thinker," "In Butterfly Time," "An Unwilling Guest," "A Souvenir," "An Old Arithmetician," "A Conflict Ended," "A Patient Waiter," "A Conquest of Humility."

The Love of Parson Lord and Other Stories. New York: Harper and Brothers, 1900. "The Love of Parson Lord," "The Tree of Knowledge," "Catherine Carr," "The Three Old Sisters and the Old Beau," "One Good Time."

A Mary Wilkins Freeman Reader. Ed. and intro. Mary R. Reichardt. Lincoln: University of Nebraska Press, 1997. "An Honest Soul," "A Conflict Ended," "An Independent Thinker," "A New England Nun," "Christmas Jenny," "Life-Everlastin'," "A Village Singer," "A Church Mouse," "A Poetess," "The Revolt of 'Mother,' " "Louisa," "Evelina's Garden," "One Good Time," "The Parrot," "Arethusa," "The Balsam Fir," "The Great Pine," "Luella Miller," "The Lost Ghost," "Eglantina," "The Revolt of Sophia Lane," "The Reign of the Doll," "The Gold," "The Old-Maid Aunt," "Old Woman Magoun," "The Selfishness of Amelia Lamkin," "The Balking of Christopher," "The Outside of the House."

A New England Nun and Other Stories. New York: Harper and Brothers, 1891. "A New England Nun," "A Village Singer," "A Gala Dress," "The Twelfth Guest," "Sister Liddy," "Calla-Lilies and Hannah," "A Wayfaring Couple," "A Poetess," "Christmas Jenny," "A Pot of Gold," "The Scent of the Roses," "A Solitary," "A Gentle Ghost," "A Discovered Pearl," "A Village Lear," "Amanda and Love," "Up Primrose Hill," "A Stolen Christmas," "Life-Everlastin'," "An Innocent Gamester," "Louisa," "A Church Mouse," "A Kitchen Colonel," "The Revolt of 'Mother.' "

The People of Our Neighborhood. Philadelphia: Curtis Publishing Company, 1898. "Timothy Sampson: The Wise Man," "Little Margaret Snell: The Village Runaway," "Cyrus Emmett: The Unlucky Man," "Phebe Ann Little: The Neat Woman," "Amanda Todd: The Friend of Cats," "Lydia Wheelock: The Good Woman," "A Quilting Bee in Our Village," "The Stockwells' Apple-Paring Bee," "The Christmas Sing in Our Village."

The Revolt of Mother and Other Stories. Ed. and afterword Michele Clark. New York: Feminist Press, 1974. "A Mistaken Charity," "A Moral Exigency," "A Taste of Honey," "Louisa," "A New England Nun," "A Gala Dress," "The Revolt of 'Mother,' " "A Church Mouse."

Selected Stories of Mary E. Wilkins Freeman. Ed. and intro. Marjorie Pryse. New York: W. W. Norton, 1983. "Two Old Lovers," "An Honest Soul," "On the Walpole Road," "A Mistaken Charity," "A Gatherer of Simples," "A Conflict Ended," "A Patient Waiter," "A New England Nun," "A Village Singer," "A Gala Dress," "Sister Liddy," "A Poetess," "Christmas Jenny," "A Solitary," "A Village Lear," "Up Primrose Hill," "A Church Mouse," "The Revolt of 'Mother.' "

Short Fiction of Sarah Orne Jewett and Mary Wilkins Freeman. Ed. and intro. Barbara H. Solomon. New York: New American Library, 1979. "A Mistaken Charity," "Gentian," "An Independent Thinker," "A Conflict Ended," "A New England Nun," "A Village Singer," "A Poetess," "Louisa," "A Church Mouse," "The Revolt of 'Mother,' " "One Good Time," "The Lombardy Poplar," "The Selfishness of Amelia Lamkin," "Old Woman Magoun."

Silence and Other Stories. New York: Harper and Brothers, 1898. "Silence," "The Buckley Lady," "Evelina's Garden," "A New England Prophet," "The Little Maid at the Door," "Lydia Hersey, of East Bridgewater."

Six Trees. New York: Harper and Brothers, 1903. "The Elm-Tree," "The White Birch," "The Great Pine," "The Balsam Fir," "The Lombardy Poplar," "The Apple-Tree."

The Uncollected Stories of Mary Wilkins Freeman. Ed. and intro. Mary R. Reichardt. Jackson: University Press of Mississippi, 1992. "Emmy," "Juliza," "A Tragedy from the Trivial," "The Prism," "The Hall Bedroom," "Humble Pie," "The Slip of the Leash," "For the Love of One's Self," "The Witch's Daughter," "The Horn of Plenty," "A Guest in Sodom," "The Doll Lady," "The Blue Butterfly," "Friend of My Heart," "Criss-Cross," "Sweet-Flowering Perennial," "The Cloak Also," "Mother-Wings," "The Jester," "The White Shawl."

Understudies. New York: Harper and Brothers, 1901. "The Cat," "The Monkey," "The Squirrel," "The Lost Dog," "The Parrot," "The Doctor's Horse," "Bouncing Bet," "Prince's-Feather," "Arethusa," "Mountain-Laurel," "Peony," "Morning-Glory."

The Wind in the Rose-Bush and Other Stories of the Supernatural. New York: Doubleday, Page and Company, 1903. Reprinted with an afterword by Alfred Bendixen. Chicago: Academy Chicago, 1986. "The Wind in the Rose-Bush," "The Shadows on the Wall," "Luella Miller," "The Southwest Chamber," "The Vacant Lot," "The Lost Ghost."

The Winning Lady and Others. New York: Harper and Brothers, 1909. "The Winning Lady," "Little-Girl-Afraid-of-a-Dog," "The Joy of Youth," "Billy and Susy," "The Selfishness of Amelia Lamkin," "The Travelling Sister," "Her Christmas," "Old Woman Magoun," "Eliza Sam," "Flora and Hannah," "A New-Year's Resolution."

Uncollected Adult Short Stories

"About Hannah Stone." *Everybody's* 4 (January 1901): 25–33.

"The Auction." *Woman's Home Companion* 36 (October 1909): 7–8, 93.

"Away from the Sunflower Ranch." *Boston Evening Transcript: The Holiday Transcript* (December 1890): 4.

"Betsey Somerset." *Harper's Bazar* 26 (18 March 1893): 205–7.

"The Boomerang." *Pictorial Review* 18 (March 1917): 22–24, 44.

"The Bright Side." *Harper's Monthly* 146 (April 1923): 630–44.

"The Brother." MS. (c. 1927). Reference from Foster, 213.

"A Brotherhood of Three." *Harper's Weekly* 41 (18 December 1897): 1248–50. Also in *Illustrated London News* 111 (18 December 1897): 879–81.

"The Cautious King, and the All-Round Wise Woman." *Harper's Weekly* 53 (26 June 1909): 22–24.

"The Christmas Ghost." *Everybody's* 3 (December 1900): 512–20.

"A Christmas Lady." *Ladies' Home Journal* 27 (December 1909): 17–18.

"D.J.: A Christmas Story." *Mail and Express Illustrated Saturday Magazine* (New York; 5 December 1903): 14–15, 22, 30. Also in *Advance* 46 (17 December 1903): 766–69.

"A Devotee of Art." *Harper's Bazar* 27 (27 January 1894): 69–71.

"Down the Road to the Emersons." *Romance* 12 (November 1893): 3–24.

"An Easter-Card." *Everybody's* 4 (April 1901): 372–77.

"Emancipation." *Harper's Monthly* 132 (December 1915): 27–35.

"Eunice and the Doll." *Boston Evening Transcript* (13 December 1897): 8; (14 December 1897): 10. Also in *Pocket Magazine* 5 (March 1898): 1–41 and in *Best Things from American Literature,* ed. Irving Bacheller. New York: The Christian Herald, 1899, 369–82.

"Far Away Job." *Woman's Home Companion* 36 (December 1909): 6–7, 72–75.

"The Fighting McLeans." *The Delineator* 75 (February 1910): 113–114, 150–52.

"General: A Christmas Story." *10 Story Book* 1 (January 1902): 10–15.

"The Gift of Love." *Woman's Home Companion* 33 (December 1906): 21–22, 73.

"The Happy Day." *McClure's* 21 (May 1903): 89–94.

"The Home-Coming of Jessica." *Woman's Home Companion* 28 (3 November 1901): n.p. Also in *The Home-Coming of Jessica* [by Mary E. Wilkins]; *An Idyl of Central Park* [by Brander Matthews]; *The Romance of a Soul* [by Robert Grant]. New York: Crowell and Kirkpatrick, 1901, 3–17.

"Honorable Tommy." *Woman's Home Companion* 43 (December 1916): 15–16, 68.

"How Charlotte Ellen Went Visiting." *Boston Evening Transcript* 1 (November 1897): 10; (2 November 1897): 8. Also in *New York Ledger* 54 (14 May and 21 May 1898): 17–18 each issue.

"Hyacinthus." *Harper's Monthly* 109 (August 1904): 447–58. Also in *Quaint Courtships,* ed. William Dean Howells and Henry Mills Alden. London: Harper and Brothers, 1906, 75–107.

"The Jade Bracelet." *Forum* 59 (April 1918): 429–40.

[Jane Lennox.] Undated MS., privately owned. Reference from Foster, 142–43.

"Josiah's First Christmas." *Collier's* 44 (11 December 1909): 9–10.

"Julia—Her Thanksgiving." *Harper's Bazar* 43 (November 1909): 1079–82.

"The Little Green Door." *New York Times* (13–15 April 1896): 9 each issue. Also in *Pocket Magazine* 3 (July 1896): 56–90 and in *New York Ledger* 52 (25 April 1898): 16–17.

"The Long Arm." By Mary E. Wilkins and J. Edgar Chamberlin. *Pocket Magazine* 1 (December 1895): 1–76. Also in Mary E. Wilkins et al. *The Long Arm and Other Detective Stories*. London: Chapman and Hall, 1895, 1–66.

"A Meeting Half-Way." *Harper's Bazar* 24 (11 April 1891): 273–75.

"Mrs. Sackett's Easter Bonnet." *Woman's Home Companion* 34 (April 1907): 5–7.

"The Mystery of Miss Amidon." *Boston Evening Transcript* (22 December 1900): 18.

"Nanny and Martha Pepperill." *Harper's Bazar* 28 (14 December 1895): 1021–23.

"A Narrow Escape/How Santa Claus Baffled the Mounted Police." *Detroit Sunday News* (25 December 1892): 12.

"An Old Valentine." *Home-Maker* 8 (February 1890): 367–74. Also in *Romance* 9 (February 1893): 50–64.

"One." MS. (c. 1928). Reference from Foster, 213.

"Other People's Cake." *Collier's* 42 (21 November 1908): 14–15, 32, 34, 36–37.

"The Other Side." *Harper's Bazar* 24 (26 December 1891): 993–95.

"The Price She Paid." *Harper's Bazar* 21 (10 March 1888): 158–59.

"The Prop." *Saturday Evening Post* 190 (5 January 1918): 12–13, 109–10.

"A Protracted Meeting." *Housewife* 6 (February 1891): 6; 6 (March 1891): 6.

"The Proud Lucinda." *Harper's Bazar* 24 (7 February 1891): 101–3.

"The Pumpkin." *Harper's Bazar* 33 (24 November 1900): 1863–71.

"The Return." *Woman's Home Companion* 48 (August 1921): 21–22, 83.

"The Rocket." Undated MS, also entitled "One Old Lady." Manuscript and Archives Division, New York Public Library.

"Rosemary Marsh." *Harper's Bazar* 30 (11 December 1897): 1026.

"A Rustic Comedy." *Ladies' Home Journal* 8 (March 1891): 7–8.

"Santa Claus: Two Jack-Knives." *Springfield* [Mass.] *Sunday Republican* (15 December 1901): 24.

"The Saving of Hiram Sessions." *Pictorial Review* 16 (May 1915): 20–21, 70–72.

"The School-Teacher." *Harper's Bazar* 28 (6 April 1895): 262.

"The School-Teacher's Story." *Romance* 13 (February 1894): 5–18.

"Serena Ann's First Valentine." *Boston Evening Transcript* (5 February 1897): 9. Also in *New York Ledger* 53 (13 February 1897): 6–7 and in *English Illustrated* 17 (June 1897): 235–42.

"Serena Ann: Her First Christmas Keeping." *Hartford Daily Courant* (15 December 1894): 10.

"The Shadow Family." *Boston Sunday Budget* (1 January 1882): n.p..

"She Who Adorns Her Sister Adorns Herself." *Harper's Bazar* 38 (May 1904): 456–60.

"A Slayer of Serpents." *Collier's* 44 (19 March 1910): 16–17, 19, 36, 38.

"Something on Her Mind." *Harper's Bazar* 46 (December 1912): 607–8.

"Sonny." *Lippincott's* 47 (June 1891): 776–85. Also in *Romance* 8 (November 1892): 13–27.

"Starlight." *Woman's Home Companion* 35 (December 1908): 19–20, 74.

"The Steeple." *Hampton-Columbian* 27 (October 1911): 412–20.

"The Story of Little Mary Whitlow." *Lippincott's* 21 (May 1883): 500–504.

"A Stress of Conscience." *Harper's Bazar* 25 (25 June 1892): 518–19. Also in *Illustrated London News* 100 (25 June 1892): 785–87.

"The Strike of Hannah." *Woman's Home Companion* 33 (November 1906): 9–10, 50–52.

"A Study in China." *Harper's Bazar* 20 (5 November 1887): 766–67.

"Susan: Her Neighbor's Story." *Harper's Bazar* 32 (23 September 1899): 801, 804.

"Susan Jane's Valentine." *Harper's Bazar* 33 (17 February 1900): 132–33.

"Sweet-Williams." *Harper's Bazar* 28 (25 May 1895): 418.

"Tall Jane." *St. Louis Republic* (25 October 1891): 5. Also in *Detroit Sunday News* (25 October 1891): 12.

"Thanksgiving Crossroads." *Woman's Home Companion* 44 (November 1917): 13, 58, 60.

"A Thanksgiving Thief." *Ladies' Home Journal* 9 (November 1892): 1–2.

"Two for Peace." *Lippincott's* 68 (July 1901): 51–70.

"Two Friends." *Harper's Bazar* 20 (25 June 1887): 450–51.

"Uncle Davy." *Detroit Sunday News* (10 January 1892): 10.

"An Unlucky Christmas." *Harper's Bazar* 29 (12 December 1896): 1037–39.

"A Wandering Samaritan." *Cosmopolitan* 2 (September 1886): 28–33.

"A War-Time Dress." *Cosmopolitan* 25 (August 1898): 403–16.

"Wrong Side Out." *10 Story Book* 1 (July 1901): 10–16.

Works in Other Genres

The Adventures of Ann: Stories of Colonial Times. Boston: D. Lothrop, 1886. Reprinted with an additional story, *In Colonial Times, The Adventures of Ann.* Boston: D. Lothrop, 1889. Children's stories.

An Alabaster Box, by Mary Wilkins Freeman and Florence Morse Kingsley. New York: D. Appleton and Company, 1917. Novel.

An Alabaster Box. Directed by Chester Withey. Vitagraph Company of America, 1917. Motion picture.

The Butterfly House. New York: Dodd, Mead and Company, 1912. Novel.

By the Light of the Soul. New York: Harper and Brothers, 1907. Novel.

Comfort Pease and Her Gold Ring. New York: Fleming H. Revell, 1895. Children's story.

The Cow with the Golden Horns and Other Stories. Boston: D. Lothrop, 1884. Children's stories.

The Debtor. New York: Harper and Brothers, 1905. Novel.

Decorative Plaques. Boston: D. Lothrop, 1883. Children's poems.

"Doc" Gordon. New York: Authors and Newspapers Association, 1906. Novel.

Selected Bibliography

Eglantina: A Romantic Parlor Play. Ladies' Home Journal 27 (July 1910): 13–14, 38. Play.
False Evidence (based on *Madelon*). Metro Motion Picture Company, 1919. Motion picture.
Giles Corey, Yeoman. New York: Harper and Brothers, 1893. Play.
The Green Door. New York: Moffat, Yard and Company, 1910. Children's story.
The Heart's Highway, A Romance of Virginia in the Seventeenth Century. New York: Doubleday, Page and Company, 1900. Novel.
The Jamesons. New York: Doubleday and McClure Company, 1899. Novel.
Jane Field. New York: Harper and Brothers, 1893. Novel.
Jerome, a Poor Man. New York: Harper and Brothers, 1897. Novel.
Madelon. New York: Harper and Brothers, 1896. Novel.
Once Upon a Time and Other Child-Verses. Boston: D. Lothrop, 1897. Children's poems.
Pembroke. New York: Harper and Brothers, 1894. Novel.
The Pilgrim's Progress. Adapted by Mary E. Wilkins and William Dinwiddie. New York, 1915. Motion picture.
The Portion of Labor. New York: Harper and Brothers, 1901. Novel.
The Pot of Gold and Other Stories. Boston: D. Lothrop, 1892. Children's stories.
Red Robin, a New England Drama. Copyrighted in 1892 and 1893, n.p. Play.
The Shoulders of Atlas. New York: Harper and Brothers, 1908. Novel.
The Whole Family: A Novel by Twelve Authors. Mary Wilkins Freeman, William D. Howells, Henry James, et al. New York: Harper and Brothers, 1908. Chapter in novel.
The Yates Pride: A Romance. New York: Harper and Brothers, 1912. Brief novel.
Young Lucretia and Other Stories. New York: Harper and Brothers, 1892. Children's stories.

Nonfiction

Author's preface. *A Humble Romance and Other Stories.* Edinburgh: David Douglas, 1890, v–vi.
"An Autobiography." In "Who's Who—and Why: Serious and Frivolous Facts about the Great and the Near Great." *Saturday Evening Post* 190 (8 December 1917): 25, 75.
"Emily Brontë and *Wuthering Heights*." In *The World's Great Woman Novelists*, ed. T. M. Parrott. Philadelphia: The Booklovers Library, 1901, 85–93.
"The Girl Who Wants to Write: Things to Do and to Avoid." *Harper's Bazar* 47 (June 1913): 272.
"Good Wits, Pen and Paper." In *What Women Can Earn: Occupations of Women and Their Compensation,* ed. Grace H. Dodge et al. New York: Frederick A. Stokes, 1899, 28–29.
"He Does Not Want a Fool." *Delineator* 72 (July 1908): 80, 135.

"How I Write My Novels: Twelve of America's Most Popular Authors Reveal the Secrets of Their Art." *New York Herald* (25 October 1908): magazine section, 3–4.

"If They Had a Million Dollars: What Nine Famous Women Would Do If a Fortune Were Theirs." *Ladies' Home Journal* 20 (September 1903): 10.

"Introductory Sketch" in Biographical Edition of *Pembroke*. New York: Harper and Brothers, 1899, iii–vii.

["My Maiden Effort."] In *My Maiden Effort: Being the Personal Confessions of Well-Known American Authors As to Their Literary Beginnings*. Garden City, New York: Doubleday, Page and Company, 1921, 265–67.

"New England, 'Mother of America.' " *Country Life in America* 22 (July 1912): 27–32, 64–67.

"We Are with France." In *For France*, ed. Charles H. Towne. Garden City, N.Y.: Doubleday, Page and Company, 1917, 336.

"A Woman's Tribute to Mr. Howells." *Literary Digest* 44 (9 March 1912): 485.

Secondary Works

Books

Foster, Edward. *Mary E. Wilkins Freeman*. New York: Hendricks House, 1956.

Glasser, Leah Blatt. *In a Closet Hidden: The Life and Work of Mary E. Wilkins Freeman*. Amherst: University of Massachusetts Press, 1996.

Hamblen, Abigail Ann. *The New England Art of Mary E. Wilkins Freeman*. Amherst, Mass.: Green Knight Press, 1966.

Kendrick, Brent L., ed. *The Infant Sphinx: Collected Letters of Mary E. Wilkins Freeman*. Metuchen, N.J.: Scarecrow Press, 1985.

Marchalonis, Shirley, ed. *Critical Essays on Mary Wilkins Freeman*. Boston: G. K. Hall, 1991.

Reichardt, Mary R. *A Web of Relationship: Women in the Short Stories of Mary Wilkins Freeman*. Jackson: University Press of Mississippi, 1992.

Westbrook, Perry D. *Mary Wilkins Freeman*. New York: Twayne, 1967. Rev. ed., 1988.

Critical Articles and Chapters in Books

Apthorp, Elaine Sargent. "Sentiment, Naturalism, and the Female Regionalist." *Legacy: A Journal of American Women Writers* 7 (Spring 1990): 3–21.

Bader, Julia. "The Dissolving Vision: Realism in Jewett, Freeman, and Gilman." In *American Realism: New Essays*, ed. Eric J. Sundquist. Baltimore: Johns Hopkins University Press, 1982, 176–98.

Blum, Virginia L. "Mary Wilkins Freeman and the Taste of Necessity." *American Literature* 65 (March 1993): 69–94.

Brand, Alice Glarden. "Mary Wilkins Freeman: Misanthropy as Propaganda." *New England Quarterly* 50 (March 1977): 83–100.

Church, Joseph. "Reconstructing Woman's Place in Freeman's 'The Revolt of "Mother." ' " *Colby Quarterly* 26 (September 1990): 195–200.

Crowley, John W. "Freeman's Yankee Tragedy: 'Amanda and Love.' " *Markham Review* 5 (Spring 1976): 58–60.

Cutter, Martha J. "Beyond Stereotypes: Mary Wilkins Freeman's Radical Critique of Nineteenth-Century Cults of Femininity." *Women's Studies* 21 (1992): 383–95.

———. "Frontiers of Language: Engendering Discourse in 'The Revolt of "Mother." ' " *American Literature* 63 (June 1991): 279–91.

Daniel, Janice B. "Freeman's 'A Church Mouse.' " *Explicator* 53 (Fall 1994): 43–44.

DeEulis, Marilyn Davis. " 'Her Box of a House': Spatial Restriction As Psychic Signpost in Mary Wilkins Freeman's 'The Revolt of "Mother." ' " *Markham Review* 8 (Spring 1979): 51–52.

Donovan, Josephine. "Mary E. Wilkins Freeman and the Tree of Knowledge." In Donovan, *New England Local Color Literature: A Women's Tradition*. New York: Frederick Ungar, 1983, 119–38.

———. "Silence or Capitulation: Prepatriarchal 'Mothers' Gardens' in Jewett and Freeman." *Studies in Short Fiction* 23 (Winter 1986): 43–48.

Dwyer, Patricia M. "Diffusing Boundaries: A Study of Narrative Strategies in Mary Wilkins Freeman's 'The Revolt of "Mother." ' " *Legacy: A Journal of American Women Writers* 10 (Fall 1993): 120–27.

Elbert, Monika M. "Mary Wilkins Freeman's Devious Women, *Harper's Bazar*, and the Rhetoric of Advertising." *Essays in Literature* 20 (Fall 1993): 251–72.

Fisken, Beth Wynne. "The 'Faces of Children That Had Never Been': Ghost Stories by Mary Wilkins Freeman." In *Haunting the House of Fiction*. Lynette Carpenter and Wendy K. Kolmar, eds. Knoxville: University of Tennessee Press, 1991, 41–63.

———. " 'Unusual' People in a 'Usual Place': 'The Balking of Christopher' by Mary Wilkins Freeman." *Colby Library Quarterly* 21 (June 1985): 99–103.

Gardner, Kate. "The Subversion of Genre in the Short Stories of Mary Wilkins Freeman." *New England Quarterly* 63 (September 1992): 447–68.

Getz, John. " 'Eglantina': Freeman's Revision of Hawthorne's 'The Birth-mark.' " In *Critical Essays on Mary Wilkins Freeman*. Shirley Marchalonis, ed. Boston: G. K. Hall, 1991, 177–84.

———. "Mary Wilkins Freeman and Sherwood Anderson: Confluence or Influence?" *MidAmerica: Yearbook of the Society for the Study of Midwestern Literature* 19 (1992): 74–86.

Glasser, Leah Blatt. "Mary E. Wilkins Freeman: The Stranger in the Mirror." *Massachusetts Review* 25 (Summer 1984): 323–39.

———. " 'She Is the One You Call Sister': Discovering Mary Wilkins Freeman." In *Between Women: Biographers, Novelists, Critics, Teachers, and Artists Write About Their Work on Women.* Carol Ascher et al., eds. Boston: Beacon Press, 1984, 187–211.

Grasso, Linda. " 'Thwarted Life, Mighty Hunger, Unfinished Work': The Legacy of Nineteenth-Century Women Writing in America." *ATQ* n.s. 8 (June 1994): 97–118.

Hirsch, David H. "Subdued Meaning in 'A New England Nun.' " *Studies in Short Fiction* 2 (Winter 1965): 124–36.

Johns, Barbara A. " 'Love-Cracked': Spinsters As Subversives in 'Anna Malann,' 'Christmas Jenny,' and 'An Object of Love.' " *Colby Library Quarterly* 23 (March 1987): 4–15.

Johnsen, Norma. "Pieces: Artist and Audience in Three Mary Wilkins Freeman Stories." *Colby Quarterly* 29 (March 1993): 43–56.

Klemans, Patricia A. "The Courageous Soul: Woman As Artist in American Literature." *CEA Critic* 43 (May 1981): 39–43.

Koppelman, Susan. "About 'Two Friends' and Mary Eleanor Wilkins Freeman." *American Literary Realism* 21 (Fall 1988): 43–57.

Levy, Babette M. "Mutations in New England Local Color." *New England Quarterly* 19 (Summer 1946): 338–58.

Luscher, Robert M. "Seeing the Forest for the Trees: The 'Intimate Connection' of Mary Wilkins Freeman's *Six Trees*." *ATQ* n.s. 3 (December 1989): 363–81.

Maik, Thomas A. "Dissent and Affirmation: Conflicting Voices of Female Roles in Selected Stories by Mary Wilkins Freeman." *Colby Quarterly* 26 (March 1990): 59–68.

———. "Mary Wilkins Freeman's 'Louisa': Liberation, Independence, or Madness?" *North Dakota Quarterly* 60 (Fall 1992): 137–48.

Marchalonis, Shirley. "Another Mary Wilkins Freeman: *Understudies* and *Six Trees*." *ATQ* n.s. 9 (June 1995): 89–101.

———. "The Sharp-edged Humor of Mary Wilkins Freeman: *The Jamesons*—and Other Stories." In *Critical Essays on Mary Wilkins Freeman.* Shirley Marchalonis, ed. Boston: G. K. Hall, 1991, 222–34.

Matthiessen, F.O. "New England Stories." In *American Writers on American Literature.* John Macy, ed. New York: Horace Liveright, 1931, 339–413.

McElrath, Joseph R. "The Artistry of Mary E. Wilkins Freeman's 'The Revolt.' " *Studies in Short Fiction* 17 (Summer 1980): 255–61.

Meese, Elizabeth. "Signs of Undecidability: Reconsidering the Stories of Mary Wilkins Freeman." In Meese, *Crossing the Double-Cross: The Practice of Feminist Criticism.* Chapel Hill: University of North Carolina Press, 1986, 19–38.

Morey, Ann-Janine. "American Myth and Biblical Interpretation in the Fiction of Harriet Beecher Stowe and Mary E. Wilkins Freeman." *Journal of the American Academy of Religion* 55 (Spring 1987): 741–63.

Moss, Mary. "Some Representative American Story Tellers: Mary E. Wilkins." *Bookman* 24 (September 1906): 21–29.

Oaks, Susan. "The Haunting Will: The Ghost Stories of Mary Wilkins Freeman." *Colby Library Quarterly* 21 (December 1985): 208–20.

Orr, Elaine. "Reading Negotiation and Negotiated Reading: A Practice with/in 'A White Heron' and 'The Revolt of "Mother." ' " *CEA Critic* 53 (Spring/Summer 1991): 49–65.

Pennell, Melissa McFarland. "The Liberating Will: Freedom of Choice in the Fiction of Mary Wilkins Freeman." In *Critical Essays on Mary Wilkins Freeman*. Shirley Marchalonis, ed. Boston: G. K. Hall, 1991, 207–21.

Pryse, Marjorie. " 'Distilling Essences': Regionalism and 'Women's Culture.' " *American Literary Realism* 25 (Winter 1993): 1–15.

———. "The Humanity of Women in Freeman's 'A Village Singer.' " *Colby Library Quarterly* 19 (June 1983): 69–77.

Reichardt, Mary R. " 'Friend of My Heart': Women As Friends and Rivals in the Short Stories of Mary Wilkins Freeman." *American Literary Realism* 22 (Winter 1990): 54–68.

———. "Mary Wilkins Freeman: One Hundred Years of Criticism." *Legacy: A Journal of Nineteenth-Century American Women Writers* 4 (Fall 1987): 31–44.

———. " 'The Web of Self-Strangulation': Mothers, Daughters, and the Question of Marriage in the Short Stories of Mary Wilkins Freeman." In *Joinings and Disjoinings: The Significance of Marital Status in Literature*. JoAnna Stephens Mink and Janet Doubler Ward, eds. Bowling Green, Ohio: Popular Press, 1991, 109–19.

Romines, Ann. "Freeman's Repetitions: The Housekeeper and Her Plot." In Romines, *The Home Plot: Women, Writing, and Domestic Ritual*. Amherst: University of Massachusetts Press, 1992, 91–127.

———. "A Place for 'A Poetess.' " *Markham Review* 12 (Summer 1983): 61–64.

Sherman, Sarah W. "The Great Goddess in New England: Mary Wilkins Freeman's 'Christmas Jenny.' " *Studies in Short Fiction* 17 (Spring 1980): 157–64.

Thompson, Charles Miner. "Miss Wilkins: An Idealist in Masquerade." *Atlantic Monthly* 83 (May 1899): 665–75.

Toth, Susan Allen. "Defiant Light: A Positive View of Mary Wilkins Freeman." *New England Quarterly* 46 (March 1973): 82–93.

———. "Mary Wilkins Freeman's Parable of Wasted Life." *American Literature* 42 (January 1971): 564–67.

Tutwiler, Julia R. "Two New England Writers—in Relation to Their Art and to Each Other." *Gunton's Magazine* 25 (November 1903): 419–25.

Warner, Sylvia Townsend. "Item, One Empty House." *New Yorker* 42 (26 March 1966): 131–38.

Westbrook, Perry D. "The Anatomy of the Will: Mary Wilkins Freeman." In Westbrook, *Acres of Flint: Sarah Orne Jewett and Her Contemporaries*. Rev. ed. Metuchen, N.J.: Scarecrow Press, 1981, 86–104.

Wood, Ann Douglas. "The Literature of Impoverishment: The Women Local Colorists in America 1865–1914." *Women's Studies* 1 (1972): 3–40.

Bibliography and Reference Works

Blanck, Jacob. N. "Mary E. Wilkins Freeman." *Bibliography of American Literature* 3 (1959): 324–43.

Boren, Lynda S. "Mary Wilkins Freeman." In *Dictionary of Literary Biography: American Realists and Naturalists*, vol. 12. Donald Pizer and Earl H. Harbert, eds. Detroit: Gale, 1982, 183–91.

Mainiero, Lina, ed. "Mary E. Wilkins Freeman." *American Women Writers* 2 (1980): 82–84.

Poupard, Dennis, ed. "Mary (Eleanor) Wilkins Freeman." *Twentieth Century Literary Criticism* 9 (1983): 59–80.

Pryse, Marjorie. "Mary E. Wilkins Freeman." In *Modern American Women Writers*. Elaine Showalter, ed. New York: Charles Scribners, 1991, 141–53.

Index

The Author

Mary R. Reichardt is associate professor of English at the University of St. Thomas in St. Paul, Minnesota, where she teaches courses in American literature. She also works as a freelance instructor, consultant, and editor for business and professional writing. She received her Ph.D. from the University of Wisconsin–Madison in 1987, writing her dissertation on the short stories of Mary Wilkins Freeman. Since that time, her research on Freeman has been extensive, yielding articles published in such journals as *Legacy* and *American Literary Realism* and in such collections of essays as *Joinings and Disjoinings: The Significance of Marital Status in Literature* and *Critical Essays on Mary Wilkins Freeman.* She is the author of *A Web of Relationship: Women in the Short Stories of Mary Wilkins Freeman* (1992) and the editor of *The Uncollected Stories of Mary Wilkins Freeman* (1992) and *A Mary Wilkins Freeman Reader* (1997).

The Editors

Gary Scharnhorst is professor of English at the University of New Mexico, coeditor of *American Literary Realism,* and editor in alternating years of *American Literary Scholarship: An Annual.* He is the author or editor of books about Horatio Alger Jr., Charlotte Perkins Gilman, Bret Harte, Nathaniel Hawthorne, Henry David Thoreau, and Mark Twain, and he has taught in Germany on Fulbright fellowships three times (1978–1979, 1985–1986, 1993). He is also the current president of the Western Literature Association and the Pacific Northwest American Studies Association.

Eric Haralson is assistant professor of English at the State University of New York at Stony Brook. He has published articles on American and English literature—in *American Literature, Nineteenth-Century Literature,* the *Arizona Quarterly, American Literary Realism,* and the *Henry James Review,* as well as in several essay collections. He is also the editor of *The Garland Encyclopedia of American Nineteenth-Century Poetry.*